VIRGINIA WOOLF S RENAISSANCE
WOMAN READER OR COMMON READER

DUSINBERRE, JULIET

# VIRGINIA WOOLF'S RENAISSANCE

# Virginia Woolf's Renaissance

Woman Reader or Common Reader?

Juliet Dusinberre

University of Iowa Press, Iowa City

For Bill

*and for*

David Ellerton 1975–95

*Resurgat*

# Contents

# Acknowledgements

I have in the course of writing this book incurred formidable debts to both institutions and individuals. I would like to thank the British Academy for giving me one of its first assignments of Short Research Leave, which enabled me to double a period of study leave from Girton College. The generosity of both institutions enabled me to complete the work. Without the support of Girton College over a long period the project could not have been undertaken or finished. I also acknowledge with gratitude its financial help towards publication expenses.

I would like to thank Frances Gandy and the Girton College Library, and in particular the archivist, Kate Perry, for making material relating to Virginia Woolf's visit to the College in 1928 available to me. My thanks are also due to Cambridge University Library, to the British Library Manuscript Division, to Helen Bickerstaffe in the Manuscript section of the University of Sussex Library, and to the staff of the Henry W. and Albert A. Berg Collection of English and American Literature in the New York Public Library.

Chapter 2 appeared in a slightly different form under the title 'Virginia Woolf and Montaigne' in *Textual Practice*, 5:2 (1991): 219–41, and is printed here with acknowledgements to the editors, then Terence Hawkes, and now Alan Sinfield. The anonymous Readers for the Journal gave me my first real backing for this venture. I am extremely grateful to Terence Cave and Warren Boutcher for detailed and constructive criticism of the Montaigne work. Hero Chalmers and members of the Oxford University graduate seminar, 'Women, Text and History, 1500–1750', and James Shapiro and members of the graduate seminar at Columbia University, New York, all commented on earlier versions of the Montaigne chapter.

A number of the ideas in this book were tried out on James Simpson and Anne Fernihough, whose interest and encouragement sustained me throughout, and who gave specific advice on both the Montaigne and the Pepys chapters. Jill Jondorf kindly suggested modifications and corrections to my translations of Madame de Sévigné's *Lettres* in Chapter 4. Some aspects of my work on Sir

John Harington have been discussed at graduate seminars at the Universities of Kent, Sussex and Cambridge, and at the International Shakespeare Conference at the Shakespeare Institute in Stratford-upon-Avon in August 1992. I am grateful to Sally Greene, Chair of the 1994 MLA Session on 'Virginia Woolf and the Renaissance', who brought to my attention Pauline Scott's unpublished paper – delivered at that session – on Virginia Woolf's *Orlando* and Ariosto's *Orlando Furioso*.

Chapter 6 is a revised version of 'Bunyan and Virginia Woolf: A History and a Language of Their Own', published in *Bunyan Studies* 5 (Autumn, 1994): 15–46, and my warm thanks are due to W. R. Owens and Stuart Sim for expert editing. I would also like to thank Arthur Kinney for advice on this chapter. Any infelicities and errors which remain are my own.

All quotations from the Holograph Reading Notes are published by the kind permission of Quentin Bell and Angelica Garnett, the Society of Authors and the Woolf Estate, and from the Curator and Trustees of the Henry W. and Albert A. Berg Collection, the New York Public Library, Astor, Lenox and Tilden Foundations. Quotations from the Monks House Papers in the Manuscript section at the University of Sussex Library are also printed with the permission of Quentin and Angelica Bell, the Society of Authors and the Woolf Estate. Excerpts from *The Diary of Virginia Woolf*, Volume Three: 1925–1930, edited by Anne Olivier Bell, copyright © 1980 by Quentin Bell and Angelica Garnett, *The Diary of Virginia Woolf*, Volume Five: 1936–1941, edited by Anne Olivier Bell, copyright © 1984 by Quentin Bell and Angelica Garnett, and from *The Letters of Virginia Woolf*, Volume I: 1888–1912, edited by Joanne Trautmann and Nigel Nicolson, copyright © 1975 by Quentin Bell and Angelica Garnett, are reprinted by kind permission of Quentin and Angelica Garnett and the Woolf estate, Chatto & Windus Ltd, and Harcourt Brace & Company.

I would like to thank Edward and Martin Dusinberre for unfailing interest, support and goading, particularly in 1994–5. Without William Dusinberre I could not have written any books, for women readers or anyone else. His scrupulous criticism, unstinting generosity and faith in the end product has sustained me throughout the work. To all the common readers – friends, relations, students, colleagues, scholars, members of adult classes, women and men – who have contributed in innumerable ways to my awareness of traditions of reading and writing, I offer this book with affection and gratitude.

Juliet Dusinberre
Girton College, Cambridge

# Abbreviations

## MANUSCRIPT COLLECTIONS

Berg    *Holograph Reading Notes, Henry W. and Albert A. Berg Collection, the New York Public Library*

MHP    *Monks House Papers, University of Sussex Library, Manuscript Section*

## By VIRGINIA WOOLF:

CR I    *The Common Reader: First Series*
CR II   *The Common Reader: Second Series*
O       *Orlando*
PA      *A Passionate Apprentice: The Early Journals 1897–1909*
RO      *A Room of One's Own*
TG      *Three Guineas*

## By JOHN BUNYAN:

GA      Bunyan, *Grace Aboundingy*
PP      Bunyan, *The Pilgrim's Progress*

## By SIR JOHN HARINGTON:

OF      Ariosto, *Orlando Furioso*, translated by Sir John Harington

## JOURNALS:

JEGP    *Journal of English and Germanic Philology*
MLQ     *Modern Language Quarterly*
MLR     *Modern Language Review*
NLH     *New Literary History*
N&Q     *Notes & Queries*

PQ      *Philological Quarterly*
PMLA    *Proceedings of the Modern Language Association*
SB      *Studies in Bibliography*
SEL     *Studies in English Literature*

# 1

# Virginia Woolf's Renaissance: Amateurs and Professionals

## WOMEN AND LITERARY TRADITION

The single most dramatic departure in literary studies in the last three decades of the twentieth century has been the recovery of women as readers and as writers. Literary studies in the late twentieth century have been characterised by women's awareness of themselves not as surrogate male readers, but as *women* readers. Virginia Woolf's *A Room of One's Own*, first published in 1929, with its insistence on the conditions which have governed women's relation to the written word, and its impassioned plea for a rewriting of history and culture along the female line, now looks like a prophetic foreshadowing of late twentieth-century feminist activity.[1] Its sequel, *Three Guineas* (1938), written under the shadow of encroaching war in Europe – a much more virulent attack on patriarchy as the catalyst to the Second World War – proposes a banding together of outsiders, men and women, against the dominant culture of their time. These two works grew from long meditations on the relation of women to culture, which were in evidence from the outset of Woolf's writing career as a journalist in the first decade of the twentieth century, through the publication of the two volumes of *The Common Reader* (in 1925 and 1932). Virginia Woolf always wanted to remap for women the whole male-dominated territory of literary culture.

Woolf was extraordinarily daring and unusual for her time in making her assumptions about culture explicit. She stated that she used the past for a purpose, as an empowering model for herself as woman writer,[2] and particularly as a writer not of fiction but of criticism and literary history. Her conviction that the history of language determined the history of writing and reading; her realisation of the significance of the printing press – fascinating to her in her own role as printer – in creating new readers; her insistence that great writers emerge from webs of

culture created by readers, writers, education, patrons; her recognition that the body has been ignored in the search for the
mind; all these concerns make her critical enterprise crucial for
women readers.

Woolf's real confrontation with the male literary establishment
took place when she thought of herself not as a novelist but as
a literary critic. Born to the purple as the daughter of Leslie
Stephen, one of the most eminent and respected of Victorian men
of letters, she constituted herself from early on in life as a cultural dissident, a woman who might be described as one of the
'disaffected participants in the literary tradition'.[3] As critic she
was forced to confront her lack of formal education, her amateur status as a 'lady' writer in a world of professional men, the
prejudices implicit in the gender constructions of her time, and
the absence of any established tradition of female literary scholarship. She combated that disabling awareness with a defiant belief
that all that was needed was pen and paper, personal courage
and formal inventiveness. After all, 'for ten and sixpence one
can buy paper enough to write all the plays of Shakespeare – if
one has a mind that way.'[4] But she knew that traditions empower as well as disable, and that women could not hope to be
great writers without the subsoil of ordinary – or 'obscure' –
talent which nurtures the exceptional: 'The extraordinary woman
depends on the ordinary woman.'[5] Throughout her entire career
as a writer Woolf searched diligently for cultural ancestors, men
and women who might constitute an alternative tradition to which
both she and other women writers, past and future, might belong.

In the two volumes of *The Common Reader*, Virginia Woolf identified the emergence of women as readers and writers. When she
looked back at her *Common Reader* essays in the late thirties she
expressed distaste for their urbanity and discursiveness – what
she called her 'tea-table training'.[6] She felt that her anxiety to
establish herself as a literary critic in a man's world had caused
her to underplay her hand, and that only after *A Room of One's
Own* had she gained the courage to speak out about what she
was doing in her critical writing.[7] At her death in 1941, she was
working on a third volume of *The Common Reader* which she called
her 'Common History', a book which would trace women's relation to an oral tradition in the vernacular, which had been su-
perseded by the written word once the printing press was
established. Of this project two draft essays exist, entitled 'Anon'

and 'The Reader', which construct a cultural mythology, identifying a transition between the unnamed singer in the oral tradition – sometimes man and sometimes woman – and the named
writer and individualised reader of books in print. Women, in
Woolf's model of cultural history, were excised from the record
when writing took over from speaking and singing. This transition, which occurred gradually, was complete at some point during
the sixteenth century.[8] The projected work directed Woolf with
renewed intensity to a period she had always found particularly
congenial, the late English Renaissance, which she characterised
as a time of emerging voices, an emergent vernacular, and a new
sense of the past.

The sixteenth and seventeenth centuries represented for Virginia Woolf a key aspect of her revolt against the nineteenth
century. She discovered, by leap-frogging two centuries, writing
which was still malleable, as prose was shaped to new modes
for new readers. The novel was unborn, but its predecessors were
everywhere, in Montaigne's essays, in letters and diaries and
strange hybrid writings such as Sir Thomas Browne's *Religio Medici*
and Burton's *Anatomy of Melancholy*. The transition from manuscript to print culture, from oral utterance to written word, and
from public theatre to private reading, embodied for Virginia
Woolf her own need to reach behind the traditional models of
masculine education which dominated the literary world into
which she had been born. In September 1921 when the first *Common Reader* was beginning to germinate in her mind, she returned
eagerly to her writing after an enforced break, rejoicing in the
'recovery of the pen' which was both a repossession, and a re-
entry into vitality: 'Thus the hidden stream was given exit, & I
felt *reborn*' (*Diary*, 2. 134, my italics). The metaphor of rebirth,
*renaissance*, occurred to her as she embarked on the exhilarating
project of *The Common Reader*. The Renaissance had been a period
of unique rebirth of culture. In her own reading of sixteenth-
and seventeenth-century literature Virginia Woolf connected herself
with a life which included her own rebirth as writer and reader
through the recovery of female forebears.

The sense of rebirth was not just, of course, occasioned by
reading women writers. Woolf's critical project was always two-
fold: the reading by women of literature written by men, and
the discovery of women as writers and readers. Her own distinctive viewpoint was to inform all her writings on male authors,

so that received critical judgements, and with them accepted notions of how to write, became subjugated to an idiosyncratic renegotiation of the past through a woman's vision. Often, as in the cases of Montaigne and Donne, this process involved analysing the extent to which the male writer felt himself to be ill at ease with his own relation to culture, and particularly to the gender boundaries created by his own time. Montaigne and Donne occupy key positions at the beginning of the two volumes of *The Common Reader*. But when, in the late 1930s, Woolf contemplated the third volume, the 'Common History', she returned to the early modern period with an intensified awareness of the immense changes it had witnessed and created, and other writers surfaced in her mind as part of this process: Bunyan, Pepys, Madame de Sévigné. Writing after 1660, they are all chronologically too late to carry any credence as Renaissance writers, a term which has expired by 1625, with the end of James I's reign.

Joan Kelly-Gadol's celebrated question: 'Did Women have a Renaissance?' has usually been answered decisively in the negative. The Italian Renaissance affected a handful of well-born women, both in Italy, France, and, in the Elizabethan period, in England,[9] but the vast majority were unaffected by the rebirth of classical learning, as were also the vast majority of working men. But if the chronological boundaries of the Renaissance were to be redrawn to reach further into the seventeenth century, the picture might be very different. Most intellectual historians would hardly wish to talk about 'the Renaissance' as having any definable meaning as late as 1660. Yet in 1660, with the Restoration of that extremely un-Renaissance monarch, Charles II, Milton had still to write *Paradise Lost*, Bunyan had not yet composed *The Pilgrim's Progress*, Pepys's *Diary* had received only its first entries, and Dorothy Osborne's letters were just seven years old. These writings all bear witness to the new world brought into being by the multiple changes wrought in the sixteenth-century Renaissance in Northern Europe, itself a late manifestation of the expansion of learning and art witnessed in *quattrocento* Italy.

If one argues that women had no Renaissance, working men must join them in that exclusion. Bunyan's case offers a particularly striking possibility of revision: that for women and working men there is a much later 'Renaissance' discernible in the mid-seventeenth century in a sector of society whose members were initially untouched by the educational ferment of the earlier

period. The same revision affects many other writers, both men
and women, whose Renaissance defies traditional chronological
boundaries. Like Virginia Woolf, they also were reborn in the
life of the pen, even if it was a later manifestation of the rebirth
which animated Montaigne and Donne.

Virginia Woolf's Renaissance encompasses two different phenom-
ena: her affinity on many different levels with the early modern
period, and her own sense of being reborn through the creation
of an alternative tradition of reading and writing whose roots
go back to the Elizabethans and beyond. This book will explore
both aspects of her Renaissance. It spans her reading and writing about particular authors, and her identification of the areas
in which the late Renaissance period spoke to her own condition, not just as a modernist writer casting aside the traditions
of the nineteenth century, but as a woman writer, painfully aware
of the absence of a female literary tradition. In suggesting such
a tradition I shall, as Woolf herself does, carry the idea of a Renaissance into the late seventeenth century, so that the heirs of
Montaigne and Donne – male and female – can be seen as clearly
as the original writers. Montaigne's *Essays* were the single most
important force in suggesting new forms of thinking and writing which proved to be open to women writers, just as his original most devoted reader had been in fact a young woman, Marie
le Jars de Gournay. This is not, however, a study of literary influence, nor is it primarily a study of interaction between Woolf's
critical writings and her novels.[10] It engages with Woolf's theories about the relationship between different periods and different forms of writing, and how this affects the emergence of women
as readers and writers.

Woolf believed, as did T.S. Eliot, that writers need a tradition
and that tradition nourishes the individual talent. But what was
for him, in the famous essay 'Tradition and the Individual Talent',[11] a lucid interaction between the voices of the past and the
individual voice of the poet in the present, for Woolf was complicated by the fact that the voices of the past were predominantly male voices. This dilemma affected her not as a novelist
– as she was well aware of her many eminent female fore-
runners in that art – but as a literary critic and journalist. Her
solitariness in those roles, and the masculinist assumptions that
surrounded them, fired her to scrutinise the past for a tradition
which might belong to women. Locating women's exclusion from

dominant culture in the history of education, of language and of literary forms, Woolf turned to the sixteenth and seventeenth centuries as a time when 'professional' writers emerged at the expense of an 'amateur' tradition. For her one of the most difficult and ongoing struggles had always lain in the uneasy territory she herself occupied somewhere between amateurism and professionalism.

In her early twenties Virginia Woolf rebelled against the rigid boundaries between amateur and professional in her father, Leslie Stephen's, literary world. She claimed in *A Room of One's Own* that the first woman professional was the Restoration playwright, Aphra Behn: 'It is she – shady and amorous as she was – who makes it not quite fantastic for me to say to you tonight: Earn five hundred a year by your wits'.[12] But although the earning of money always remained intensely important to her as testimony of her own professional standing, she queried the terms of male professionalism. Her discontent was fuelled by her perception that Montaigne and a number of Elizabethans writers did not recognise the rigid division between amateur and professional – and its concomitant relegating of women to a leisure class – which went virtually unquestioned in her own world.

Woolf's career as a writer demonstrates a dilemma which has dogged women throughout the twentieth century as they gain access to various forms of professional life. The standard orthodoxy of a patriarchal society has been that the professional and the private must be kept separate; Shakespeare's Antony wreaks destruction on himself and his supporters when he allows his passion for Cleopatra to invade the sphere of public duty. The public world has historically belonged to men, and their success in it has usually depended on the degree to which women, as symbols of personal life, have been excluded from that public domain. When male educators in Renaissance Italy undertook the tuition of aristocratic women, they did not envisage their pupils' entry into a public sphere of activity, such as would have constituted an appropriate climax to the Humanist education of young men.[13] Renaissance women themselves recognised that their choice lay between the reclusive solitary life of a scholar, and domestic roles.[14] In neither activity had they any access to a public arena of their own. Elizabeth I, one of the few women who did have such access, negotiated her own special charter of rights as a woman ruler, which depended on a cunning manipulation of her anomalous position as a woman who nevertheless wielded supreme power in a patriarchal society.

When Virginia Woolf was born in 1882 a very small number of women had gained entry to a higher education which had been for centuries available to their male relatives, although not, of course, to working men, nor to those who did not conform to the Church of England. The subsequent slow but sure entry of women into the male-dominated professions – medicine, law, politics, the universities – Woolf observed during her life. She knew from her reading how much was owed to pioneering Victorians such as Octavia Hill and Sophia Jex-Blake, among many others. Her cousin Katherine Stephen became Principal of Newnham College, Cambridge. Her first reviewing and journalism was undertaken for Margaret Lyttelton, editor of the clerical journal, *The Guardian*. Her own doctor was a woman, Elinor Rendel. The sacrifices of personal life demanded by women in the professions were everywhere apparent. It was unthinkable that a married woman, let alone a woman with children, could continue in her chosen career. The public sphere continued to exact a price from women which it did not exact from men, that it must be entered at the expense of domesticity, a word which in its semantic root contains the concept of being confined to the home.

Yet for writers this is a complex rather than a simple distinction. Writing has often been done at home, by men as well as women. Many men have pursued careers not related to the literary works for which they are renowned: from Sir Philip Sidney, diplomat and soldier, to John Donne, Dean of St Paul's, to Keats, medical student, Trollope, civil servant, and in Woolf's own circle, T.S. Eliot, bank clerk, a position from which his friends released him through their own financial subsidy so that he could concentrate on writing poetry. In these cases, the opposition between professional and amateur becomes confused. What is a professional writer, if such a person is paid to do another kind of activity? Sidney, and Donne after him, would both have scorned the notion of writing for money as the debasing activity of the hack, the attitude which the Elizabethan Orlando takes, in Virginia Woolf's novel, towards Nick Greene, a second-rate playwright, and which she herself took to his late Victorian counterpart, Sir Edmund Gosse. Yet Woolf's claim in *A Room of One's Own* that 'Money dignifies what is frivolous if unpaid for' (*RO*, p. 65) is a modern one which Renaissance men would not have understood.

Woolf's uneasiness with the professional label never deserted her. On the one hand she coveted professionalism; on the other she felt threatened and repelled by it. She said of her friend Molly Hamilton, Labour MP for Blackburn: 'Odd to me that life should require "professional women"' (*Diary*, 2. 35). In January 1931 Virginia Woolf was asked to talk to the London/National Society for Women's Service about her professional experiences. This request provoked in her two contradictory impulses. The first was to deny that she had professional experiences: 'It is true I am a woman; it is true I am employed; but what professional experiences have I had? It is difficult to say.' The second was to see herself as part of a tradition of professionals: 'For the road was cut many years ago – by Fanny Burney, by Aphra Behn, by Harriet Martineau, by Jane Austen, by George Eliot – many famous women, and many more unknown and forgotten, have been before me, making the path smooth, and regulating my steps.'[15] Her self-deprecating tone is belied by the energetic language of John the Baptist. But she immediately undercuts her own pride in women's professionalism. She told her female audience that when she received a cheque for 'one pound seven and sixpence'[16] for her first review, she spent it not 'upon bread and butter, rent, shoes and stockings, or butcher's bills', but on buying a beautiful Persian cat.[17] She knows that the cat spells amateurishness, because she doesn't need the money in order to live. She plays at being professional, just as Montaigne plays at being amateur. That ludic disregard for the insignia of professionalism is part of a pioneer spirit shared by her listeners, the Co-operative Guild women: 'You call out, as the old and established societies at Westminster and Oxford and Cambridge cannot call all those sympathies which, in literature, are stimulated by the explorers who set out in crazy cockle shells to discover new lands, and found new civilisations. And your enterprise is not 'in literature'; it is in being—an enterprise which makes it less easy to describe with the fluency of a flowing pen, but far more interesting.'[18] At fifteen she had been fascinated by Hakluyt, the Elizabethan traveller: 'I used to read & dream of those obscure adventurers and no doubt practised their style in my copy books' (*Diary*, 3. 271); later those explorations seemed to her to symbolise in Montaigne and Sir Thomas Browne voyages into the life of the mind.[19] Women have to renegotiate the relation between writing and living.

The only professional experience Virginia Woolf would admit to was the celebrated 'killing the Angel in the House', – the ritual slaughter of the lady who 'sacrificed herself daily'. This lady advised Virginia Woolf to flatter and deceive and never to 'let anybody guess that you have a mind of your own. Above all, be pure'. Woolf kills this phantom, although 'she was always creeping back when I thought I had despatched her. . . . Killing the Angel in the House was part of the occupation of a woman writer'. For all women writers the phantoms remain. She exhorted her audience: 'You have won rooms of your own in the house hitherto exclusively owned by men. . . . But this freedom is only a beginning. The room is your own, but it is still bare.'[20] The murderous impulse is resuscitated in contemporary feminism in Hélène Cixous's 'The Laugh of Medusa': 'We must kill the false woman who is preventing the live one from breathing.'[21] The professional experience marries writing and being.

Many of Virginia Woolf's early experiments with professional literary criticism show her adopting a male voice, but as she became more confident she discarded the surrogate male reading, and looked instead for a road into past writing which would belong to women. She urged them to read for themselves, to make the book into a room of their own. Her way into an alternative tradition highlighted the extent to which many male writers themselves contravened the accepted norms of professional life. Behind the playfulness, the Persian cat and the serious statement about literature and being, lies a conviction that it is not enough to pretend to male professionalism. One must set out in one's cockle-shell in quest of an alternative vision. Many male writers in the early modern period were themselves adventurers on those seas – Montaigne, Donne, Sir John Harington, and later Bunyan and Pepys, as well as women like Lady Anne Clifford, a great business-woman and landowner for whom reading was a part of living. As Woolf progressed from early reviewer to literary critic, she became convinced that the key moment of change for women occurred during the Elizabethan period. The vitality of the Elizabethan past nourished for her the pioneer energy of the present.

When Virginia Woolf immersed herself in Elizabethan writing she perceived the fluid boundaries between the amateur and the professional, and the different values associated with them. Her brother Thoby gave her the essays of Montaigne in 1903 (in partnership with Bacon's *Essays*) as a twenty-first birthday present. Montaigne always constructs himself as amateur writer in a world of professionals, doodling away in his tower while others pursue serious business.[22] What does he write about? That least respectable of literary subjects, himself and his vagaries. Even the form he invented,[23] the *'essai'* – a trial – reeks of amateurism and impermanence. The ideal reader he hoped to find turned out to be a young woman who would also be caught up in the confusion surrounding women and serious study: Marie de Gournay, the future editor of the essays, ridiculed by her contemporaries for excessive erudition.

Some women might in that earlier period have been able to read books with less awareness of the inhibiting fact of womanhood than Virginia Woolf experienced in the twentieth century. As she gathered together books to take with her to the country in the summer of 1903, Virginia tried out her own imitation of Montaigne in a little sketch called 'The Country in London'. As she packs her books, she exclaims: 'What right have I, a woman, to read all these things that men have done?'[24] It was not a question which Lady Anne Clifford, three hundred years earlier, had felt obliged to ask herself, as Virginia Woolf recognised when she constituted Lady Anne as a representative woman reader both in the essay on Donne in the second volume of *The Common Reader*, and in her notes for the projected 'Common History': 'A great heiress, infected with all the passion of her age for lands and houses, busied with all the cares of wealth and property, she still read good English books as naturally as she ate good beef and mutton.' Not French, because her father would not allow her to learn any language but her own vernacular. 'It is proof,' declares Virginia Woolf, 'of the respect in which reading was held that a girl of fashion should be able to read an old corrupt poet like Chaucer without feeling that she was making herself a target for ridicule as a blue-stocking'.[25] Marie de Gournay was not so fortunate, no doubt because she was not so wealthy and aristocratic.

Montaigne's extraordinary female reader, the woman who responded to the pleas voiced in his *Essays* that they would find for him a friend to replace his lost comrade Etienne de la Boétie, is curiously absent from Woolf's record, as though she sensed a resemblance too close for comfort between herself and the Frenchwoman. De Gournay lurks behind one of the most famous passages in *A Room of One's Own*, the portrait of Shakespeare's sister, Judith Shakespeare: 'She was not sent to school. She had no chance of learning grammar and logic, let alone of reading Horace and Virgil. She picked up a book now and then, one of her brother's perhaps, and read a few pages. But then her parents came in and told her to mend the stockings or mind the stew and not moon about with books and papers' (*RO*, p. 49). Like Shakespeare's imaginary sister, Marie de Gournay inhabited a world inhospitable to the talented woman. Her mother had no taste at all for a learned daughter, who in the solitude of the family estate at Gournay-sur-Aronde taught herself Latin – usually in the small hours – by comparing French and Latin texts. Later she was to acquire, like Virginia Woolf, a private teacher of Greek.[26] The talents and intellectual drive which would have been channelled and disciplined by competition and the companionship of like minds had Marie been a boy, exposed her, from childhood to old age, simultaneously to the excessive admiration of her contemporaries and to their ridicule of her eccentricity. The later of de Gournay's two short essays on women, entitled *Grief Des Dames* (1626), is an impassioned outburst against the scorn with which men greet any attempt at serious disputation from a woman: 'C'est une femme qui parle.'[27] What right has a woman . . .?

Nevertheless, despite Woolf's consciousness of the difficulties which women encountered in the early modern period, she returned to it throughout her writing life as a place where literary ancestors along the female line could be found. When she sketched, in the last few months before her suicide in March 1941, her plans for a new literary history which would map an alternative culture highlighting the interaction of women as readers and writers, the changes which took place in the sixteenth and seventeenth centuries struck her as crucial for women. Lady Anne Clifford reading to calm her soul in a hostile and combative male world, in a room in which texts were nailed to the wall, was, for Woolf, a female Montaigne (*CR II*, pp. 30–2). If she herself looked more like the eccentric bluestocking Marie de Gournay, there was one big difference. Woolf was not planning to edit Montaigne, but to allow him pride of place as the first named author in the book of essays entitled *The Common Reader* which was to establish her as a professional critic.

Virginia Woolf lifted the phrase 'the common reader' from Johnson's 'Life of Gray', quoting in the Preface to her first volume

Johnson's exact words: '"I rejoice to concur with the common reader; for by the common sense of readers, uncorrupted by literary prejudices, after all the refinements of subtilty and the dogmatism of learning, must be finally decided all claim to poetical honours."'[28] Johnson's meaning becomes clear if the sentence quoted by Woolf is viewed within the context of the whole essay on Gray, a man whom Johnson considers to be pedantic, vain and effeminate; as a poet 'he has a kind of strutting dignity, and is tall by walking on tiptoe'.[29] The only poem Johnson admires is the 'Elegy Written in a Country Churchyard', which generates emotions every reader can share. Johnson's common reader, apprehending through the heart rather than through the mind, perceives in the poem a merit which rests not on the rhetoric of learning, but on truth of feeling. Johnson creates an ideal reader who is both himself, the reader of his 'Life of Gray', and the common readers of the future, whose judgement will outlast that of the contemporary pedant. Whether these readers include women is not clear. The despised professionals are evidently men, because Johnson refers explicitly to Gray's standing as a university professor. The common reader is a judicious man-in-the-street.

In the Preface to *The Common Reader* Woolf redraws Johnson's portrait of the ideal reader in unflattering terms: 'The common reader, as Dr Johnson implies, differs from the critic and the scholar. He is worse educated, and nature has not gifted him so generously. He reads for his own pleasure rather than to impart knowledge or correct the opinions of others.' Johnson would already have dissented, as he thought the common reader well-educated, as Johnson himself was – hands smudged with Fleet Street ink - in the school of life. Woolf's reader lays no claim to either kind of education, but tries to construct some 'rickety and ramshackle' theory of art. His methods travesty professionalism: 'Hasty, inaccurate, and superficial, snatching now this poem, now that scrap of old furniture. . . . His deficiencies as a critic are too obvious to be pointed out.' However, observes Woolf, with an ironic smile, as the great Doctor has granted this nobody 'some say in the final distribution of poetical honours' (p. 1), he must be allowed his opinions. The male pronoun, 'he', masks the true identity of the new common reader. She is a woman.[30]

The gender transformation is clear in the original draft for the Preface, entitled 'Byron and Mr Briggs', which depicts a common reader of Byron's letters. Woolf analyses the act of reading in terms of the reader's trying to make sense of the whole, but breaks off abruptly: '"He", do we say? . . . In the colour of each judgment . . . in the shape of each sentence, in the tilt of the whole, it is obvious . . . that he is a woman.'[31] But in the final version Woolf disguised the reader's change of sex, which is instead disseminated throughout the whole volume of *The Common Reader*. The hasty and inaccurate reader is also the writer, Virginia Woolf. The concealed change was to determine every aspect of her literary criticism.[32]

T.S. Eliot declared in 1923 in an essay on 'The Function of Criticism', that 'criticism . . . must always profess an end in view, which, roughly speaking, appears to be the elucidation of works of art and the correction of taste'.[33] Dr Johnson and Woolf's father, Leslie Stephen, would both have agreed with him. But Woolf never wanted to speak with the single authoritative voice of the male world. At the end of 1924 she determined to dedicate *The Common Reader* to Strachey: 'And that's the last of my books to be dedicated, I think. What do we talk about? I wish I could write conversations' (*Diary*, 2. 326). The idea of the book as a dialogue between reader and writer remained with her from the earliest essays in *The Common Reader* to her last jottings, in 1941, on the 'Common History'.

On 30 November 1916, Virginia Woolf had published an unsigned article in the *Times Literary Supplement*, called 'Hours in a Library', a title which contained its own coded message, because Leslie Stephen had used it for his collected critical essays on English literature. Virginia Woolf's relation to her father's criticism was complex; she often admired his critical writing and shared some of his views.[34] But equally she was at war with his implicit assumptions about women and writing, most strongly in evidence in his essay on Charlotte Brontë whom he patronises for young ladyishness. The first volume of Stephen's *Hours in a Library*, published in 1874, opens with an essay on Defoe, which begins: 'According to the high authority of Charles Lamb, it has sometimes happened that. . . .'[35] Leslie Stephen begins with the high authority of Charles Lamb, and it might be that his daughter ought to begin with the high authority of Sir Leslie. Instead, she sets up an opposition in the opening paragraph between the ordinary reader and the learned man, between scholar and layman, amateur and professional:

A learned man is a sedentary, concentrated solitary enthusi-
ast, who searches through books to discover some particular
grain of truth upon which he has set his heart. If the passion
for reading conquers him, his gains dwindle and vanish between his fingers. A reader, on the other hand, must check the
desire for learning at the outset; if knowledge sticks to him
well and good, but to go in pursuit of it, to read on a system,
to become a specialist or an authority, is very apt to kill what
it suits us to consider the more humane passion for pure and
disinterested reading. (Essays, 2.55)

She reiterated this attack on authority in 'How Should One Read
a Book?', the concluding essay to *The Common Reader* Second Series:
'To admit authorities, however heavily furred and gowned, into
our libraries and let them tell us how to read, what to read,
what value to place upon what we read, is to destroy the spirit
of freedom which is the breath of those sanctuaries' (*CR II*,
p. 258). That note had already been sounded in her impassioned
outburst in *A Room of One's Own* against her exclusion from a
Cambridge College Library: 'Lock up your libraries if you like;
but there is no gate, no lock, no bolt that you can set upon the
freedom of my mind' (*RO*, p. 76). The echo of the Lady defying
Comus in Milton's masque gives Woolf's protest its intellectual
roots in the period she loved the best. She warns the reader against
relying on the critic, even such critics as Coleridge, Dryden and
Johnson: 'They can do nothing for us if we herd ourselves under
their authority and lie down like sheep in the shade of a hedge'
(*CR II*, p. 269). A woman reader does not start with high authorities, but *converses* with the writer, creating dialogues in the
place of an authoritarian discourse.

The more she delved into the writings of the past the more
Virginia Woolf became convinced that gender was the single most
significant factor in determining the reader's reaction to the words
on the page. She insisted that gender difference is culturally
determined, the product of history, education, upbringing, class.
The fact that many of her friends were homosexual or bisexual,
including the two closest, Lytton Strachey and Vita Sackville-
West, made her more acutely aware of the artificiality and tem-
porality of the conventions surrounding 'masculinity' and
'femininity'. But she also recognised, more than she has often
been credited with, that differences of class separate women from

other women more effectively than gender can divide them from men of the same class. Some of her deepest emotional, artistic and intellectual affinities were with male writers of the past who participated in her own consciousness of exclusion from dominant professional male culture.

In examining her own reading of some male writers and the sources of her sense of communion with them, Woolf discovered in the early modern period women writers whom she could bring to life by giving them readers. The lives and writings of the obscure remained a major part of *The Common Reader* enterprise, just as the recovery of 'Anon' animated the projected 'Common History', which she thought of as a third *Common Reader*. Women began to write in significant numbers in the seventeenth century. As she read their writings, Woolf considered the relation of tradition to the individual talent, but it was an alternative tradition in which talent had to struggle against prejudices which remained to a significant degree unchanged in her own time.

Virginia Woolf would not have accepted a division between the study of women writing and reading, to which she devoted so much time and energy, and women's revisionary reading of male-authored texts, which some feminist critics reject as a conservative attempt to render palatable to women readers the productions of patriarchy.[36] Her own difficulties and strivings for new directions were reflected in the writings of sixteenth- and seventeenth-century men as much, if not more, than in the writings of women.

This book discusses what Woolf was trying to achieve in her rewriting of literary history, and offers a critique of her whole project in the light of a reading of key writers and significant areas in her critical enterprise, sometimes considering writers she might have included but did not. Her mode of writing criticism and literary history, although illuminated in the late twentieth century by a number of feminist scholars, has never acquired credibility within a mainstream critical establishment. Her projected literary history consists only of a collection of sketches, but they extend and develop ideas present even in her earliest critical writing. There have been no serious attempts to consider the authenticity of her proposals for an alternative cultural tradition which would accommodate women both as writers and readers.

Virginia Woolf never pretends to be an Elizabethan. For her, the Elizabethans were moderns. As she reads them she pioneers a new critical voice, discussing those emergent literary forms – essays, letters, diaries – which could not readily be assimilated to models of high culture. In her search for common readers not educated in a male classsical tradition she recovers and creates women readers.

## THE PERSONAL AND THE PROFESSIONAL

Montaigne's fusion in his *Essays* of literature and being speaks to a dilemma which dogged Virginia Woolf's rebirth as a writer. In 1903, eight years after the death of her mother, she and her siblings knew that Leslie Stephen had cancer; another year passed before he died in February 1904. The summer of 1904 saw Virginia Woolf's second severe attack of mental illness, the first having followed her mother's death in 1895. It also witnessed the beginning of her career as a writer. The personal and the professional were from the start of her career inextricably intertwined.

In the 1903 diary which contains so much evidence of her imitations of Montaigne, Woolf elaborates on a newspaper report of a young woman's having drowned herself in the Serpentine, with a note attached to her clothing on which was written: '"No father, no mother, no work."'[37] Around this melancholy figure Woolf weaves her own narrative, of a middle-aged married woman whose husband has left her and whose children either die or desert her. The woman's thoughts turn again to the loss of her parents, hardly valued while she had them:

> That sorrow I say is bitter enough in youth with the world before one & its promise; but in middle age one knows that the loss is one that nothing can heal & no fresh tie renew. . . . If your father & mother die you have lost something that the longest life can never bring again. . . . There was one thing left which might make life endurable . . . & that was work. (p. 213)

Woolf is anxious not to sully her fictional character with pennypinching: 'I do not believe that she coupled this word with the sacred names of father & mother in any merely material sense – by work she meant bread & butter, but she also meant something nobler. She had learnt perhaps the self respect & purity that come from work, & the blessed peace with which it deadens sorrow.' No one gave the woman work, and, 'slipping off the weight that had been too much for her, she sank in the waters'. She is the first of Woolf's suicides.

Nearly forty years later Woolf saw her own work slipping away from her as she anticipated another war which would mean no more books and no more readers, and her answer was the same as the woman's in the newspaper report. But in 1903 her answer to loss was work. A desperate letter to Violet Dickinson, the last to be written in May 1904 before her madness, exclaims: 'Oh my Violet if you could only find me a great solid bit of work to do when I get back that will make me forget my own stupidity I should be so grateful. I *must* work.'[38] As she recovered from her second serious breakdown the idea of work was her lifeline.

Work was to be in Woolf's experience inseparable from personal loss. She thought of calling *To the Lighthouse* an 'elegy' and claimed that it had laid the ghosts of her parents. *The Waves* she wanted to dedicate to Thoby, who died of typhoid in 1906. *Jacob's Room* is written from the experience of Thoby's death; *The Voyage Out* dramatises the isolation she felt at Vanessa's marriage shortly afterwards. Her career as critic, journalist and polemical writer also took root in a period of personal disaster following her father's death. Her initial impulse towards professional writing was to embrace history and criticism: the kind of literary life which her father had himself led.

In October 1904, Leslie Stephen's biographer, Frederick Maitland, asked Virginia to write a note on her father to be incorporated into the biography. Encouragement in the enterprise came to her from Leslie Stephen's Quaker sister, Caroline Emilia, who offered her access to family records. Her aunt, always nicknamed 'Nun', 'has a very good hoard of diaries, of her own and her Mothers. Her Mothers are the most amusing and interesting. She kept records of all her children said and did from the time they were born till 1873' (*Letters*, 1. 146). The sources of family history were prolix: 'I have to go through 2 vols: of extracts from Father's and Mother's letters to each other. They are so private that Fred wont look at them himself, and I have to decide what he ought to see and possibly publish' (1. 148). The intermeshing of private and public created her first professional dilemma.

Virginia crossed swords a month later with Jack Hills, widower of her stepsister, Stella Duckworth, over the propriety of publishing private letters. He admonished her in 'an emphatic solicitorial letter' not to '"publish anything too intimate" etc. etc. etc. ending, however, that he knew my views were totally wrong, and he should dislike whatever I did."' Woolf retorted vehemently

> that I probably cared 10,000 times more for delicacy and re-
> serve where my own Father and Mother are concerned than
> he could; and declaring that anyhow if I made a selection, it
> was to be final. Then comes a letter of 8 sheets; all abuse of
> my principles of selection; ridiculing the idea that *I* should set
> myself up to judge what it was good for the world to know
> etc etc etc. and repeating as usual that whatever I did, was
> sure to be wrong. (*Letters*, 1. 151)

Her rage is both personal and professional, because Hills doubts her fitness for the task. Caroline Emilia Stephen championed her niece: 'Happily the Quaker has mounted her warhorse too, and strongly disapproves of the "very unintelligent behaviour" she calls it of Mr Jack Hills' (1. 152). Woolf's Note was ultimately printed in Maitland's biography as by 'one of his daughters'. The family diaries with the accounts of Leslie's childhood, the intimate letters, the quarrel over proprieties, the support of her aunt, all lead to an area in which Virginia Woolf is for the first time a professional writer.

Woolf's admiration for Maitland's working methods gave her a new concept of professionalism – 'He would read 4 volumes to write two words, and think nothing of it' – and a new inter-est in history: 'I am going to produce a real historical work this summer; for which I have solidly read and annotated 4 volumes of medieval English' (*Letters*, 1. 202). Her research into the let-ters and diaries of her own family made her aware of the pri-mary sources of history and of the role of the historian as interpreter of vast quantities of miscellaneous and forgotten records. Her immediate interest was stimulated by her own ex-periments in the teaching of history to young working women at the adult evening institute, Morley College.

## HISTORY OR FICTION?

Woolf was asked initially to teach literature at Morley College, but by the summer of 1905, when she was working with Maitland, she was teaching history classes: 'Tomorrow also is my working women, for whom I have been making out a vivid account of the battle of Hastings. I hope to make their flesh creep! Aint it ridiculous—teaching working women about the ancient Britons!' (*Letters*, 1. 191). Somebody (probably Maitland) had suggested to her that she might eventually write history (*Letters*, 1. 167–8). She approached the teaching of history with a new sense of professional vocation.

From the start Woolf was ill at ease with academic history. She was afraid of boring her Morley College pupils with the dryness of Greek history and relieved when 'they beg me to lecture steadily at English History next term "from the beginning"' (*PA*, p. 255). But history gave her a sense of being a professional not created by literature: 'I have got a ticket for Dr Williams Library across the square, and describe myself as a "journalist who wants to read history" and so I do feel a professional Lady'. Her method of teaching history came under fire from the Morley College authorities as too impressionistic. However, her report on her teaching shows her moving towards that radical redefinition of history to encompass women's lives which she would develop in *A Room of One's Own*. In 'Women and Fiction' she laments that the raw material for women's history 'lies at present locked in old diaries, stuffed away in old drawers, half-obliterated in the memories of the aged.... For very little is known about women. The history of England is the history of the male line, not of the female.'[39] Only when the daily conditions of women's lives were known, could the conditions of their writing, or lack of writing, be understood: 'The immense effect of environment and suggestion upon the mind, we in our psychoanalytical age are beginning to realize. Again, with memoirs and letters to help us, we are beginning to understand how abnormal is the effort needed to produce a work of art, and what shelter and what support the mind of the artist requires' (p. 45). These ideas were germinating in her mind in 1905 when she still thought she might become a historian.

Woolf wrote of her teaching method: 'I tried to make the real interest of history – as it appears to me – visible to them.... I do not know how many of the phantoms that passed through that dreary school room left any image of themselves upon the women; I used to ask myself how is it *possible* to make them feel the flesh & blood in these shadows? So thin is the present to them; must not the past remain a spectre always?'[40] The poverty of the present, the lack of a whole vision, made history seem like 'disconnected fragments . . . to people who have absolutely no power of receiving them as part of a whole, & applying them to their proper ends' (p. 204). Later she was to read the life of Mary Astell, the late seventeenth-century pioneer of women's education who complained vociferously that the history of men had no meaning for her as a woman. The search for a whole looks forward to the common (woman) reader's haphazard longing for a complete literary map.

Woolf's Morley College teaching gave her a vision of women trapped in silence, living lives for which there were no records. The collections of letters, memoirs and family diaries, and journal which she herself was engaged in writing in 1905, were foremost in her consciousness when she and Vanessa spent their holiday at Blo' Norton Hall in Norfolk in the summer of 1906. In Norfolk Woolf wrote one of her earliest surviving stories, the unpublished and untitled work, '[The Journal of Mistress Joan Martyn]'.[41] The story bears witness to her meditation on her own ambitions as a professional writer, which she contemplated realising in a new kind of history.

The story's heroine, Rosamond Merridew, recalls Woolf's cousin Rosamond Stephen, whom she described in the 'Warboys Diary' of 1899 as 'tinged strongly with the usual Stephen solidity & cumbersomeness; so that her attempts to be winsome & frolicsome are oddly & ludicrously out of harmony with her appearance' (*PA*, 149). Her heroine, Rosamond Merridew, shares both this mixture of jocose earnestness and Rosamond Stephen's interest in ecclesiastical history, noted by her niece when the family moved from Hyde Park Gate: 'A terrible stamping and screaming going on in the Studio announced Rosamond, who was tumbling books out of the shelves, & choosing ecclesiastical history' (*PA*, 245). In other times and other circumstances Rosamond Stephen, eccentric Victorian lady without a function, might have been metamorphosed into Rosamond Merridew, professional medieval scholar.

Woolf's Rosamond Merridew declares complacently that she is 'not absolutely unknown in one or two secluded rooms in Oxford & Cambridge'. She has exchanged 'a husband & a family & a house in which I may grow old for certain fragments of yellow parchment'.[42] Rosamond's recognition of her own transference of maternal passion to the offspring of her pen makes her enquire into aspects of history which other historians spurn:

> A sudden light upon the legs of Dame Elizabeth Partridge sends its beams over the whole state of England, to the King upon his throne; She wanted stockings! & no other need impresses you in quite the same way with the reality of mediaeval legs; & therefore with the reality of mediaeval bodies, & so, proceeding upward step by step, with the reality of mediaeval brains. (p. 241)

Rosamond encounters the criticism of her method meted out to Woolf by the Morley College authorities: digression and lack of source material: 'It is well known that the period I have chosen is more bare than any other of private records: unless you choose to draw all your inspiration from the Paston Letters you must be content to imagine merely, like any story teller. And that, I am told, is a useful art in its place; but it should be allowed to claim no relationship with the sterner art of the Historian' (p. 242). History must not be confused with fiction.

Rosamond is undaunted; she visits old houses, asking to look at family papers, and in this way comes across Martyn Hall, and the long-preserved diary of Mistress Joan Martyn. In doing so, she discovers in their owner an attitude to history the reverse of her own antiquarianism. For Mr Martyn the records of his family forebears are 'company': 'I often think I shouldn't know how to pass the time, if it weren't for my relations.' Rosamond is quick to identify the contemporaneousness of this position: 'All generations seemed bathed in his mind in the same clear and equable light: it was not precisely the light of the present day, but it certainly was not what we commonly call the light of the past' (p. 250). The people of the past were as solid, as much flesh and blood, as he was himself. If challenged he would have claimed that 'the fact that they have been dead for four or five centuries makes no more difference to them, than the glass you place over a canvas changes the picture beneath it' (p. 251). Mr Martyn embodies Virginia Woolf's view that history must be fleshed out and the phantoms made real so that the barriers between past and present are rescinded. With this introduction, Rosamond opens the journal of Mistress Joan Martyn, and the rest of Woolf's story consists of that daily record.

The nature of time, and the contemporaneousness of narrative, underpin Joan's journal. Various discrepancies in dates are central to Woolf's vision of the story, as foreshadowed in Mr Martyn's refusal to accept that the past is separated and closed off from the present. Joan reads aloud to her mother from Lydgate's account of Helen of Troy in the poem called 'The Palace of Glass'. Joan thinks that her mother is like Helen, and Sir John, the priest, believes that the story is not of Troy but of Arthur and the knights of the Round Table. When Joan stops reading for lack of light, they all discuss the troubled state of the country, but Joan muses that 'for all I can see, we are not worse now than we have always been; and we in Norfolk today are much the same as we were in the days of Helen, wherever she may have lived. Was not Jane Moryson carried off on the eve of her wedding only last year?'. The reality of the story of Helen is not in doubt, even if the story 'is old; my mother says it happened long before her day; & these robbings & burnings are going on now' (p. 254). But when Joan goes to bed in her old, cold room, she pulls back the curtain in a new reverie: 'With my cheek leant upon the window pane I like to fancy that I am pressing as closely as can be upon the massy wall of time, which is for ever lifting & pulling & letting fresh spaces of life in upon us. May it be mine to taste the moment before it has spread itself over the rest of the world!' (p. 254). The tasting of the moment and the perception of the thin film which divides the present from the past, catapult the reader without warning into Woolf's famous attack in 'Modern Fiction' on the realist fiction of Bennett and Galsworthy: 'Life is not a series of gig lamps symmetrically arranged; life is a luminous halo, a semi-transparent envelope surrounding us from the beginning of consciousness to the end' (*CR I*, p. 150). Woolf's aesthetic is intimately connected in this early story with her own experiences as diarist. The everyday impressions, the arresting of the moment, and the record of dailiness are the stuff of diaries, as she was aware not only from her own journal, but from her lifelong fascination with Pepys. Virginia Woolf makes out of Joan's diary account of an ordinary mind on an ordinary day, a new kind of fiction.

Towards the end of the story Joan and her father discuss the importance of the diary both as a record of family history, and a guarantee of personal immortality. But Joan is filled with discontent: 'For, truly, there is nothing in the pale of my days that needs telling: & the record grows wearisome. And I thought as I went along in the sharp air of the winter morning, that if I ever write again it shall not be of Norfolk & myself, but of Knights & Ladies & adventures in strange lands' (p. 267). The ending of '[The Journal of Mistress Joan Martyn]' shows Woolf turning aside impatiently from Rosamond Merridew's antiquarian researches, into fictions which are by implication a more real form of history, as Philip Sidney declared in *An Apology for Poetry*. '[The Journal of Mistress Joan Martyn]' defies Morley College's disapproval of its author's 'unprofessional' methods of teaching history. Woolf uses the story to question the boundaries which divide professional and amateur, personal and public. It becomes a manifesto for her sense of an alternative history along the female line which more than twenty years later she would urge on the female students of Newnham and Girton. The diary, a form which is neither literature nor history, provides her with the long-sought-after source material.

## LITERATURE AND BEING: QUAKER INHERITANCE

One of the early champions of Woolf's movement into a professional world was the unlikely figure of her aunt Caroline Emelia Stephen. It is easy to underestimate the significance of Woolf's relationship with 'Nun' in her subsequent development as a writer because she often impatiently satirised her Quaker maiden aunt. Caroline Emelia Stephen was associated in Virginia Woolf's mind with the constraints of her convalescence after Leslie Stephen's death, when Woolf expressed her irritation at being excluded from the newly settled freedom of Gordon Square with outbursts against the restrictive somnolence and improving Victorianism of her aunt's Cambridge house. But as she became more confident and less self-absorbed, Virginia observed her aunt with increasing curiosity.

Virginia Woolf's version of Caroline Emelia Stephen's life in the obituary she wrote for her differs significantly from Quentin Bell's. Bell dismisses Caroline Emelia as an 'intelligent woman who fell, nevertheless, into the role of the imbecile Victorian female' who suffered an unhappy love affair and solaced herself in religion. According to Woolf 'Nun' lost her health in nothing so romantic, but in that Victorian female occupation of nursing her mother through a protracted final illness.[43] Woolf baulked at the 'respectful lamentations' demanded by obituary-writing, ex-postulating: 'If one could only say what one thinks, some good might come of it' (*Letters*, 1. 390). She had already uncompro-misingly said what she thought about her aunt in the early 'Warboys Diary' (1899) and in a number of letters. Her aunt's spirit would, however, prove tenacious, and haunt both *A Room of One's Own* (1929) and *Three Guineas* (1938).[44]

Caroline Emelia Stephen cherished Virginia's gradual progress into a professional world. She wanted her niece to fulfil her tal-ents in a worthy fashion.[45] Woolf wrote to Madge Vaughan – her first letter on Gordon Square writing paper – from her aunt's home in Cambridge:

> I got sat upon as usual by the Quaker—(who thinks it right to criticise her relations, and *never* to praise them) for 'journal-ism'—She thinks I am going to sell my soul for gold, which I should willingly do for gold enough, and wants me to write a solid historical work!! People do take themselves so seriously: she sits and twiddles her fingers all day long, but she exhorts me to realise the 'beauty of hard work' as she says profoundly (*Letters*, 1. 165).

Her exasperation and wounded vanity – she complained that the Quaker's tolerance was worse than criticism because she was incapable of enthusiasm – caused her momentarily to neglect the two books on Quakerism which made Caroline Emelia an author in her own right.[46] Woolf, mercurial and volatile, found the coolness and slow pace of Quakerism a curb on her spirit. She wanted to be a worker where her aunt seemed to epitomise the life of the Victorian lady with nothing better to do than grow fat eating marzipan. But real as these feelings were, they were not the whole story.

Caroline Emelia's advice to her niece to undertake serious writ-ing, perhaps history, did not go unheeded. Virginia sent Violet Dickinson a short piece in November 1904: 'The Quaker's words bear fruit; and I think I may as well send this to Mrs Lyttelton [editor of *The Guardian*] to show her the kind of thing I do' (*Let-ters*, 1. 154). Caroline Emelia was as capable as Virginia herself of observing that the Stephen family confined its education to males and that talented women must do what they could to find an outlet. As Woolf became less prickly and insecure about her writing she looked at her aunt's life with a more tolerant eye. The figure of her aunt, which she, like the young Quakers described in her obituary, sometimes found maternal, connected her with a past which belonged to women. Her claim in *A Room of One's Own* that women think back through their mothers[47] was in her own case more materially possible through her living Stephen aunt than through the powerfully mythologised mother who had died when she was only thirteen. When she looked at Caroline Emelia she found, not the tiresome Victorian guardian of propriety for a rebellious young woman, but a woman who had tried in her own way to break out of the constrictions of conventional Victorian womanhood.

During a visit to her aunt at Cambridge in 1906, when she was convalescing from her madness, Woolf described her long talks with 'Nun': 'The Quaker was charming and wise and humane, and less of an inspired prophetess than usual. . . . She dived into the ample recesses of her mind, and spun stories of her souls adventures and disasters; but she has swum through them all' (*Letters*, 1. 230). A letter to Madge Vaughan at about the same time is more expansive about her aunt:

We talked for some 9 hours; and she poured forth all her spiritual experiences, and then descended and became a very wise and witty old lady. I never knew anyone with such a collection of stories which all have some odd twist in them—natural or supernatural. All her life she has been listening to inner voices, and talking with spirits: and she is like a person who sees ghosts, or rather disembodied souls, instead of bodies. . . . She is a kind of modern prophetess. (1. 229)

Her niece observes that Caroline Emelia has created her own inner reality in defiance of the outer realities of other people. Inner voices at this moment were not so terrifying to Virginia as they would have been just after her madness, but she could hardly have forgotten that they described an experience she knew only too vividly. Caroline Emelia had written that 'unchanging inner realities must dominate outward'. The pursuit of the inner world creates the alternative vision on which Woolf herself would insist in her many attacks on Victorian realism. Her aunt 'had come to dwell apart, among "things which are unseen and eternal"'. The quotation is from Caroline Emelia's own work.[48] In June 1906

Woolf countered Madge Vaughan's complaint that her writing lacked heart: 'My only defence is that I write of things as I see them. . . . My present feeling is that this vague and dream like world, without love, or heart, or passion, or sex, is the world I really care about, and find interesting. For, though they are dreams to you, and I cant express them at all adequately, these things are perfectly real to me' (*Letters*, 1. 226). Her aunt in her religious vision attacked a materialist version of reality in terms easily transfered to the secular aesthetics of the novelist.

When Woolf declared in *A Room of One's Own* that 'a woman must have money and a room of her own if she is to write fiction' (p. 6), the aunt who left money is not a fiction, any more than is the cat which in 'Professions for Women' Woolf claims she bought with her first earnings. Both were sober history. In 1909 Caroline Emelia left her £2500. Her niece's letter to her brother-in-law Clive Bell ungraciously describes the will as disappointing, but this is a sop to the Bells' disappointment in Vanessa and Adrian's legacy each of £100, rather than a comment on the much larger one left to herself. The title, *A Room of One's Own*, she had used when writing to Madge Vaughan in Giggleswick, Yorkshire, from her aunt's house in Cambridge, proposing that on her next visit to the Vaughans she should stay in lodgings: 'I thought that 2 rooms of my own, would give me greater freedom' (1. 162).[49] Just before she left for Giggleswick she noted that the Stephen offspring were overdrawn because of her illness and that she didn't want Mrs Lyttelton's 'candid criticism; I want her cheque!' (*Letters*, 1. 154). A few days later she wrote exultantly that *The Guardian* editor had commissioned an article: 'I am too delighted to have a chance of turning an honest penny to mind what I do for it' (1. 155). The wish to make money was always central to her desire for work, whatever she might have felt – and written – about the ennobling character of work independent of its financial incentives.[50] She wrote proudly to her cousin Emma Vaughan: 'I am realising the ambition of our youth, and actually making money' (1. 180).

Virginia Woolf knew that writing for money did not always result in professional excellence. A year later, when she was more established as a journalist, she told Violet: 'I have had such a run of work as is not remembered for I cant say how many years; books from the Times, the Academy, the Guardian— it must be confessed that I write great nonsense, but you will understand that I have to make money to pay my bills. The Quaker wont see it; and talks with deep significance of *serious* work, not *pot boilers'* (1. 210). Caroline Emelia's legacy meant that she would not have to keep penny-pinching through reviewing, and in 1909, with that added financial security, she began her first novel, *The Voyage Out*. If its heroine was a young women brought up in the claustrophobic confines of a house owned by two Victorian maiden aunts, her creator had nevertheless, through the generosity of her Stephen maiden aunt, found the means to embark on her own voyage into the uncharted waters not of history, but of fiction.

When Virginia Woolf composed *A Room of One's Own* for a Cambridge audience, the Cambridge aunt with the gift for story-telling and turn for the supernatural returned to haunt her: 'When . . . one reads of a witch being ducked, of a woman possessed by devils, of a wise woman selling herbs . . . then I think we are on the track of a lost novelist. . . . Indeed, I would venture to guess that Anon, who wrote so many poems without signing them, was often a woman' (pp. 50–1). But she had also, in the manuscript draft for 'Women & Fiction' (the lecture given at Cambridge which would become *A Room of One's Own*) described herself and her role in terms of her own later creation of 'Anon':

I am not a lecturer – a professor. I am a writer a strolling
  *mendicant* peddlar, the sort of person who
went in the middle ages from village to village
selling [reels of] laces & coloured [ballads?]; who
gossiped with the women at the cottage doors.[51]

Caroline Emelia was part of a tradition she wanted to recover for women, of which she felt herself to be a descendant. Woolf remembered her aunt again in *Three Guineas* in the women prophets of the early Christian Church who had been the forerunners of the anonymous poets and singers who owned the oral tradition before the advent of the printing press. In September 1928 she wrote of her own gift in almost religious language, contrasting public and private, outer and inner reality, as her Quaker aunt, 'Nun', had done:

This has been a very animated summer: a summer lived almost too much in public. Often down here I have entered into a sanctuary; a nunnery; had a religious retreat; of great agony

once; & always some terror: so afraid one is of loneliness: of
seeing to the bottom of the vessel. That is one of the experiences I have had here in some Augusts; & got then to a consciousness of what I call 'reality': a thing I see before me;
something abstract; but residing in the downs or sky; beside
which nothing matters; in which I shall rest & continue to exist.
Reality I call it. (*Diary*, 3. 196)

In October 1928, just a month after writing this diary entry, Woolf
delivered at Cambridge the lecture on 'Women and Fiction' which,
in its later form as *A Room of One's Own*, acknowledged the extent of her aunt's influence on her own writing career. Caroline
Emelia Stephen's life and the timely legacy she left her niece
prompted Virginia Woolf to reassess her own professionalism,
in order to find a new way of reconciling writing and being.

During those intensely formative years between the death of
her mother in 1895, her stepsister in 1897, her father in 1904,
and her brother in 1906, Virginia Woolf questioned the ways in
which work might take her out of the prisonhouse of personal
loss. Quakers, with their strong tradition of social reform, do
not hold that practical life should or can be separated from spiritual
life. Woolf wrote to Violet Dickinson in December 1906 of her
new-found pleasure in housekeeping:

> I think it really ought to be just as good as writing, and I
> never see—as I argued the other day with Nessa—where the
> separation between the two comes in. At least if you must put
> books on one side and life on t'other, each is a poor and blood-
> less thing. But my theory is that they mix indistinguishably.
> (1. 272)

The intertwining of the humdrum with the creative was authorised
within Quaker thought and can be seen as clearly in Roger Fry's
instinct for craftsmanship in the establishment of the Omega
workshops as in Woolf's concern not only with the relation between the literary and the domestic, but between writing and
printing. Nearly twenty years later she expressed the same inte-
grating principle more confidently:

> Somehow the connection between life & literature must be made
> by women: & they so seldom do it right. There was Hussey

stalking beside me to the London Library (though I wished to be alone) & mincing out highly intelligent remarks beneath the horses noses, about seeing things like God & setting the cap on, & I so much rather she'd talk about her cat, her cook, or her weekly bills. But, of course, she didn't praise me. (*Diary*, 2. 184)

Her distaste for a professionalism bought at the price of women's special modes of entry into writing from their own history in language and culture, never deserted Virginia Woolf. Her own professionalism, hard-won, and always in some sense, provisional, challenged equally the literary world she had inherited from her father and the world of her Cambridge-educated friends.

## WOMEN AND PRINTING

On 27 November 1927 Virginia Woolf overheard a 'brighteyed young woman' announce that she wanted to become a printer: '"They say there's never been a woman printer; but I mean to be one"' (*Diary*, 2. 213). Virginia Woolf secured Marjorie Joad for the Hogarth Press, while preserving her own special position, as she believed, as first woman printer. Printing was then, as now, a male-dominated industry. But Woolf's pioneer activities as a woman printer had at least one Renaissance forerunner.

Most of the learned women of the Renaissance belonged to a Humanist traditon unsullied by contact with trade, but not all, as Merry E. Wiesner has demonstrated in the case of Jeanne Giunta who was a publisher in Lyon in the mid-sixteenth century. Giunta's writing combines a concern with trade with the wish to be re-membered by posterity, which is a hallmark of Humanist schol-arship. This curious mixed mode springs from the fact that printing 'brought together individuals who were artisans, entrepreneurs, and scholars'.[52] The printshop environment is fleshed out in Natalie Zemon Davis's description of the printed book in the early modern period as a 'carrier of relationships'. Davis denies that print de-stroyed oral culture, arguing that reading aloud gave people who read in groups subjects to talk about. The history of the printing of nursery rhymes, fairy tales and early children's books offers a prime example of her claim that 'artisans, tradesmen, and women composed themselves a few of the books they read'. She sketches a picture of the print-shop itself: 'I am thinking not merely of the discussion of copy among scholar-printers, authors, and editors, but of reading in snatches that could reach out to the journeymen and to the spouses and daughters helping to hang up the freshly printed sheets.'[53] This vignette portrays a world in which private and public, commercial and intellectual, marry. The commercial aspects of printing introduce into the allegedly pure world of male learning the practical and economic aspects of book production with which twentieth-century scholars have become reluctantly familiar.

Stephanie Jed has traced the history of a tradition in which Humanist learning is distanced from the commerce of book production. She distinguishes in fifteenth-century Florence between two different types of writing, characterised by different kinds of handwriting: the humanistic and the mercantile.[54] Humanist learning seemed able to create pure scholarship unsullied by the processes of production, or by its passage through the hands of different readers, where mercantile writing proclaimed its own practical provenance. The two could not be confused. The long survival of scribal manuscript culture in the seventeenth century evinces a distaste on behalf of its writers for dabbling in the book market. The same sense of literary and philosophical texts rising above the conditions of their own production is strong in British literary culture in the late eighteenth century. In his study of this phenomenon in the eighteenth century James Raven refers to the question put to the Free Debating Society of Birmingham in July 1774: '"Why is Trade and Commerce in a manner incompatible with polite literature?"'[55] The question could equally well have been asked in the Elizabethan period. But, as Elizabeth Eisenstein has pointed out, the activity of printing brought scholars and artisans into closer contact, diminishing the divide between the writer and the producer of the book. Nevertheless in public consciousness that division remains, so that in contemplating the Renaissance period historians are apt to assume that 'printing and Protestantism seem to go together naturally, as printing and the Renaissance do not'.[56] Is Tyndale a Humanist martyr for his learning, or a Protestant martyr for his dissemination of the vernacular Bible in print?

Print breaks down the writer's dependence on an exclusive known group of intimate readers, the kind of group in which both Donne and Harington circulated their manuscript poetry.

It was not just a group of like minds, but of people who shared an educational and social background.[57] Donne may have had a Catholic upbringing, Harington may always have played the part in Elizabeth I's court of court jester, and have sought in vain for office under James I, but both progressed from the university to Lincoln's Inn, and moved in the same circle, consisting of men in public life and educated aristocratic women. Ben Jonson, despite his superior classicism (Donne and Harington both identify themselves in upper-class mode as lazy scholars) was a working playwright from humble origins. By printing his works Jonson could nullify his own sense of exclusion from that charmed circle, which he both admired and envied, considering Donne the greatest poet of his time. Print bypasses those cliques of initiates, and offers a readership which may harbour a more broadly based group of unknown kindred spirits,[58] as Montaigne hoped when he sent his essays forth into the world, and as Bunyan also expected when he decided to print *The Pilgrim's Progress*. When Bunyan published his Second Part he claimed in his verse prologue that his 'Pilgrim' had found friends, both rich and poor in France, Flanders, Holland, Ireland, Scotland and New England.

The printed work does not declare the social class of its author, as sixteenth-century handwriting still did. When, in 1600, Sir John Harington sent a presentation copy of his *Orlando Furioso* to his mother-in-law, Lady Jane Rogers, he signed his name, as all of his class would have done, in Italic script, although his scribe copied the letter in secretary, the hand used for business transactions and often taught to women. By the mid-seventeenth century the established hand was a variant of the 'sweet Roman hand' used by Olivia – and successfully copied by her maid Maria in order to gull Malvolio in *Twelfth Night*. That itself may be a sign of the influence of print, that writing could no longer mirror class distinction once print produced a text not inscribed with the marks of its author's social background. This must also be a significant factor in the history of women's writing. Print is silent about the gender of the writer. But even more significantly the advent of print in the Renaissance opened the book to common readers, not just men-in-the-street, but also women.[59]

Another democratising element in the arrival of print lay in its necessitating cheaper writing materials, paper instead of parchment, which enabled the 'recording of more sermons, orations,

adages, and poems. It contributed greatly to the keeping of more
diaries, memoirs, copybooks, and notebooks'.[60] Sir John Harington's
father transcribed a large and valuable collection of Tudor poetry apparently for his own pleasure,[61] and his son continued to
keep family records in a haphazard and lively manner. Montaigne
stated that his father, very precise about his family records, re-
gretted never having kept a journal. This looks forward not only
to Pepys's *Diary* but to his love of maps, his insistence on the
keeping of Navy records, and his meticulousness about accounts,
public and private. Cheap paper made it possible for more private letters (as well as diaries) to be written, just as print enabled people to learn to read and write who had not before done
so, amongst whom must be numbered many women who had
learnt their own language but not Latin. Women from the first
were educated in practical matters for the management of house-
holds; when they first entered formal education, it was commercial rather than classical.[62] This did them no favours in the world
of male learning, which had a long history of rising above the
muddy waters of the book trade.

Into those waters Virginia Woolf energetically plunged when
she and Leonard Woolf bought, on 25 January 1915, her thirty-
third birthday, the printing press which marked the inception of
the Hogarth Press. Madness intervened, and the record of the
Press's life was resumed two years later. The afterlife of Virginia
Woolf within literary history and the history of the Bloomsbury
group has seen a virtually complete blotting-out of the Hogarth
Press, except as a polite, slightly eccentric hobby for Virginia,
and a means for Leonard to domineer over his employees, mostly
young men from public schools and Cambridge willing to tie
parcels under the Woolfs' aura. Most of the records of the Hogarth
Press were destroyed in the Blitz. But even the introduction to
the valuable *Checklist of the Hogarth Press* demonstrates the assumptions which have relegated the Hogarth Press to a footnote
on high culture, despite the fact that all Virginia Woolf's works
from 'The Mark on the Wall' (1917) onwards appeared under its
imprint. Mary Gaither writes:

> It sometimes happens that a small, independent publisher hold-
> ing to high and exacting standards of intellectual content and
> aesthetic form, with only a secondary concern for making a
> profit, earns a secure reputation for publishing books that voice

the foremost literary, social, and political ideas of the day, a reputation that may go beyond even that enjoyed by larger and older houses. Such publishers were Leonard and Virginia Woolf at the Hogarth Press.[63]

The high literary ideals must be separated from the compromising wish to make money. What has the stream of commerce to do with the stream of consciousness? Leonard Woolf, according to John Lehmann 'did in the end infect Virginia to a certain degree with his own attitude towards money'.[64] Lehmann joined the Press as an apprentice in 1931–2, graduated to manager, and in 1938 bought out Virginia's share in the partnership. Yet his statement bears no investigation. From the start Virginia Woolf was overjoyed by the money the Press brought her, and relished it as a commercially viable business.

In her biography of Fry Virginia Woolf juxtaposes with evident glee the business and artistic aspects of Fry's Omega enterprise. In the Fitzroy Square house where the Pre-Raphaelites had congregated,

Georgian and Victorian ghosts were routed. Two Post-Impressionist Titans were mounted over the doorway; and inside everything was bustle and confusion. There were bright chintzes designed by the young artists; there were painted tables and painted chairs; and there was Roger Fry himself escorting now Lady So-and-so, now a business man from Birmingham, round the rooms and doing his best to persuade them to buy.[65]

Money seems to sit more easily in the art world than in the literary one, perhaps because in painting there is no equivalent to the arrival of printing with its capacity for mass production. Of that mass production the true artist has always fought shy. But writers, while longing for huge sales, must – if they are part of a literary rather than a popular culture – covet wide readership and fame, and only incidentally enjoy the money which goes with them. Is it respectable to envy the millions earned by hack writers selling their novels in railway bookstalls? Not in circles where 'art' is supposed to be above commerce. This attitude has a long history in British culture, as James Raven has demonstrated. It is there, discernibly, in the separation between the Humanist and the mercantile in fifteenth-century Florence. But the distinction between learning and commerce, philosophy and the market-place, is muddied by the introduction of print, and the muddy waters are particularly evident when the writer is himself a printer, as was the case with Samuel Richardson in the eighteenth century.

Terry Eagleton has explored the intertwining in Richardson's life and work between business and literature: 'He remained more concerned with disciplining his apprentices than in discussing fine art.'[66] Eagleton argues that 'the relationship between master-printer and apprentices blurred any hard distinction between the domestic and the industrial' (p. 9). One is already in the territory between public and private which Merry Wiesner saw as the new ground from which women became articulate in sixteenth-century Lyon, making it possible for Jeanne Giunta to be a printer. For Eagleton Richardson's career represents a significant step in the feminising of culture. His joint role as printer and novelist makes him a natural forerunner of Virginia Woolf.

For Woolf the Hogarth Press mingled the creative and the commercial in precisely the manner spurned by Humanist high culture, and encouraged by the advent of print. That interaction between business and art, the book as an emanation of the spirit and a material object, fascinated and stimulated her. She had written in her *Diary*, eight years before her proud claim to Marjorie Joad that she herself was the first woman printer, a trenchant criticism of her friend Lytton Strachey and his clan:

> When I think of a Strachey, I think of someone infinitely cautious, elusive & unadventurous. To the common stock of our set they have added phrases, standards, & witticisms, but never any new departure; never an Omega, a Post Impressionist movement, nor even a country cottage, a Brunswick Square or a printing press.

Her own heritage is different: 'We Stephens' (and it is worth remembering how critical she was of the Stephen family: Rosamund, Dorothea, Caroline Emelia, her own father) 'yes, & even Clive, with all his faults, had the initiative, & the vitality to conceive and carry our wishes into effect because we wished too strongly to be chilled by ridicule or checked by difficulty' (*Diary*, 1. 236). For her the Hogarth Press ranked with Roger Fry's Omega workshop, as a bold new creative venture.

The idea of print, and Virginia Woolf's own operation as a printer, is as central to *The Common Reader* as the idea of the woman reader and writer. Vanessa Bell's dust-jacket for the book shows a woman reading with her hand curled round a pen. The design, the print, the material object of the book, is inseparable from its project in literary history of recovering women as readers and writers. As D.F. McKenzie has written: 'Every society rewrites its past, every reader rewrites its texts, and, if they have any continuing life at all, at some point every printer redesigns them.'[67] The remarkable fact about Virginia Woolf, often ignored in the determination to keep high culture unsullied by trade, is that she herself, through her role as printer, acknowledged that new ideas were inseparable from the medium through which they would reach new readers. She knew that when she printed her own works she was part of an alternative tradition in which outsiders from high culture – whether by choice or necessity – could speak with a free voice to readers beyond the pale of high culture.

Woolf's own journey was to be from high culture to trade, a voyage on which she embarked with mixed feelings. In a dismissive review (in 1906) of a book called *The Author's Progress* she had declared that 'all that goes to make a book successful independently of the book itself may be learnt in his pages' (*Essays*, 1. 116). *The Author's Progress* grows out of the unpalatable economic reality that books are sold as boots are sold. Read the book and you'll know all you need to know about what goes into making them, except how to write them. In her Morley College report she spoke of a young woman hack journalist who was 'a writing machine'; but as she herself entered professional journalism she encountered an environment in which the production of words bore little resemblance to the high art of literature: 'I had 2 proofs of Reviews this morning, which were very badly printed, so I was in need of your proof correcting book, which I have left at home' (*Letters*, 1. 169). She knew that book production could garble an author's work, as when she wrote to Violet to send her another copy of her work published under the pseudonym 'Antony Harte', 'as my copy is all wrongly bound, and numbered, and the same pages are repeated'. She finished her postcard in true Grub Street fashion: 'Dont cut a poor devil out whose trying to make a living by her pen' (*Letters*, 1. 175). They were both in the trade together. She complained of her article on 'Street Music' that 'Leo [Maxse] prints badly' (*PA*, p. 239). A couple of days later she noted: 'Wrote like the little Printers devil I am, all the morning at my Times review' (*PA*, p. 240). She began to savour production as the mark of a new kind of professionalism. When she says that she 'pegged away at my review' (p. 240), she sounds like Jo March, the journalist sister in Louisa May Alcott's *Little Women*.

Jo March was mannish, and the mannish tone of Virginia's injunction to Violet Dickinson not to cut her emphasises her Stephen professional lady's sense that trade is something which dirties the hands: a place for pot-boilers rather than serious writing. In her review of *The Author's Progress* she wrote: 'The root of the matter is that the confusion between art and trade must always be ugly' (*Essays*, 1. 115–16). However, this 'lady's' distaste for trade, which was no doubt congenial to the high Church readers of *The Guardian*, was not, for Woolf, the whole story. She relished her early brushes with trade and wrote to Lady Robert Cecil, herself secretly writing a novel: 'Now would you like some Grub Street Shop? You are in the trade too' (*Letters*, 1. 211). Woolf enjoyed the consciousness that in the world of *real* ladies her own position was nearer to that of a Grub Street hack than an aristocratic amateur. In *Orlando* she implied that blue blood was a distinct disadvantage in the profession of letters, a disadvantage she observed in Vita Sackville-West despite her admiration for her. She fought ladyishness by becoming immersed in the inky and sticky processes of printing and bookbinding.

From the start Woolf asked herself whether her printing press would be the activity of an amateur or a professional. On 9 October 1917 her cousin Emma Vaughan sent her her old bookbinding equipment and she recorded her first batch of printing: 'We took a proof of the first page of K[atherine]. M[ansfield].'s story, The Prelude. It looks very nice, set solid in the new type' (*Diary*, 1. 56). The next few months contain records of printing activities and of the problems related to finding assistants for the work. The Woolfs received both further machines and advice from a professional printer, who caused them some irritation: 'The truth is he takes us for amateurs, who needn't be treated seriously' (*Diary*, 1. 104). Woolf flounces out: 'These chilly half animate over-worked little creatures can't be taken seriously. They don't attach the same meaning to promises, even written & stamped promises, that we do' (*Diary*, 1. 102). Leonard and Virginia certainly had teething troubles with their printing, interspersed even in the early days with the intense satisfactions of mastering a new skill in a totally different tradition of activity.

The personal and the professional continue to jostle each other in the first volume of the *Diary*, as when Woolf records in her usual way the onset of menstruation, which she saluted, in keeping with the culture of well-bred young women, by lying down all day: 'Owing to the usual circumstances, I had to spend the day recumbent. However this is much mitigated by printing, which I do from my bed on the sloping table' (*Diary*, 1. 66). The recumbent lady with the female complaint is trumped by the tradeswoman.

As the Woolfs became more adept at printing, and their business flourished, Virginia set down some of the joys of her new contact with the trade. Her business concerns have a solidity, and their achievements a tangible material reality which was a welcome antidote to novel-writing. The sense of herself as a lady-novelist in an amateur tradition became less disabling when she could re-tool herself as a business woman with her hands dirtied by trade:

> Then, being at a low ebb with my book—the death of Septimus,—I begin to count myself a failure. Now the point of the Press is that it entirely prevents brooding, & gives me something solid to fall back on. Anyhow, if I can't write, I can make other people write: I can build up a business. (*Diary*, 2. 307–8)

She did encounter, especially from her sister Vanessa, criticisms which reminded her unpleasantly of the little printer's sense that they were amateurs who could not be taken seriously:

> Nessa & I quarrelled as nearly as we ever do quarrel now over the get up of Kew Gardens, both type & woodcuts; & she firmly refused to illustrate any more stories of mine under those conditions, & went so far as to doubt the value of the Hogarth Press altogether. An ordinary printer would do better in her opinion. This both stung & chilled me. Not that she was bitter or extreme; its her reason & control that give her blame its severity. Anyhow I left in rather a crumpled condition. (*Diary*, 1. 279)

It is hard not to feel the elder sister's jealousy of the younger in this quarrel, but also the old childish sense that Vanessa had access to exciting and exclusive materials which made her art more real. Virginia Woolf always tried to compete with her sister by means of a writer's paraphernalia of ink-pots and nibs, and perhaps felt some satisfaction in upstaging her with the sensational clutter of the Hogarth Press. She wrote in February 1926: 'The publishing season is about to begin. Nessa says Why don't you give it up? I say, because I enjoy it. Then I wonder, but do I?' (*Diary*, 3. 60). The irritating implication of her sister's suggestion that her printing is a hobby, pursued by amateurs, which can be abandoned at will, echoes the professional printer's scepticism.

Woolf believed that the manual labour of producing the book interacted with the mental labour of writing it: 'I enjoy my printing afternoons, & think it the sanest way of life—for if I were always writing, or merely recouping from writing, I should be like an inbreeding rabbit,—my progeny becoming weakly albinos.' (*Diary*, 2. 326–7). Earlier, housekeeping at Gordon Square had seemed to her to perform the same function. But she also observed that the printing press spelt control over the editors to whom she had been subject in the early years of her journalism.

With supreme practical intelligence Virginia Woolf recognised what many women have observed in more recent times, and which has resulted in the pioneering work of Virago and other women's presses, that control over the means of production was essential if women were to be free to say in their own way what they found important, as opposed to what men found important. Woolf wrote jubilantly in September 1925:

> How my handwriting goes down hill! Another sacrifice to the Hogarth Press. Yet what I owe the Hogarth Press is barely paid by the whole of my handwriting. Haven't I just written to Herbert Fisher refusing to do a book for the Home University Series on Post Victorian?—knowing that I can write a book, a better book, a book off my own bat, for the Press if I wish. To think of being battened down in the hold of those University dons fairly makes my blood run cold. Yet I'm the only woman in England free to write what I like. (*Diary*, 3. 42–3)

It was to be a hard-won freedom, wrested from the male establishment with blood, tears, sweat and toil.

On 8 October 1917, at the beginning of their Hogarth Press venture, Virginia and Leonard Woolf made an outing to London:

> We walked through Gough Sqre; Dr Johnson's house is a fine, very well kept place, not so shabby as I expected. A little square, folded in behind Chancery Lane, & given over to printing presses. This is the best part of London to look at—not I now think to live in. Carrying my manuscript to the Times I felt like a hack much in keeping. (*Diary*, 1. 56)

The ghost of Leslie Stephen seems to accompany her into Gough Square to look at Johnson's house. But how it has changed, he murmurs: it's a place for printing presses and journalistic hacks now, not for the cream of the critical world. And his daughter retorts: I belong here: I have a printing press of my own; my hands are dirty where yours were clean. I am a hack carrying my manuscript to the *Times Literary Supplement*; and I have a right in Johnson's square which he himself would have recognised, a man who was not a gentleman and whose hands were inky.

Dr Johnson's common reader was a man-in-the-street, whose natural judgement was capable of redressing the ivory-tower affectations of an academic world to which Johnson himself did not belong. This exclusion Woolf was proud to share with him, as she prepared for her own printing press the volumes of literary criticism which would prove her 'credentials' as a professional writer (*Diary*, 4. 77). If in her hands Johnson's common reader became a woman, so, as she strolled Gough Square, she might have seen herself as wresting from Johnson himself his mantle of authority.

In her diaries, as in her letters, Woolf tried to define a new relation between amateur and professional which would suit women. As she read the diarists, letter-writers and essayists of that most fluid of periods, the late northern European Renaissance, she observed that those forms of writing offered women new voices. She used her reading to fashion modes of expression which would make her a different kind of professional writer, who could reach out to a new audience, not common readers but women readers.

# 2

## Virginia Woolf and Montaigne: Them and Us

### A FEMALE GENRE

Virginia Woolf gave Montaigne the first single-author essay in the first volume of *The Common Reader*. Her fascination with the French writer had been evident in a very early review, printed in 1905, on 'The Decay of Essay-writing' – a title which infuriated her as a tame editorial version of her own choice, 'A Plague of Essays'. In it she laments the proliferation of printed matter brought about by the growth of literacy. In the greed for new forms, the essay emerges: 'It is true that it is at least as old as Montaigne, but we may count him the first of the moderns.'[1] Woolf attacks the essay form for encouraging egotism. The essayist exposes 'personal peculiarities' under 'the decent veil of print' (p. 26). When her jaundiced view of essays appeared in *The Common Reader* twenty years later, considerably expanded, the attack on personality was intensified: 'We are nauseated by the sight of trivial personalities decomposing in the eternity of print' (*CR I*, p. 217). The blame on the market is more forthright: 'To write weekly, to write daily, to write shortly, to write for busy people catching trains in the morning or for tired people coming home in the evening, is a heart-breaking task for men who know good writing from bad' (p. 219). Her discontent arises from her sense that her own writing is sometimes vitiated by being too personal.

One of the peculiarities for which Woolf castigated herself was her propensity for writing in 'images'. Her remedy on one occasion was to reach for the eighteenth-century essayist, David Hume, a philosopher much admired by Leslie Stephen[2]: 'I must somehow get Hume's Essays & purge myself' (*Diary*, 2. 56). Hume identifies the essay as a 'female' genre.

Hume contrasts the civilised intercourse of learning and sociability in the eighteenth century with the separation of the

40

'learned' and the 'conversable' which he associates with the seventeenth. The two worlds need to be conjoined by 'the fair sex'. Hume never doubts women's inferiority to men in both mental and physical strength. The proof of a civilised world is that men, despite their obvious superiority, defer to women where barbarians tyrannise over them. The presence of women elevates sociability amongst men.[3] In 'Of Essay-Writing' Hume observes that women 'of sense and education . . . are much better judges of all polite writing than men of the same degree of understanding'. They must not be deterred by 'the common ridicule that is levelled against learned ladies', and induced to abandon reading and study. Men, announces Hume encouragingly, respect the literary judgement of women – at least 'of such books as lie within the compass of their knowledge' (pp. 570–1). He would like women to increase that compass by wide reading. They would then be better qualified for their natural role as mediators of the ideal civilised union between society and the academy. Behind the veil of his own masculine language of the 'fair sex' Hume courts the woman reader, in a form of writing – that of the essay – which exemplifies the marriage of learning and sociability, in being approachable but improving, like a well-bred woman. Hume repudiates, as Leslie Stephen does later, the gender divisions of his own time, but in a language saturated with those divisions. Nevertheless, he is not writing about women for the male reader, but addressing himself palpably to women readers, to whom he believes the essay as a genre belongs.

When Woolf blamed the frivolity of the essay on the mass market, she knew that the form evoked the belle-lettriste lady-like ambience which she detested. She insisted in *The Common Reader* that, far from being a display of personality, 'the art of writing has for its backbone some fierce attachment to an idea' (p. 221). As she prepared her own book of essays she worried about falling prey to the habits of writing she condemned: 'Do I write essays about myself?' (*Diary*, 2. 248). She wanted to find a new method of composition: 'For plans, I have immediately to write a dialogue on Conrad' (*Diary*, 2. 259). The Conrad essay was an experiment which she hoped to replicate in *The Common Reader*, which consisted of literary criticism in the form of a conversation between a man and a woman: 'So I think a *trial* should be made' (*Diary*, 2. 261, my italics). The word is Montaigne's: an '*essai*', or 'trial'. The conversational form recalls Hume's claim that the essay makes the learned world 'conversable'. Woolf wanted to inject the text of male literary criticism with conversation, the oral rather than the written. The Conrad 'trial' fell flat, however. It seems to have suffered from the 'side-long' propensity for which she later condemned all her critical essays, for no one noticed its experimental nature. Resolving in future to be more 'definite and outspoken', Woolf lighted on the title which would remain with her; of 'The Common Reader'. The Conrad conversation became subsumed into a wider purpose both of rejecting the single authoritarian voice, and of acknowledging the significance of gender difference in the reader's response to the book.

During 1922 and 1923 Woolf's *Diary* shows her mulling over the project of *The Common Reader* while saturating herself with Montaigne's essays, which, as in the early diaries, she often imitates in the actual diary entries, referring to the operations of her 'soul', as the unconventional element which sits in judgement on the conventionalities of everyday social life (as she would do later in her own essay on Montaigne): 'Soul, you see, is framing all these judgments, & saying as she sits by the fire, this is not to my liking, this is second rate, this vulgar; this nice, sincere, & so on. And how should my soul know?' (*Diary*, 2. 236). At the end of 1923 she was 'doing Hardy, & Montaigne & the Greeks & the Elizabethans' (*Diary*, 2. 278). In January 1924 she reviewed the Cotton translation of Montaigne, which Thoby had given her in 1903, in preference to Florio's. She quoted Montaigne in French in both in the review and in *The Common Reader*, but the *Diary* suggests some fudging: 'Now, I must tackle my Montaigne quotations, since thats demanded by some Cockney in charge of the Supt' (*Diary*, 2. 287).[4] In preferring the translation to the original she was true to her own alternative tradition of women readers.

## THE ART OF READING

Montaigne's essays occupy a curious place in the educated culture of England in the late twentieth century. Most of the reading public has heard of them, and would be able to date their author within a hundred years. Most specialists in English literature have read one or two of them in John Florio's contemporary translation (1603), and could quote parts of 'Of Cannibals', even if only from the Appendix in Frank Kermode's classic Arden edition of *The Tempest*. The same scholars speak with reasonable authority about Montaigne's impact on late sixteenth-century writing and thinking, as most people could now speak about Freud, or Nietzsche, or Derrida. Such is the process of cultural dissemination. However, unlike Freud, or Nietzsche or Derrida, Montaigne is fairly near to being, for most specialists and for all the general reading public, a dead duck. No doubt Montaigne's works still live in France, but his French is for English readers a powerful deterrent to real familiarity. Even in translation the reader is daunted by the essayist's endless references to classical texts no one has read or wants to read, and very few people have even heard of. This situation was markedly different at the beginning of the twentieth century, when Virginia Woolf called him the first of the moderns and André Gide declared that the *Essays* spoke to him almost as if he had written them himself: 'So much have I made him my own ... it seems he is my very self. ... How many of his phrases, empty for others, are addressed to me quite specially.'[5] Virginia Woolf's opening paragraph on Montaigne conjures up a dizzying hall of mirrors: Montaigne gazing at a self-portrait of the King of Sicily, and demanding why the pen might not also create a self-portrait; and Woolf herself, as part of a crowd standing in front of that portrait and 'seeing their own faces reflected in it' (*CR I*, p. 58). Gide's communion with Montaigne – a Catholic conservative aristocrat reared in the classical culture of Renaissance Humanism – is surprising enough, but Woolf's is even more so, across barriers of gender.

Both writers could be said to read Montaigne from an urgent need to communicate the sense of a self at odds with its own time and culture. For Gide Montaigne is a friend, a sympathetic voice which speaks to the solitude of his emotional world. Woolf's recognition of Montaigne is more reserved: many people see their faces mirrored in his, but whether hers is one of them is never, in *The Common Reader* essay, quite clear. The depth of her relation to him emerges only from a perusal of her own writings on the art of reading.

In 'How Should One Read a Book' which concludes the second volume of *The Common Reader* (1932) Woolf presents her celebrated dictum that the reader must be the writer's 'fellow-worker and accomplice' (p. 259). In an earlier essay entitled 'Reading' Woolf sketches herself in the act of reading. Books become people longing to be heard, displaced by each new generation of male writers:

If I looked down at my book I could see Keats and Pope behind him, and then Dryden and Sir Thomas Browne – hosts of
them merging in the mass of Shakespeare, behind whom, if
one peered long enough, some shapes of men in pilgrims' dress
emerged, Chaucer perhaps, and again – who was it? some un-
couth poet scarcely able to syllable his words; and so they
died away.[6]

Woolf proceeds to the letters and records of the obscure, who
are always women, and are given their own essay in *The Common Reader* First Series where 'they shuffle, they preen, they
bridle. . . . The divine relief of communication will soon again
be theirs' ('The Lives of the Obscure', *CR I*, p. 107). 'Reading'
ends with Sir Thomas Browne, the English writer who in the
1640s saw his own face mirrored in Montaigne's. Readers and
writers have in 'Reading' become indistinct, uniting in the book.
The writer longs to *tell*, and thus to share the life of the reader.
Woolf herself reads as a writer who must communicate with
her own reader in a language which she shares with the male
writers of the past. In 'Reading' the book itself partakes of the
view from the window by which she reads it: the tennis game
in the garden is over, the light fades and the moths flutter, 'hanging
an inch or two above the yellow of the Evening Primroses, vi-
brating to a blur. It was, I supposed, nearly time to go into the
woods' (*Essays*, 3. 150). In closing her book Woolf opens for her
own reader another volume, from whose pages one of that line
of poets lingering in the garden, speaks to her:

> When through the old oak forest I am gone
> Let me not wander in a barren dream,
> But when I am consumed in the fire,
> Give me new phoenix wings to fly at my desire.[7]

The configuration, in Keats's sonnet 'On sitting down to read
King Lear once again', of reading, the work of art, the imagination, death, immortality and the individual consciousness, feeds
into Woolf's own essay on 'Reading' at the moment when she
seems not to be reading, but writing. Through the echoes of language Woolf declares the impossibility of constructing a tradition of writing and reading which excludes those male poets
shadowing each other in the garden. Both her novels and her

essays share an awareness of intertextuality, of language as a tissue of inherited discourses, which moves her beyond any simple definition of the feminist critic as recuperator of male writings.[8] She uses reading to write herself, 'to put herself into the text'. She could have written, as well as Hélène Cixous, that 'it's not to be feared that language conceals an invincible adversary, because it's the language of men and their grammar'.[9] Woolf believed with Cixous that a woman writer must remake the language of men in her own image.

Woolf's entry into Montaigne's text in her essay in *The Common Reader* suffers from a self-conscious complicity evident in her imitation of his manner. The result is a peculiarly distancing pastiche which leaves her reader sensible of some trickery. But when she writes in 'Reading' about her own mode of reading, then Woolf silently enlists Montaigne in the politics of discourse. Why does not Mrs Woolf stick to the point; talk about the book not the view from the window; stop reminiscing and digressing; stop fantasising about herself; control her reluctance to generalise? Why does she force the reader to wonder whether time is being wasted on the perusal of a discourse so rambling and self-indulgent, so lacking in structured argument or anything resembling scholarly evidence? Woolf, like Montaigne, writes as she would be read, against the grain of traditional male education and culture, reading, as he himself did, in order to inscribe herself in language.[10]

In the late twentieth century women readers might argue that feminist thought, in challenging a twentieth-century bourgeois humanist view of the autonomous human subject who controls meaning and discourse, must relegate Montaigne's *Essays* to the compost-heap of cultural archaeology. It is easy to equate modern bourgeois humanism with that rather different phenomemon, Renaissance Humanism,[11] and as a consequence to consider Montaigne's essays as relics of a period which uncompromisingly fostered the belief that a human self *could* be constructed and communicated. This tempting conflation of modern views of humanism with a sixteenth-century version of it misrepresents not only Montaigne's view of the human subject[12] but also that of many of his contemporaries. Nevertheless, the *Essays* exist within traditions of writing and thinking whose symbolic structures are predicated on the exclusion of women.[13] Montaigne's remarks about women in general are notoriously dismissive, inscribing the standard assumptions of his age about the 'otherness' of the woman through which the norms of maleness may be consti-tuted. Most of the time women, children, madmen and the com-mon people jostle each other in his *Essays* for precedence in credulity, ignorance and irrationality. At other times Montaigne observes that he himself is one of *'le vulgaire'*[14] and even, some-times, a child and a woman. But these more subtle perceptions of sameness do not inhibit him in his demonstrations of difference.

Why then read him? Virginia Woolf's answer is by no means simple. On the one hand, she doubts his enterprise: 'For beyond the difficulty of communicating oneself, there is the difficulty of being oneself. This soul, or life within us, by no means agrees with the life outside oneself' (*CR I*, p. 59). On the other, she sees it as a valid attempt to create a new space within language for a private world of human consciousness, which can accommodate gender difference. The woman reader has access to Montaigne's text because he testifies to division and fragmentation within the human psyche (hence Gide's comparison of him to Freud), rather than to an ideological commitment to the 'whole man' commonly associated with Renaissance Humanism. Woolf sug-gests that Montaigne's essays offer a psychological space which will harbour later women writers. As she perceived when she imitated him in her *Diary*, his (female) soul is constantly at odds with the ceremonies and conventions of a world perceived to be outside it, whose normative maleness it sharply interrogates.[15] Moreover the pervasive irony of Montaigne's text calls into ques-tion the stability of his own discourse. The indirectness of Montaigne's mode of writing thus mirrors that of Woolf herself, who, in a literary criticism sanctioned by a male literary estab-lishment, forces received literary traditions to declare their in-herent maleness. In refusing to accept as possible an ungendered practice of reading, Woolf redraws the tree of literary inherit-ance, proposing an alternative genealogy along the female line. The genesis of this tradition can, in her view, be discovered in works ostensibly inhospitable to women, of which one of the most notable instances is that of Montaigne's *Essays*.

In the two lectures later published as *A Room of One's Own* Virginia Woolf offered her reluctant women undergraduate au-dience a startling programme of new study in which women would no longer be invisible. Women were to write not only novels, but history, science, biography. They were to write it not on a male model, but on a female one, so that women readers might read not what the male world found interesting, but what they themselves perceived as the central concerns of living. In her critique of a male-dominated cultural history Woolf boldly challenges the entire realist empirical tradition on the grounds that the reality it describes is transparently of its own making.

The young women she addressed were not at all ready for that challenge. They did not perceive an attack on the realist tradition as relevant to a feminism which declared that they could be trained to write empirically just as effectively as men could, and could thus, as scholars, be indistinguishable from the male breed of scholar. They could not endorse what seemed on the face of it to be a conservative rather than a radical proposal, that women should rejoice in their difference from men. It sounded altogether too much like the segregation and inferiority they were fighting against. Those first female undergraduate audiences pigeon-holed Mrs Woolf as an upper-class lady of letters who patronised them and was not on their wavelength.[16] They did not recognise a sister in her, and it must be said that she did not recognise that blood relation with them either. As a woman who had never been to school because family money was spent on the public school and university education of brothers, she represented other women of her class, but she could not represent the plight of the majority of women in her society. The privileges she enjoyed – educated company, the privacy of her own room (even at Hyde Park Gate), sufficient inherited money to move out of the family home and set up house independently with her sister, masses of books, a private tutor in Greek – made her seem, to those women, and to many men and women subsequently, like the heroine of *The Cherry Orchard*, a creature whose suffering, if real, is rarefied. But in Woolf's distance from the educational establishment of her own age lies a clue to her easy entry into Montaigne's intellectual environment.

Walter J. Ong argues persuasively that the childhood learning of Latin in the Renaissance period, which coincided with the male child's removal from the home circle dominated by his mother, into the male world of school, represented a *rite de passage* from childhood to maturity. The study of Latin was seen as a process of toughening a child both mentally and physically – as its pedagogy was usually accompanied with flogging – in order that he might enter a masculine adult world. The teaching of rhetoric through disputation encouraged combative habits of mind which could later be fed into practical skills on the battlefield. Even in a peacetime environment the persuasive arts of rhetoric were part of a structure of competitive public display which the young male child learnt as soon as he entered school and which became as natural to him as breathing. The study of Latin, and to a lesser extent Greek, was inseparable from a masculinising of culture which determined the conceptual shape of adult life. The sequestration of girls from a Latin culture available to boys represented more than loss of educational opportunity. Debarring women from the learning of Latin and from the school environment automatically debarred them from the habits of mind which dominated mainstream culture.[17]

Virginia Woolf's resentment of her exclusion from her brothers' educational world, both at school and at Cambridge, always expressed itself in terms of an exclusion from Latin and Greek. Her determination to nullify that deprivation took the form of a rigorous programme of self-instruction and private lessons with her Greek tutor, Janet Case. But this access to private study did not satisfy her sense of disabling exclusion from the clash of minds in the classroom, which Ong believes to be a significant element in the formation of the competitive bias of Western culture. Woolf, formidably well-read in the classics – as can be seen from the essay in *The Common Reader* ironically entitled 'On Not Knowing Greek' – never ceased to devalue her own acquaintance with classical literature as amateurish. The essay 'On Not Knowing Greek' does not, in discrediting an alleged masculine superiority, neutralise the acid of inferiority which determines its title. Woolf feared, perhaps more than she admitted, the scorn of the educated male establishment of scholarship and literary criticism.

It would not be difficult to claim Montaigne for that scoffing world of educated men. In the essay 'Of Three Employments' Montaigne expresses a Jonsonian contempt for ladies' pretensions to learning: 'The learning that cannot penetrate their souls hangs still upon the tongue'. If women must vie with men in knowledge, they should confine themselves to poetry, a diversion proper for them: ''Tis a wanton, subtle, dissembling, and prating art, all pleasure and all show, like themselves' (IV. 226, 227). Learning belongs to a hierarchy of authority to which women and common people should submit, and from which they are properly excluded.

From the exclusion of women from the world of secular learning Montaigne moves to theology. The translators of the Bible into the vernacular devalue it for the ignorant. The Bible ought not to be a household book: 'Neither is it decent to see the Holy Book of the holy mysteries of our belief tumbled up and down a hall or a kitchen' ('Of Prayers', II. 219). Making it common will turn it into fiction. Moreoever, the translated Bible encourages presumption in its readers: 'The very women and children nowadays take upon them to lecture the oldest and most experienced men about the ecclesiastical laws' ('Of Prayers', II. 221). The world of Marie de Gournay's 'C'est une femme qui parle', is copiously represented in the *Essays* both she and Woolf so passionately admired.

Yet the stability of Montaigne's own stance in any dialogue, whether about the capacities of women, about religion, the relation of learning to wisdom, or even about himself, is extremely open to question, and his attitude to the vernacular is a case in point. Certainly, in the choice of the vernacular for the *Essays*, Montaigne could be seen as part of a widespread championing of the vernacular during the course of the sixteenth century – in the poets of the Pléiade, in Ramus's educational reforms, in vernacular translations of the Bible. The most famous works of More and Erasmus – *Utopia* and *The Praise of Folly* – were written in Latin, but they were well known in English translation by the middle of the sixteenth century. Montaigne declares himself a second-generation Humanist, who has moved on from his father's excessive veneration for the classics and consequent insistence on an impeccable Erasmian Latin education for his son. In the new enthusiasm for the vernacular in the latter part of the sixteenth century women were important as patrons: John Florio's translation of Montaigne is dedicated to Lucy, Countess of Bedford in language which explicitly invokes translation into the vernacular as a feminine literary form,[19] just as Montaigne himself was to translate Raimond de Sebonde's work with a female readership in mind.[20]

Nevertheless, the notion that the vernacular belonged historically to women, and should therefore be relegated to second place in the hierarchy of learning, died hard. Women had always been the guardians of a vernacular oral tradition of story-telling, ballads and singing.[21] Literature in the vernacular continued to be categorised by many Humanists as 'women's literature', whether its character was devotional or entertaining – Rabelais' *Gargantua and Pantagruel* or the despised medieval romance. Ramus's Scholastic detractors at the University of Paris declared that his works were of as little value as Rabelais' fictions. Moreover, despite Humanist educational ideals, the primacy of Latin within schools remained largely unchallenged, even if Ramist reforms dispensed with some of the aridities of Scholastic disputation.[22] The Learned Latin of the Humanist classroom involved a privileging of the written word, which belonged to an exclusively male educational environment. By contrast basic literacy in one's own native tongue remained, as in More's time, within the province of women in the home, who taught children to read their own language before they entered the male world of school in order to learn Latin. In Ong's view the learning of the vernacular throughout the sixteenth century represented for the male child a transitional stage which must be put away with the putting-away of childish things, among them the woman-dominated home environment. Sir Thomas More's attempts to make the home learned by teaching Latin to his wife and daughters remained part of a Utopian programme.

A comparable educational principle was adopted, however, in the impeccably old-fashioned Humanist household in which Michel de Montaigne was brought up. Montaigne's father decreed that the only language the infant Michel was to hear was Latin, and his mother and the servants were taught enough Latin that all communications with the child could be conducted in that language until he was old enough to have a resident tutor – a German who knew no native French. Latin, therefore, instead of being the language of initiation into adulthood, remained for Montaigne, throughout his life, the language of primary emotion associated with infancy. He observes in 'Of Repentance' that Latin was always more natural to him than French and that he understood it better. When, during Montaigne's adult life, his father fell into a sudden swoon, his son exclaimed impromptu in Latin, although he had not for many years spoken the language. When he was seven years old he read Ovid for fun in the original Latin in place of stories in his own language. He was sent to school in order to have the companionship of other children and the initiation process of leaving home, but this was not, as in most cases in his time, tied to the learning of Latin, but rather to the unlearning of that language and to the learning of his own vernacular, both of which were achieved at school.[23]

For Montaigne, therefore, the learning not of Latin but of the vernacular was associated with a *rite de passage* to adult life. The choice of the vernacular for the *Essays* represents a movement into a language world which has for the essayist a complex ambience within the range of attitudes available to him in his own culture. His remarks on the Bible and poetry, as well as on the female readership which he courts for his own writing, suggest that he considered the vernacular as the homeground of women rather than men. His own decision to write in French, when Latin was to him the more natural language of communication, is symptomatic of his ambivalence towards the masculine culture implicit in this period in the learning of school Latin. Latin, the language of Montaigne's nursery years, was never associated for him with the ritual floggings of school life and he retained throughout his life a horror of violence as a spur to learning, imitating instead his own father's pioneering gentleness with children.[24] The correction of error should be 'in the form of conference, and not of authority' ('Of the Art of Conferring', V. 37–8, 39). He disliked the competitive arena of disputation as the main mode of instruction: 'To make of a man's wit and words competitive parade is, in my opinion, very unbecoming a man of honour.' Nor can this dislike be interpreted simply as a conventional Humanist attack on the old-fashioned methods of Scholastic pedagogy. Ramus and other Humanist educators also came within the scope of Montaigne's disapproval.[25]

Montaigne projects his own reading of the classics as belonging to a private rather than a public world, to home and leisure rather than to the active public life for which Ramus (and, following him, Sidney in *An Apology for Poetry*) believed it trained a man. The learning of Latin meant, for the infant Montaigne, entry into the sphere of story-telling and the imagination, as, Ong argues, it also did for the young Lady Jane Grey, pupil of Roger Ascham. Lady Jane preferred to read Plato rather than to go hunting, where a comparable young man would have enhanced his manhood by doing both.[26] Montaigne, a dedicated horseman, certainly did both. But for the essayist the study of the classics did not automatically represent entry into the male adult world of action, any more than it did for the learned aristocratic women of Renaissance Italy, fostered but feared – as Marie de Gournay herself was – by Humanist educators.[27] Coaxed into a love of Latin through his father's gentle 'mothering' instruction (supplemented in infancy by a Latin-speaking mother and servants – what would one give for their comments on the arrangement?) Montaigne shared with Lady Jane Grey, with Marie de Gournay, and with Virginia Woolf a sense of the classical languages as gateway to fantasy, freedom, and individuality. For such women the classics presented a curious cultural cross-coding, of an educational empire belonging to men, but entered in clandestine fashion as an escape rather than as a discipline for adult life. They neither suffered from nor enjoyed the combativeness of group training in the classics.

## REJECTING AUTHORITY

The alternative values which Montaigne associated with a rejection of traditional Roman culture are nowhere clearer than in his views on male power politics and aggression. Like Virginia Woolf he witnessed a society in which the battles studied by the schoolboy as he conned his Caesar and learnt Roman ideals of heroism, were translated into a horrifying new reality. In some moods Montaigne could, just as well as Keith Douglas, have written 'Aristocrats':

> How can I live among this gentle
> obsolescent breed of heroes, and not weep?[28]

In 'Of the Recompenses of Honour' he attacks the concept of valour, 'that by which the strongest and most valiant have mastered the weaker' (II. 307), and likens the overvaluing of valour in a man to a similar overvaluing of chastity in a woman.[29] He loathed the structures by which society enforced power: 'I disrelish all dominion, whether active or passive' ('Of the Inconvenience of Greatness', V. 30), as fervently as Virginia Woolf or any of her friends could have done.

This dislike of authoritarianism extended to his attitude to books, and the use to which they were put in traditional education: 'A mere bookish learning is a poor, paltry learning.' A schoolboy would find him wanting in a schoolboy's learning, but the schoolboy would be floored by a challenge to 'natural understanding' ('Of the Institution of Children', I. 194, 182). It is tempting to say that Montaigne meant by this evasive phrase a characteristic which he shares with the women and common people who were busy throwing their Bibles round the kitchen and contradicting their betters. Quoting a long speech of Cicero's, Montaigne exclaims: 'Does not this man seem to speak of the condition of the ever-living and almighty God? Yet, as to the effect, a thousand little country-women have lived lives more equal, more sweet and constant than his' ('Apology for Raimond de Sebonde', III. 99). An artificial, learned and bookish eloquence is simply a means by which the ruling classes enforce their authority over the commons, and by which men assert their ascendancy over women. Montaigne repudiated the mastery implicit in a concept of professional training. No writer has ultimate authority even over his own works, which belong to the reader, both present and to come. Fortune allows us to discern felicities 'beyond the intention, but even without the knowledge of the workman'. A careful reader 'often discovers in other men's writings other perfections than the author himself either intended or perceived, a richer sense and more quaint expression' ('Various Events from the same Counsel', I. 154). Montaigne's choice of Fortune, the feminine pagan deity, in preference to the masculine hand of Providential casuistry, was challenged by the Papal censor in 1581. The essayist's attack on a too-easy access to the Bible in the vernacular was added to the essay 'Of Prayers' as part of a defence, offered to, and accepted by the authorities, of his invocation of Fortune. He excused his use of the word as a layman's reluctance to trespass on theological ground,[30] thus associating himself with the lay readers (male and female) of the vernacular Bible, whom he simultaneously attacks.

Montaigne as a reader always claims rights over the author's own text: 'I do turn over books; I do not study them. What I retain I no longer recognise as another's' ('Of Presumption', III. 348). Ben Jonson castigated such habits of reading as a form of plunder which led to 'raw, and undigested' writing: 'Such are all *Essayists*, even their Master Mountaigne.'[31] His jibe is that of the professional towards the amateur, the *common* reader of Virginia Woolf's Preface to the first *Common Reader*, running up some ramshackle building and calling it a theory of art. Jonson's scorn locates both Montaigne and the provisional form he writes in – the essay – in the hemisphere of the collegiate women in *Epicoene*, whose learning is all on the tongue and not in the soul. Montaigne, licensing his own free reading of other authors, liberates his own text in the service of his readers. The refusal either to claim or admit authority over the written word moves the essayist even in his own time, as Jonson seems to imply, into a woman's world.[32]

No one would have been quicker to recognise this shift than Woolf herself, who attacked the authority of critics as the death of liberty for the reader. But freedom to read is equally freedom to write.[33] When John Gross in *The Rise and Fall of the English Man of Letters* (1969) defined Woolf's criticism as a 'brilliant circular flight' leading nowhere,[34] he might have been describing Montaigne's manner of writing.

In the structure of his *Essays* Montaigne defies Ramus's principles of pedagogy, in which logical divisions are constructed and an argument pursued to its conclusion. His writing is 'an irregular and perpetual motion, without model and without aim' ('Of Experience', V. 254), which rejoices in its own lack of direction: 'Other men's thoughts are ever wandering abroad, if they will but see it; they are still going forward.... For my part I circulate in myself' ('Of Presumption', III. 357). The linear progress of the Ramists, based on a formal male schoolroom pedagogy of logic and rhetoric, is totally alien to him.

Woolf's mode of writing is, according to this way of thinking, a feminine one. But what was in Montaigne's period recognised as Ramist 'method', has, by the time it reaches the twentieth century, been transferred to mental qualities. A man can observe the rules of logical argument better than a woman, because his mind, not his education, is constructed that way. Montaigne was perfectly cognisant of a fact already lost to Woolf's society, that logic and linear progress are the artificial constructs of male education. The circular method is related to an oral mode: to telling, rather than to writing down. As Ong has pointed out, it is extremely hard to memorise a prolonged scientific analysis. Montaigne saw no reason why a circular manner of proceeding should not be as valuable as a linear and logical progression, nor why it should not be equally the property of the male mind. Interestingly, this covert argument which Montaigne conducts with the foremost French rhetorician of his time is in the twentieth century still at the heart of French feminist thought, as exemplified in the works of Hélène Cixous and Luce Irigaray.[35]

Virginia Woolf hated lecturing because she felt it was an authoritarian male mode of discourse.[36] She would have hated it even more if she could have heard the reading out loud of articles about to be published which in the late twentieth century has virtually replaced genuine oral presentation. Linear logical written argument is too dense to translate well into a discourse spoken to an audience. The late twentieth-century emphasis on the publishing of lectures and papers has virtually killed a form of writing in which the accents of the spoken voice could be heard. Montaigne's writing belongs self-confessedly to an oral tradition of using the vernacular. 'The things I say are better than those I write', he observes in 'Of Quick or Slow Speech' (I. 50), an essay which explores writing as a form of speaking in preference to the different kinds of speech promised in its title. He enlists the vernacular as a spoken communication between equals, as was instantly recognised by those he would hardly, if challenged, have designated his equals: Marie de Gournay, and her twentieth-century counterpart, Virginia Woolf. Woolf discerned in Montaigne's speaking voice the potential for new forms of writing in which the voices of hitherto silent women would begin to be heard.

When, in *A Room of One's Own*, Virginia Woolf requested a feminine sentence in place of the Johnsonian period which she offers as a paradigm of the masculine, she invoked as her feminine model Jane Austen, who never went to school or studied the classics. It is easier to understand this celebrated – or indeed notorious – demand within the context of the cultural status of Latin, which remained virtually unchanged for people of her class from the sixteenth to the twentieth centuries. Woolf wrote in *Three Guineas*, as Marie de Gournay could equally have written in the last quarter of the sixteenth century, that 'culture for the great majority of educated men's daughters must still be that which is acquired outside the sacred gates, in public libraries or in private libraries, whose doors by some unaccountable oversight have been left unlocked. It must still, in the year 1938, largely consist in reading and writing our own tongue.'[37] When the study of English literature took on formal status in the nineteenth century it belonged to the dispossessed: women, working men, dissenters. Dr Kennedy of Latin Primer fame declared that he had not time to teach English at Shrewsbury and that furthermore it would whittle away his classical empire to do so. In *A Room of One's Own* Virginia Woolf correctly identifies the Johnsonian period as an attempt to give the vernacular, for those who had no access to the classics, the status of a classical language. Becky Sharp's impudent rejection in *Vanity Fair* of the great Doctor's Dictionary as a parting present (reluctantly rendered) from Miss Pinkerton's Academy for Young Ladies, says volumes about her repudiation not just of male culture, but of the watered-down version of it served up for women. From the early days of the newly founded Oxford English School in the 1890s the problem was to attract male students.[38] There were – and still are – far more women than men wanting to read English Literature at university. Some of those indignant female listeners to Woolf's lecture in 1928 felt that she was trying to instruct them in literary matters on which they were more expert than she. The vernacular invites egalitarianism, as anyone involved in the teaching of English literature may perceive. Indeed, it would be possible to see the specialised discourses of literary criticism in the academy of the late twentieth century as an historically continuous attempt to elevate the study of literature in the vernacular above the motley multitude to whom it has traditionally belonged: women, the working class, children and madmen, what Montaigne would have called *le vulgaire*.

Woolf delicately satirises Montaigne's attitude to *le vulgaire*, which is as ambivalent as her own. Patrician as he is, and deeply versed in the classics, he nevertheless continually constitutes himself, from his introductory preface onwards, as a writer not worthy of the reader's serious attention.[39] The *humilitas* topos of the practised rhetorician, which Montaigne himself scorns as 'a certain sort of crafty humility that springs from presumption' ('Of the Resemblance of Children to Fathers', III. 138), was to become peculiarly the province of women writers. In the poem 'Salve Deus Rex Judaeorum' (1611) the Jacobean poet Aemilia Lanyer laments her lack of formal education:

> Not that I learning to my selfe assume,
> Or that I would compare with any man:
>> But as they are Scholars, and by Art do write,
>> So Nature yeelds my Soule a sad delight.[40]

Where for men the figure is purely rhetorical, for women it expresses genuine lack of confidence at entering male territory. Lanyer's protestation of inadequacy provides her with the reassurance which enables her to write. However, Montaigne's own writing suggests a sense of the psychological release inherent in the *humilitas* topos. He speaks of a lack of confidence attendant

on his social and intellectual isolation – a condition Marie de
Gournay, as also Woolf herself, would have recognised. For all
his easily-documented relegation of women to second-class citi-
zenry mentally, intellectually and socially, Montaigne often wonders
whether he does not belong with them in that second-class arena.
In the essay entitled 'Of the Art of Conferring' he demands why
a master of arts, well-versed in learning, does 'not captivate women
and ignoramuses, with admiration at the steadiness of his reasons and the beauty of his order?... Strip him of his gown, his
hood, and his Latin ... you will take him for one of us, or worse'
(V. 44). 'One of us' appears here to be, yes, *really*, one of *us*.
Women and ignoramuses, and Monsieur Mountaigne.[41]

## MONTAIGNE AND GENDER

This dilemma, of charting where he himself belongs within gender division, goes to the heart of Montaigne's project of self-
portraiture. On the one hand he defines himself traditionally as
a being whose maleness is identified by the exclusion of female-
ness: the woman's mental inferiority, her incapacity to provide a
man with the equal companionship offered by other men, the
feebleness of her emotional life, her irrationality. All these exclu-
sions belong to a long tradition of identifying as feminine all
those aspects of the human psyche which detract from man's
capacity to transcend bestiality. Those qualities which man is better
without belong to the 'other', a symbolic space named 'woman'
which is easily accommodated to actual women within society
and culture. That it need not be so accommodated, intelligent
men in this period are often aware, but they still have no language, other than that of banishing the woman within themselves,
to express the divided aspects of human nature which are enu-
merated within the symbolic dualism of gender.[42]

Humanism inherited from Aristotle, and ultimately from
Pythagoras, a system of binary oppositions which constructed
man on principles of gender division.[43] Montaigne largely underwrites these oppositions, but he repeatedly constitutes his own
place on that binary scale on the side traditionally allotted to
women. The basic dualisms of the philosophical tradition which
he perceived himself to have inherited could be set out in the
following way:

right/left
even/odd
man/woman
reason/fortune
knowledge/ignorance
soul/body
divine/human
universal/particular
authority/subjection
public/private
constancy/fickleness
design/haphazardness.

In all these dualities, the first-named quality is historically associated with the symbolic construction of man, a construction made possible by the exclusion of those characteristics printed second, which occupy a space which is called woman. Renaissance Humanists made further distinctions in rejecting Scholasticism, which they identified as oppositions between words and things, doctrine and experience, cleric and layman, professional and amateur. Montaigne has his own programme of oppositions, which derive from a general Humanist context, between rules and irregularity, society and solitude, valour and discretion, cruelty and gentleness, virtue (pain) and vice (pleasure). Montaigne's self-constitution, both symbolic, cultural and social, places him in an arena which his culture, deriving its assumptions from classical authority, defined as woman.

It would be possible to argue that Montaigne's noted jibes at women stem from a deep sense of sameness which he shares at a subconscious level with the woman reader. He expresses some arch awareness that his *Essays* will appeal to women: 'I am vexed that my Essays only serve the ladies for a common piece of furniture, and a piece for the hall; this chapter will make me part of the water-closet. I love to traffic with them a little in private; public conversation is without favour and without savour' ('Upon Some Verses of Virgil', IV. 263).[44] The sexual metaphor is unmistakable. Montaigne was too much man-of-the-world not to realise that the readership for vernacular writings, as Florio admits in the fulsome Preface to Lucy, Countess of Bedford, at the head of his translation of the *Essays*, was in large part female, and must be propitiated. Montaigne writes in the 'Apology for Raimond de

Sebonde' that his motive in translating Sebonde's original is that 'many people take a delight in reading it, and particularly the ladies, to whom we owe the most service' (III. 25). As a writer Montaigne courts intimacy, and in particular the intimacy of women: will they wrap a pat of butter in his essays and send it to market?

On a deeper level this flirtation with female readers masks his own profound, if barely conscious, sense of difference from the norms of masculinity as constructed by his own time. Herein lies the potential secret communication embraced by Gide, in the twentieth-century writer's anatomising of his own difference from the gender structures of his society. Montaigne's scrutiny of the gender divisions which determine the cultures in which men and women construct their individuality speaks equally to the homosexual Gide,[45] to Marie de Gournay, female intellectual in a world of male intellect, and to Virginia Woolf, a woman writer searching for a tradition of feminine discourse. Montaigne apprehends, in a way that few men of his time did, that gender is *constructed*: 'Women are not to blame at all, when they refuse the rules of life that are introduced into the world, forasmuch as the men make them without their help' ('Upon Some Verses of Virgil', IV. 273). This sentence Woolf copied into her Reading Notes on Montaigne.[46] Women may observe, as well as men, that such rules are arbitrary: the gift of Fortune not of Providence.

Montaigne's most important revisions of the dichotomies he inherited are concerned with the nature of reason, the relation between body and soul (which includes attitudes to sex and to creativity), notions of virtue and pleasure, the cultural evaluation of the public and private, and of the common and the élite. He does not, however, simply endorse divisions and decide to place himself on a different side from the conventional one. Rather he aims at collapsing and conflating areas which have traditionally been described as distinct, and it is within this context that his statement that 'males and females are cast in the same mould, and that, education and usage excepted, the difference is not great' ('Upon Some Verses of Virgil', IV. 337), ought to be read. (This statement heads Woolf's Reading Notes on Montaigne, Berg XXIII). In other words, Montaigne is not trying to annex women to a notion of man, as Burckhardt claimed for Italian Renaissance educationalists.[47] Instead, he unsettles the philosophical roots of all the mental structures which most Humanists, as well as most theologians, take for granted in this period.

The essayist's attitude to creativity is a case in point. His observation that good health lies at the heart of everything virtuous and creative in human life assigns spiritual values to the world not of form (associated in Aristotelian thought with the male) but of matter (associated with the female).[48] In 'Upon Some Verses of Virgil' Montaigne declares that 'our masters are to blame, that in searching out the courses of the extraordinary emotions of the soul, besides attributing it to a divine ecstasy, love, mental fierceness, poesy, rime, they have not also attributed a part to health: a boiling, vigorous, full and lazy health, such as formerly the verdure of youth and security, by fits, supplied one withal' (IV. 258). He repudiates the Platonism of some of his contemporaries in separating the soul from the body and insists on a vital interaction between the two.[49] Later readers may perceive the way in which these images of health describe, in an unbroken line from Montaigne's time to Woolf's, the upbringing and physical condition of young men rather than of young women. Montaigne's startling statement that the creative impulse is inseparable from good health, feeds into Woolf's picture of Shakespeare's sister in *A Room of One's Own*, and explains with sublime simplicity why women, bowed down by childbirth and attendant illnesses, have only begun to write in large numbers since they have had access not only to modern medicine but to the physical training which Emily Davies, pioneer of women's higher education, realised was inseparable from their mental advancement.[50]

The twentieth-century woman reader is bound to feel that Montaigne is thus more in touch than most writers of his time with the world women have traditionally inhabited in Western society. Until the beginning of the twentieth century, and beyond it for many women, women's lives have been dominated and circumscribed by the physical conditions of life, from which men of a certain class and education have always found some means to escape. The most notable example of such a calculation is the genius women can never aspire to, William Shakespeare. Having provided himself at the age of twenty-one with a wife eight years older than himself and three children under three, he wisely observed that progress implied departure from home. Montaigne, whose wife bore him seven children, six of whom died before the age of two, retained a male condescension, typical of many men in his period, towards his own partner. He never considered her capable of the ideal companionship he had enjoyed with his friend, La Boétie, although his association with Marie de Gournay did unsettle his scepticism about women's capacity for friend-ship. But if Madame de Montaigne remains in a traditional women's slot in her husband's mind, much as Lacan's female audience seem to inhabit a world of jibes and satire strangely separate from the tone of his professional enquiries into their exclusion from male thinking, the intensity of Montaigne's ob-servation of his own life and nature forced him to admit the fluidity and cultural relativity of his own gender construction.[51] In his mirror truth and falsehood often seem to look the same way, despite Montaigne's claim that he loathes lying.[52] Woolf's friends complained bitterly that her *Diary* was full of fictions about everyone she knew. She would have retorted with Montaigne: 'Que sçais-je?' For both writers, reason and realism belong to a world susceptible to control, causality, direction and design, but that world is a man-made fiction, and Montaigne would have endorsed the claim that 'man' in this compound is gender-distinctive.

Although Montaigne refused to admit the constraint of linear or causal order into his meditations, he also elsewhere denied that his essays were formless. He obviously thought long and hard about how the reader's attention is to be wooed and held. Part of the secret communication between writer and reader con-sists in the reader's ability to follow the erratic leaps of the writer's mind. This agility Virginia Woolf requires of her readers in the essay on 'Reading', which vividly illustrates Montaigne's mode of writing. Furthermore, the subtle connections between Montaigne's *Essays* suggest the method of the first volume of *The Common Reader*, where Woolf conducts a dialogue with the women reading and writing within her text, as well as with her own women readers. The essay on Montaigne which proposes the female soul guarding over and protecting the male writer from the conventions and ceremonies which will suffocate him and her, leads Woolf into her next essay, on the Duchess of Newcastle. This isolated female aristocrat, writing in her soli-tary tower to an uncomprehending and conventional male world, bodies forth in literal form the fantastical soul of the French es-sayist conjured up by Woolf in the previous essay. The Duchess's longing for recognition, her isolation and her gifts, seem the nearest that Woolf comes to creating her own silent sketch of the other face she saw in Montaigne's mirror, that of Marie de Gournay. This mode of introduction she borrowed from 'Of Presumption', where it ushers in Marie de Gournay. Montaigne talks about women's false modesty; about his (male) tendency to over-value Latin; the theologian's dislike of curiosity (the sin of Eve?); his (female) dilettantism with books; his (womanish) irresolution in the affairs of the world, and his lack of confidence; the question of whom he is writing for; his circularity; the futility of conventional education; and suddenly, his adopted daughter Marie de Gournay: ideal reader, a soul with whom to communicate.

But how is Montaigne to communicate with Woolf, not just a woman reader, but herself a writer? One answer might lie in a mode of writing Montaigne himself had on occasion scorned as feminine, that of poetry, which boys of seventeen relinquish in favour of philosophy as a mark of entry into a tough adult masculine world. Conveniently forgetting his contempt, Montaigne claims that his *Essays* more resemble poetry than prose: 'I love a poetic progress, by leaps and skips; 'tis an art, as Plato says, light, nimble, demoniac' ('Of Vanity', V. 146–7). Woolf always sought to deny her culture's distinction between poetry and prose, creating in her own writing a harmony between the two which she perceived in Montaigne.[53]

As Woolf, both reader and writer, meandered through Montaigne, trying to find a way to express and define a being which seemed at odds with the world about her, so Montaigne meandered through the authors of the ancient world in order to reconstitute a being he acknowledged as disconcertingly fluid. He felt himself to be tolerant among fanatics; anti-belligerent amidst a culture of heroes; private and solitary in a world where only monks and women wanted to live that way; fascinated by the body and its functions within an ethical structure which relegated both to the realm of the insignificant and debasing; sceptical of the efficacy of reason over the primal drives of human nature, in a moral climate privileging reason; extraordinary only in his knowledge of his own ordinariness; abdicating authority even in his own authorship; a man vowed to variety, change and inconstancy in a world where these qualities define the feminine.

A modern woman reader can hardly read Montaigne even as Woolf read him, as a writer out of tune with his time, celebrating disjunction, disarray, dissolution and disingenuousness, in a culture devoted to unity, order, solidity and truth. Such a reader, if competent to read Montaigne's French, is not going to be tossing the *Essays* round the kitchen, let alone wrapping pats of butter in loose pages of them or using them, as their author suggests, for lavatory paper. She could hardly stand the anecdotal aspects of his work, what Gide called his 'masses of chatter' (p. 75). Nor could she truly find in those works a secret message such as communicated itself to Gide across established gender divisions. Montaigne's nonconformity has, as Gide remarked, been rendered inoffensive by the passage of time. What care we that he uses the word Fortune instead of Providence? Who cares in the late twentieth century a tuppenny hang about either of them? But if on the other hand, women readers in the late twentieth century ask, how can one read a male writer of the past, then Virginia Woolf's dialogue with Montaigne opens, in a metaphor they both used for reading, various doors.

Woolf perceived in Montaigne's rewriting of some of the discourses of Humanist culture and education the relativity of all male standards of discourse within her own culture. If that revisionary process is itself a part of Humanism – and Rabelais, Erasmus and More could all attest to their own roles in it – Montaigne's is not contained within the license allowed by his own age. Montaigne, as he himself seems to have been aware, speaks from the heart of a space he has made for himself, in defiance of gender. This space bears no relation to a Humanist liberal programme for women's education, proposing that men and women have equal souls and capacities and are viewed with impartiality by God.

God's views on this matter did not interest Montaigne any more than they interested Virginia Woolf. What concerns him is himself. That self cannot speak from, cannot begin to exist within the gender divisions of culture as he has inherited it. It can only speak from a place of dissolution of those divisions. Virginia Woolf offered the fiction of Shakespeare's sister to women undergraduates in the 1920s as a symbol of that dissolution: 'My belief is that this poet who never wrote a word and was buried at the crossroads still lives. She lives in you and in me, and in many other women who are not here tonight, for they are washing up the dishes and putting the children to bed. But she lives; for great poets do not die; they are continuing presences; they need only the opportunity to walk among us in the flesh. This opportunity, as I think, it is now coming within your power to give her' (*RO*, pp. 111–12). Her audience gazed at her uncomprehendingly. What had they to do with women who washed dishes? Or, as Montaigne might have said, with *le vulgaire*? Had they not joined, through a coveted male education, the timeless and time-honoured company of the ungendered judicious, Johnson's *common* readers? Who wanted to be returned to some ramshackle amateur environment, in order to run up a rickety theory about women's relation to the world of male creativity? Who amongst them wanted to be down-graded as a *woman* reader? They didn't need Shakespeare's sister. Shakespeare himself would do. Perhaps. As Woolf, self-condemned for the sidelong, tea-table manner, pointed out, 'perhaps' is Montaigne's favourite word: 'Such words help one to muffle up opinions which it would be highly impolitic to speak outright.... One writes for a very few people, who understand' (*CR* I. 63). *Common* readers? *Le vulgaire*? Washers of dishes? Tillers of the soil? The lousy rabble? Men? Women? Children? My cat? Am *I* one of *them*? Que sçais-je?

# 3
# Virginia Woolf Reads
# John Donne

## UNDOING THE 'MASCULINE' JOHN DONNE

We have all grown tired of the 'masculine John Donne' and various attempts have been made to undo him, both as poet and person. Strangely, the chief loathing of his masculine *persona* comes from men. He sickens Stanley Fish, exasperates John Carey, and emerges from Thomas Docherty's less personal and more sympathetic analysis as troubled and neurotic.[1] It is not the old-fashioned Victorian question of a poet's life turning his readers against what he has written, as Donne's life seems to have been one of almost blameless virtue, also rather chilling for modern readers. His youthful love of women and plays can hardly raise a disapproving eyebrow in the modern world; his passionate attachment and imprudent marriage to the seventeen-year-old Anne More must seem entrancingly warm hearted in that period of frozen wedlock, where lock is as significant as wed; his exclusion from court, attempts to gain patronage, and final apotheosis amidst much conscience-searching into one of the most eloquent preachers who has ever graced the pulpit of St Paul's, all these events ought to arouse affection and admiration rather than contempt and dislike. But the fact is that Donne's poetry excites aversion in men – who continue to own Donne in a way that female critics and scholars do not – because its multiple voices challenge readers on that issue which has become in the late twentieth century the most sensitive of all except race, that of sexual identity and gender construction.

It is impossible to read anything Donne wrote without considering the differences between men and women, how those differences have been constituted historically, how they affect behaviour, particularly in the bedroom, but also, disconcertingly, when one is on one's knees before one's Maker, whether publicly or privately. Donne himself knew this and thrust those problems relentlessly in front of his own and his readers' noses, in defiance of tender sensibilities. That is especially difficult for male readers today when masculinity has become as problematic and dubious a concept as femininity. Who wants either label, unless strictly qualified by an awareness of the artificialities and *ersatz* attributes commonly assigned to both? Not to mention the brutal history of twentieth-century masculine behaviour from which any thinking man is eager to disassociate himself. Perhaps those sensibilities were less tender in Donne's own time, although research continues to uncover the extreme complexity of gender issues in Elizabethan and Jacobean England, so that all the old easy generalisations now have to be re-examined.

Donne, who appealed to the Victorians, did not offend his adherents in the way he appears to do today, if one is to credit G. H. Lewes, who effused in 1838 about 'honest John Donne—rough—hearty—pointed and sincere. . . . Donne was in every sense a *man*'.[2] Men could take it, is the implication, but they feared for women readers when faced with such strong stuff. The Victorian editor Grosart was in a fret about publishing the nineteenth Elegy 'To His Mistress on Going to Bed' as unsuitable for family reading, and Palgrave left a number of the *Songs and Sonets* out of the *Golden Treasury* perhaps for similar reasons.[3] Twentieth-century readers used to pounce on the nineteenth Elegy with the joy[4] which adolescents felt when *Lady Chatterley's Lover* made it possible finally to discover the facts of life if one had avoided doing rabbit in biology. But even the exhilarating outpouring of Elegy XIX has become in the twentieth century distrusted and suspicious, as offensive to men as it is, or men feel it ought to be, to women. C.S. Lewis found it in 1938 distressingly titillating and therefore pornographic, a category also invoked for the poem by Carey who finds Donne's poetic voice gloatingly sadistic.[5] To her great credit Joan Bennet took issue with Lewis on the question of what women like to read, suggesting that a woman might become tired of hearing male poets going on about snowy breasts and golden hair and that it might be more interesting 'to know what it feels like to be a man in love'.[6] Virginia Woolf agreed. She found the nineteenth Elegy wonderfully liberating:

Going to bed: a sensual one, about a woman's getting naked
  License my roaving hands, & let them go

O my America! my new-found-land,
My kingdom, . . .

(Berg, XIX)

The America lines surface in a brilliantly covert manner in 'The Elizabethan Lumber Room': 'Thus we find the whole of Elizabethan literature strewn with gold and silver; with talk of Guiana's rarities, and references to that America – "O my America! my new-found-land" – which was not merely a land on the map, but symbolised the unknown territories of the soul' (*CR I*, p. 43) – and the body, she might have added.

Sensuality itself is now so hedged round with the barbed wire of political correctness that it is not respectable for a man to take pleasure in the nineteenth Elegy any more than he can admit to enjoying Petruchio's antics in taming Kate. Why? Because these works can't remain in the study: they challenge readers at the rawest points in their own lives in a way which is supremely uncomfortable, and the consequent contempt and hatred is for the betrayal of the comfort which all readers expect when they open the *Collected Works* of a long-dead poet. We trust the anodyne of time miraculously to cool even the most heated passions of the past.

Donne's contemporaries may also, however, have experienced something of that discomfort. Donne himself recognised it. His anxiety about publishing his poetry, most of which remained in manuscript until after his death, and his eagerness to associate it with a youthful Jack Donne rather than a sober Dr Donne, saluted documents of unusual intimacy.[7] Their privacy was to some extent ensured by their difficulty, so that Ben Jonson claimed that they would perish for want of being understood, and Dryden sighed with relief that ladies would not like them. For whom, then, were those passionate effusions written? For men? Apparently not. Although they were passed in manuscript to Donne's male friends, as was the custom in the early seventeenth century, many of the poems were written to please women, in some cases in hope of the rewards of patronage, but perhaps also for less calculating reasons. Many of the surviving verse miscellanies of the period which contain individual poems by Donne belonged to women.

Donne's audience for poetry, as for his other talents, was by his own account in his letters painfully restricted to his domestic circle at Mitcham. The *Songs and Sonets* cry out to be read aloud, and it is not unduly fanciful to imagine that they were initially read aloud to Anne More. What did she think of them? She was not apparently the doormat figure some male critics have sketched, and contemporary research suggests that Walton's view of the 'curiously and plentifully educated'[8] young woman with whom Donne fell in love and to whom he remained devotedly attached throughout his life, may have been more capable of responding to his love poetry than is usually allowed to be the case. Ilona Bell argues convincingly that the three letters discovered by Logan Pearsall Smith in the Burley manuscripts were addressed to Anne More. In these letters Bell demonstrates Donne's use of 'the half-playful, half-pleading language of ardent love, packed (like his poetry) with all the innuendo and boldness of private under-standing, unabashed eroticism, and extreme intimacy', quoting in particular Donne's statement: '"All that part of this sommer which I spent in your presence you doubled the heat and I lived under the rage of a hott sonn and your eyes."' Bell relates the language of the letter to the language of 'Loves growth', argu-ing that both letter and poem offer a 'radical redefinition of love'.[9] The implications for the passionate nature of Anne More as hy-pothetical reader are self-evident. Bell points out that the romance challenged 'the patriarchal social structure on which all the country's laws were founded' (p. 44). Some of Donne's *Songs and Sonets* read like impatient reworkings of Spenser's *Amoretti*, sonnets which were themselves innovations in being addressed not to the poet's mistress, but to his wife.

It is plain from the verse letters that many of Donne's female readers – Lucy, Countess of Bedford, the Countess of Huntingdon, Magdalen Herbert – must have understood and liked his verse. Donne continues writing to them, and his verse letters assume familiarity with his other poetry. His funeral sermon on Magdalen Herbert suggests that he was considered part of the family.[10] The conditions of his life encouraged intimacy in writing, an intimacy as evident in his letters to his male friends as in his poetry. It is now generally accepted that Lucy, Countess of Bedford, wrote the 'Elegye on the Lady Markham' beginning 'Death be not proud', an expostulation much more famous from *Holy Son-net* X.[11] Grierson suggests in his revised edition of Donne's poems that Donne's celebrated opening may have imitated the Countess of Bedford's poem, rather than *vice versa*, although Lucy's poem was probably an answer to Donne's.[12] Certainly Donne is unusual in allowing in 'The Dampe' an image of himself as the female paper inscribed by the woman writer, when inscription is universally ascribed in this period to the male pen, in a sexualized writing metaphor.[13] This inversion is also present in the dedicatory poem, 'To E. of D'. which accompanied six of the *Holy Sonnets*:

> See Sir, how as the Suns hot Masculine flame
>    Begets strange creatures on Niles durty slime
> In me, your fatherly yet lusty Ryme
>    (For, these songs are their fruits) have wrought the
>                                         same.[14]

Donne's poetry engages in dialogues with a woman reader, arousing in her a desire to answer back which makes the poems unlike any other love poetry in the period.

Dialogue poems were common in the seventeenth century, and many manuscript miscellanies suggest that they were commoner than the printed texts now available would imply. The dialogue form breaks down the insistent masculinist voice of the poet which has so offended modern readers; women readers then as now have registered not a single tone, but a potential intercharge which brings the woman reader into the orbit of the poet's communication, which depends for its life on her reaction. In Donne's poem, 'Breake of Day', an extra stanza exists which was written in the margin in some versions, and discussion as early as 1630 of the relation between the extra stanza and the three other verses suggests an extraordinary number of possibilities, including not only that the marginal stanza is the woman's reply to the lover's lament that she must leave, but also that the whole poem is biographical; one miscellany heads it: 'Dr Dunne to his Mistress'. The uncertainty surrounding the gender of either speaker also dates from the 1630s. Questions of the relation between gender and the poetic voice were raised in relation to this poem even though Donne's public *persona* was a 'masculine' one. In 'Breake of Day' the idea of a dialogue with a woman reader undermines the notion of a 'masculine' figure whose poetry has always been thought too difficult for women.[15]

This mode of thinking for a long time predominated over any fear of the corrupting sensuality of Donne's love poetry. Ben Jonson, like Dryden and Dr Johnson, thought Donne's writing

too clever for ordinary people, and definitely much too clever
for women. Under this presumption, masculinity becomes a range
of attributes, highly flattering to male intellect, predicated on the
mental feebleness of feminity. Men know they are clever because
women are so stupid. Some men found Donne's poetry gratify-
ing for the clarity with which it has been seen to proclaim this
soothing message. Even Johnson verges on this ground, declaring of the metaphysicals in the *'Life of Cowley'* that they were
'men of learning': 'To write on their plan it was at least necessary
to read and think.'[16] Johnson fathomed them but, like Ben Jonson,
thought no one else would. Very few men admit bafflement,
Coleridge being a disarming exception, declaring of 'Aire and
Angels': 'The first stanza is able, and reminds one of Wordsworth's
apparition-poem; the second I do not understand.'[17] Emerson made
no such demur; he reads the metaphysicals 'with a surprise and
delight as if I were finding very good things in a forgotten manuscript of my own.'[18] What woman could say the same?

Those critical terms, which encompass educated men requiring educated readers – inevitably male readers, as women didn't
in the main have opportunities for education – remain virtually
unchanged even when C.S. Lewis contrasts 'the mellifluous, luxu-
rious, "builded rhyme"' of Spenser's *Amoretti'* with the 'abrupt,
familiar, and consciously "manly" style in which nearly all Wyatt's
lyrics are written.'[19] Roughness of diction, with its implication
of intellectual power, always describes not just Donne's poetry,
but the reader who can appreciate it: a thinking *man*.

Virginia Woolf always had mixed feelings about thinking men,
and this may have goaded her in 1931 to write about a rather
different John Donne in 'Donne After Three Centuries'. She had
equally distinctive feelings about thinking women, and observed
in her essay that the women who liked Donne can't have been
in the Dryden dolly-bird mode. Woolf chose as her representative woman reader a friend of Donne's, Lady Anne Clifford (whose
*Diary* Vita Sackville-West edited in 1923) a woman who had been
tutored by the poet Samuel Daniel, and who sat in a room deco-
rated with texts, as Montaigne did, drawing comfort and inspiration not only from the French essayist but from a more
home-grown source: '"If I had not excellent Chaucer's book here
to comfort me", she wrote, "I were in a pitiable case having as
many troubles as I have here, but, when I read in that I scorn
and make light of them all, and a little part of his beauteous

spirit infuses itself in me"' (*CR II*, p. 31). Woolf observes that Lucy Harington Russell, Countess of Bedford, could hardly have been deficient in understanding if she relished the poems sent her by her protegé: 'Lady Bedford must have been a very clever woman, well versed in the finer shades of theology, to derive an instant or an intoxicating pleasure from the praises of her servant' (p. 35). The Reading Notes are less guarded: 'She must have had a good head, to understand, perhaps liked him to show off—anyhow a curious relation between them' (Berg, VIII). When Woolf thought about Donne, she meditated on his women readers. What were they like and why did they like Donne? Why did he like them? Why did she herself like him?

Virginia Woolf liked Donne because he belonged to her band of outsiders. He came on his mother, Elizabeth Rastell's side, from a distinguished old Catholic family directly descended from Sir Thomas More. Literature was in his blood through the Mores and Rastells (printers as well as writers). His clandestine marriage, for which he was dismissed from his job as Secretary to the Lord Keeper, Sir Thomas Egerton, caused him to remain an outsider until appointed Dean of St Paul's by James I after his wife's death. His married life consisted of a gruelling search for employment and financial security amidst apparent domestic happiness, however little that conjunction can be understood in the late twentieth century, in which (male) critics speculate that Donne must have grown tired of the wife who reduced him to poverty and outsider status.[20] The poet's own view, quoted in Virginia Woolf's Reading Notes, was different: 'We had not one another at so cheap a rate as yt we should ever be wearye of one another.'[21]

Donne, like Montaigne, was aware of being situated on the boundaries between notions of masculinity and femininity current in his time. He was reared in a religion which privileged the female over the male icons of Protestantism.[22] The feminine and marginal were bred into him from early childhood, together with the strength of his Catholic mother, who saw one of her sons suffer for harbouring a martyr, and who herself went into exile to escape persecution. Donne witnessed a different kind of persecution inflicted on his young wife by her irascible father, and endured with her poverty and social exile, surrounded by an ever-increasing brood of children. Woolf wrote in the final pages of the second *Common Reader*:

If we like to stay here in England, in London, still the scene changes; the street narrows; the house becomes small, cramped, diamond-paned, and malodorous. We see a poet, Donne, driven from such a house because the walls were so thin that when the children cried their voices cut through them. We can follow him, through the paths that lie in the pages of books, to Twickenham; to Lady Bedford's Park, a famous meeting-ground for nobles and poets; and then turn our steps to Wilton, the great house under the downs, and hear Sidney read the *Arcadia* to his sister. (pp. 261–2)

In this thumbnail sketch Woolf captures Donne as outsider in a world where great ladies read or are read aloud to in their mansions.[23]

Forced into an unusual proximity with wife and children Donne experienced domestic life more as a woman of his period would experience it, than as a man. He wrote: 'I see that I stand like a tree, which once a year beares, though no fruit, yet this Mast of children.'[24] Not only his poems, but in particular his prose writings, are full of images of female experience such as child-birth and breast-feeding, from 'The Good-morrow': 'Were we not wean'd till then? /But suck'd on countrey pleasures, childishly?' (p. 7), to Elegy V, 'His Picture':

> That which in him was faire and delicate,
> Was but the milke, which in loves childish state
> Did nurse it: who now is growne strong enough
> To feed on that, which to disused tasts seemes tough.
>
> (p. 78)

The *Devotions Upon Emergent Occasions*, which were reprinted in 1923 and may have been read by Virginia Woolf, draw copiously on this imagery. Donne's *Devotions* address the reader from a position of physical helplessness which effeminises the speaking subject, though in this case, as in many of the *Holy Sonnets* and Divine Poems, the movement into a woman's sphere confers dignity, not indignity as in the Elegies. Donne speaks to women from their own exclusion from power, and to some of his early women readers he was certainly audible. Katherine Thimelby, from a well-known Catholic family connected with the convent at Louvain where Donne also had connections,[25] wrote to Herbert Aston in about 1635: 'How infinite a time will it seme till I se you: for lovers hours are full eternity. Doctor Dun sayd this, but I think it.'[26]

Donne's physical and mental isolation during the years of his marriage contributed to the independence of spirit[27] which allies him to Woolf. The excitement which she finds in Donne's writing comes from her recognition that he was not only in rebellion against his elders, but disjoined from his own contemporaries, aware of 'something antipathetic to him in the temper of his time'.[28] In 'Hours in a Library' (1916) Woolf declared that 'no age of literature is so little submissive to authority as ours' (*Essays*, 1. 59), a view she expanded in 'How It Strikes A Contemporary': 'No age can have been more rich than ours in writers determined to give expression to the differences which separate them from the past and not to the resemblances which connect them with it' (*CR I*, p. 237). As Woolf got older she grew restless with the idea of being one of a group, however sustaining she had found her Bloomsbury friends, insisting instead on her own idiosyncratic vision:

> I'm to write what I like; & they're to say what they like. My only interest as a writer lies, I begin to see, in some queer individuality: not in strength, or passion, or anything startling; but then I say to myself, is not 'some queer individuality' precisely the quality I respect? Peacock for example: Borrow; Donne. (*Diary*, 2. 168).

Donne declared in a sermon preached at St. Paul's in 1622: 'I am in my Cabinet at home, when I consider, what God hath done for me, and my soule; There is the *Ego*, the particular, the individuall, I.'[29] Donne insisted on the value of the particular, as Woolf did, where other poets, as Johnson had observed, lean always towards the general. For Woolf that ability to particularise moves Donne out of a masculine world into one which has historically belonged to women, and for which they have been scorned.

Virginia Woolf's first idea for an essay on Donne would have concentrated on individualism by adopting a form specially suited to its expression. She jotted down in her Reading Notebook that 'this essay should be in the put into the mouth of Mary Bickley, an obscure woman 1845. Her diary',[30] and although she seems to have abandoned Mary Bickley almost immediately, the idea of keeping the informality of a diary in critical writing remained with her till the end of her life. Mary Bickley's diary notes on Donne might have looked more like Woolf's Reading Notes than the polished published version, 'Donne After Three Centuries'. Woolf felt drawn to Donne precisely because his poetry was not in the lyrical and melliflous tradition admired by C.S. Lewis, but approached instead the colloquialism of prose. Donne is thus allied to a tradition of the oral rather than the written. He wrote to the Countess of Montgomery: 'I know what dead carcasses things written are, in respect of things spoken.'[31] Woolf read James Russell Lowell on Chaucer, and recorded in her Reading Notes: 'Till after the time of Sh[akespea]re we must always bear in mind that it is not a language of books but of living speech that we have to deal with' (MHP/B2d). Montaigne, Chaucer, Donne, Daniel, writers both dead and alive, were claimed by Lady Anne Clifford in her *Diary* as friends; she recognised in them a shared role in making the vernacular the new instrument of a culture which would belong to women as much, or even more, than it belonged to men.

In 1916 Virginia Woolf argued in a review of 'Arthur Symons's Essays' that prose, not poetry, was the best medium 'for a life lived in little houses separated only by a foot or two of brick wall' (*Essays*, 2. 70), and was thus suited to the twentieth century.[32] Donne wrote his colloquial poetry in a little jerry-built house in Mitcham in which an obscure woman in the nineteenth century might have read them and recorded her impressions in a diary. Although Woolf's completed essay abandoned the experimental form, her urge to see Donne through female eyes remains dominant. Her work on Donne in the summer of 1931 took shape amidst half-formulated plans for an essay which would trace an alternative history and literary tradition for women in which women's relation to the oral was to take pride of place.

For Virginia Woolf Donne is not read, but heard: 'He is audible. . . . It is worth perhaps trying to analyse the meaning that his voice has for us as it strikes upon the ear.' Had she had access to some of the manuscript collections of Donne's verse she would have found grounds for reinforcing her perception of the peculiar colloquial intimacy of that verse. The line she first quotes: 'I long to talke with some old lover's ghost', arrests the reader like a living voice, 'bursting into speech' (p. 20). The same much more immediate emotional effect on both eye and ear aroused by manuscript versions attends almost all Donne's opening lines or couplets: 'Marke but this flea', 'I Wonder by my troth, what thou, and I / Did, till we lov'd?', or 'If yet I have not all thy love, / Deare, I shall never have it all'.[33] Woolf's handwritten Reading Notes on Donne create the same effect. The perfect method of writing and reading for both authors, as Woolf perhaps sensed when she thought of couching her essay in the form of a woman's diary, is through manuscript rather than the printed word.

The intimacy of handwriting undermines the 'masculinist' Donne. Print, as Woolf was to argue in 'Anon', replaces the anonymous man or woman singing and reciting and telling tales, with the author on the spine of a book. Donne never wanted his poems to ossify in that manner, but to remain part of an exchange between friends, where the speaking voice reaches the reader from the page in which it has left the writer's pen and ink, just as the diarist's entries remain private, personal, uttered as much as written. Donne feared that print would kill the real vitality of the written word, which lay in its proximity to speech, which could be better remembered and recaptured in handwriting than in the fixity of print, and was therefore better preserved in the manuscript text. Several letters stress writing as an exchange between reader and writer,[34] something which was particularly central to Donne because, isolated as he was in his family at Mitcham, writing was for him, as for many women in this period, virtually his only form of exchange. Once again Donne as writing subject occupies a position which belongs historically to women: at home, private, obliged to create companions, as both Montaigne and Virginia Woolf did, through the written word.

As a preacher Donne's public audibility is undisputed. He preached to Lady Anne Clifford at Knowle, at the funeral of Magdalen Herbert, at the weddings of notable people, at the funeral of James I, at Lincoln's Inn, repeatedly at St Paul's, and on the subject of his own death, two days before that event. But earlier in his life, in social and political exile in Mitcham, he must both have felt, and been, largely inaudible. He was doomed to privacy long after he felt this to be at all desirable, and however much his Cabinet at home proclaimed his individuality, at times it certainly seemed more like a prison than a room of his own. He wrote to Goodyer at this time:

I think sometimes that the having a family should remove me
farre from the curse of a *Vae soli*. But in so strict obligation of
Parent, or Husband, or Master, (and perchance it is so in the
last degree of friendship) where all are made one, I am not
the lesse alone, for being in the midst of them.[35]

The 'prison narratives' composed by Donne at this time were
the verse letters, many of the *Songs and Sonets*, the *Holy Sonnets*
with their persistent female persona ('Except you 'enthrall me I
never shall be free / Nor ever chaste except you ravish me'),
*Pseudo-martyr* (1609/10, his attack on Catholic veneration of
martyrdom), *Biathanatos* (1607/8, his argument for suicide) and
the satirical *Ignatius His Conclave* (1611).

Donne was in some respects less audible than the female poet,
Aemilia Lanyer, whose poems were published in 1611, and whose
poetry has been seen as creating a 'feminist space' in which she
can pursue 'the revolutionary possibility of self-definition'.[36]
Lanyer's country-house poem, 'To Cookham', in praise of the
Countess of Cumberland and her daughter, Lady Anne Clifford,
may have originated the country-house form which critics have
usually attributed to Jonson's new kind of poem, 'To Penshurst'.[37]
This kind of audibility Donne shunned as totally as he may have
desired political and social visibility, writing to Goodyer in 1614:
'One thing more I must tell you; but so softly that I am loath to
hear myself; and so softly, that if that good Lady were in the
room, with you and this letter, she might not hear. It is, that I
am brought to a necessity of printing my Poems.'[38] Lucy Russell
would no doubt not only have scorned the vulgarity of that pro-
cedure, but would also would have been incensed by the hom-
age her poet paid to so many ladies besides herself.

The circulation of manuscripts created an interchange which
can be paralleled in Virginia Woolf's circle. Her books, admit-
tedly printed (by herself), were always sent first to the inner
circle of friends: her husband, her sister, Strachey, Bell, Fry, Keynes,
Forster, for a verdict which mattered to her more intensely and
in a different way from the verdict of the *Times Literary Supplement* and other journals. The critical press was significant because it affected sales. But the verdict on quality which she heeded
was always the private verdict of the inner circle, whose read-
ings could just as well have been of manuscript copy, had her
handwriting not been so awful, and the custom of the times dif-

ferent. Donne knew his audience, just as she knew hers.[39] But Donne's audience consisted, much more than has been allowed, of well-educated women.

Virginia Woolf declared that no woman could read Donne without falling in love with him.[40] It may be that his notorious masculinity is part of that appeal, as Petruchio's is to Kate, surrounded by sycophantic suitors. Great to get away from the sonneteers, snowy breasts *et al.*, as Joan Bennet pointed out. But equally it may be that John Donne was not so masculine after all. These terms can hardly now be used as constants, containing the same meaning in one period as another. Virginia Woolf tuned in to a John Donne who seemed to live in a woman's world rather than a man's, and who recognised this fact for himself and came to relish it as a source of creativity even as he records his reluctance to accept it. Perhaps that is why called himself 'masculine'. Like Montaigne he had his doubts. Was he really one of *them*?

## TRANSLATING DONNE INTO THE FEMININE

In the address 'To the curteous Reader' at the beginning of his translation in 1603 of Montaigne's *Essays* John Florio sets up a dialogue between a learned reader and a common reader. The learned man protests against the proliferation and consequent vulgarisation of the text. The translator retorts that 'learning cannot be too common, and the commoner the better'. Translating a book offends learned men, who do not want their mistresses to be prostituted, but the translator retorts: 'Yea but this Mistresse is like ayre, fire, water, the more breathed the clearer.' 'The vulgar should not knowe all', returns the scholarly advocate, to be informed by the defendant that no one can know everything. Without translation, 'hold we ignorance the mother of devotion; praying and preaching in an unknowne tongue'. Through a melée of masculine and feminine metaphor Florio moves into a recognisable Humanist and Reformation attack on the mystification of learning and religion through the Church, the academy and the Latin language. In the dedicatory epistle to Lucy, Countess of Bedford, and her mother Lady Anne Harrington, the defective female – Florio's translation – is brought forth by a learned nurse, the translator himself, through whose mediation common readers are born and nourished. The vulgar, the word Montaigne himself uses, have become the arbiters of value. Florio, who enters the text boasting of masculine births, leaves it in the care of a community of women: the learned ladies of the dedication and unlearned common readers. Florio is aware of the unstable status not only of his translation but of Montaigne's own text. Its dissemination, how it is read, who owns it, are all part of its life and its future prospects. If Time is a man, here his operations must be wooed through great ladies – in Florio's case – and in Montaigne's, through the activities of Marie de Gournay, his 'fairespoken, and fine-witted Daughter by alliance', who was also his editor.[41] Women readers are vital to the life of the translated text, which undermines the authority of the Fathers.

The act of translation is deeply woven into Donne's thought, both secular and religious. Its images in the verse letters occupy a curious bridge between secular thought and religious language, rightly recognising learned women as the true historical intermediaries of Protestantism. But there is another element in this semantic field of originals (traditionally male) and translations (traditionally female) as applied by Donne to notions of correction and mercy. Donne shared with Montaigne a very unusual upbringing. Montaigne wrote:

> In all my first age I never felt the rod but twice, and then very slightly. I practised the same method with my children, who all of them died at nurse, except Leonora, my only daughter, and who arrived at the age of five years and upward without other correction for her childish faults (her mother's indulgence easily conceiving) than words only, and those very gentle ... I should, in this, have yet been more religious towards the males, as less born to subjection and more free; and I should have made it my business to fill their hearts with ingenuousness and freedom. I have never observed other effects of whipping than to render boys more cowardly, or more wilfully obstinate. ('Of the Affection of Fathers to their Children', II. 315)

In this passage leniency is associated with the feminine: the rule of the indulgent mother; but it is related to an idea of liberty associated by Montaigne with the masculine. Liberty, however, whether in repudiation of the severity of the Judaic God, or of the closed world of a biblical text possessed by learned male masters, is conceived as a movement into a feminine world: of love not law, of the vernacular, not Latin, the mother tongue instead of the arcane language of the Fathers. Montaigne is as perfectly aware of this as Donne is when he writes in his *Devotions Upon Emergent Occasions*:

> It is thou, thou *my God*, who has led me so continually with thy hand, from the hand of my Nurce, as that I know, thou wilt not correct me, but with thine own hand. My parents would not give me over to a *Servants* correction, nor my *God*, to *Satans*.[42]

It seems no accident that the writings of both men confound traditional distinctions and divisions between the male and the female.

For Donne Latin was the language of the Church authority which he rejected in favour of its translation, the Anglican Church and vernacular writings. His mordantly satirical attack on the Jesuits in *Ignatius His Conclave* (1611) is also an attack on this authority. His love poetry and his religious poetry relocate him in a cultural context which belongs to a new liberated feminine awareness. The dialogue mode of his love poetry, abjuring a single authoritarian voice, and the pervasive Protestant language of the verse letters to women, as well as the female *persona* adopted in much of his religious poetry, suggests that his own puberty rite was, like Montaigne's, a deliberate repudiation of the Latin tradition of the young Humanist male. Richard Helgerson has suggested that 'if Donne appears extravagant, excessive and spontaneous, it is in part at least because he wished to define himself as poet in opposition to humanist ideals of sobriety, measure, and deliberation'.[43] Spontaneity, extravagance, excess, are all terms used against women in this period and associated with oral traditions rather than with writing, and, as Helgerson argues, with the amateur rather than the professional, layman rather than priest, the undisciplined rather than the disciplined, and therefore inevitably, the uneducated rather than the educated. The language they all use is the vernacular. Donne's love of Spanish, and large library of Spanish books, including Spanish mystics[44] at a time when, as Woolf points out in her Reading Notes, 'the Spaniards were to the English what Germany was to us' (Berg, XX), form part of a European vernacular movement which embraces Montaigne, Rabelais and Ramus, and in England, Spenser, Sidney and Sir John Harington, among many others.

Like many women as well as men of his own time, Donne was forced by the inactivity of his public life into a world in which writing was as much a form of action as it was for Harington translating *Aeneid VI* in prison in 1603, for Dorothy Osborne writing to William Temple, for Bunyan dreaming out *The Pilgrim's Progress* from Bedford gaol, or, eventually, for Richardson's *Pamela*, writing her heart out under Mr. B.'s captivity. As a consequence Donne understood the ways in which the vernacular and the whole Protestant tradition of writing belonged to women and spoke particularly to them. Donne's finest elegy to a woman declares: 'Language thou art too narrow, and too weake / To ease us now' ('Death', p. 259). Yet the new accessibility of language to women is a vital part of Protestantism, as Donne knew perfectly well when he preached at St Paul's, always translating the Latin texts which peppered his sermons into the vernacular for the benefit of congregations of women and working citizens who had not received a Humanist education in the classics. The terms of religion: faith, heresy, confession, continually punctuate even the simplest communications of his verse letters. Had he had a more active life in the first decade of the seventeenth century he might never have entered an idiom which seems peculiarly adapted to women readers.

The verse letters constitute a considerable body of poems specifically addressed to women readers. Did women find Donne's communications too difficult for them? Donne would hardly have written so many to the same ladies if they had not been enjoyed and appreciated. Nor is it enough to say that his female correspondents showed his verse letters (which they didn't understand themselves) to influential men to demonstrate how suitable Donne would be for a post at court. If this was the case, they, and the letters, were singularly unsuccessful, and indeed, fantastic and vital as the verse letters are (the Duchess of Newcastle on a good day?), they are hardly the letters of a prospective government servant. They suggest instead precisely the resistance to seventeenth-century patriarchal constructs of women which Barbara Lewalski observes in the writings of Jacobean women.[45]

Grierson removed the verse letter headed 'To the Countesse of Huntingdon' from his original edition on the grounds that it was too difficult to be genuine, although he claims that he had second thoughts while the edition was in the press. In this poem

Donne takes seriously Sidney's outburst in *An Apology for Poetry* against the Petrarchan mode of the popular sonnet: 'But truly many of such writings as come under the banner of unresistible love, if I were a mistress, would never persuade me they were in love; so coldly they apply fiery speeches, as men that had rather read lovers' writings . . . than that in truth they feel those passions.'[46] Sidney, who had the experience of reading out loud to his own sister, enters in his imagination the mind of a woman reading privately to herself, and hears through that apprehended female medium not an effusion of love, but the voice of a man used to reading and reproducing the writings of other men. Donne addresses in the Countess of Huntingdon a woman satiated by verses which Sidney's hypothetical woman reader would also have scorned:

> Yet neither will I vexe your eyes to see
> A sighing Ode, nor crosse-arm'd Elegie.
>
> (p. 195)

Men should not woo until they are certain of being loved, otherwise they only teach contempt: 'The honesties of love with ease I doe, / But am no porter for a tedious woo' (p. 196). Criticism of tired love poetry also enlivens a verse letter to the Countess of Salisbury in which, daunted by her beauty, the Sun

> Growne stale, is to so low a value runne,
> That his disshevel'd beames and scattered fires
> Serve but for Ladies Periwigs and Tyres
> In lovers Sonnets.
>
> (pp. 201–22)

The poems court an intelligent reader, negotiating new modes of address through which a man may speak to a woman in a verse which repudiates the traditional terms of love poetry. Donne salutes in his female reader a woman not only capable of answering him, but sufficiently well-read to recognise the literary framework within which he writes.

The address to an intellectually sophisticated female reader determines the form of all Donne's verse letters. He speaks to Lucy, Countess of Bedford, through the metaphor of a learned text: 'For, as darke texts need notes: there some must bee / To

usher vertue, and say, *This is shee'* (p. 168).[47] The lady, to whom
so many translations and original works were dedicated, can
understand the compliment of 'If good and lovely were not one,
of both / You were the transcript, and originall' (p. 170). The
letter assumes a knowledge of Donne's poems (which he must
have shown the Countess in manuscript), rewriting 'The Sunne
Rising', in which the 'busie old sun' was banished from the lovers'
chamber:

> In this you'have made the Court the Antipodes,
> And will'd your Delegate, the vulgar Sunne,
> To doe profane autumnall offices.
>
> (p. 169)

Here the 'vulgar sun' rules over an ordinary court, where Lucy
Russell graces a superior one. But as Donne praises, he remembers Sidney's uncomfortable warning about a woman chilled by
such extravagance, and retreats from 'Poëtique rage, or flattery',
resolving on simplicity: 'The story of beauty, 'in Twicknam is,
and you' (p. 170). The verse letter which Donne sent to Lucy,
apparently accompanying the 'Elegie on Mistress Boulstred' also
recapitulates 'The Sunne Rising':

> Shee was all spices, you all metalls; so
> In you two wee did both rich Indies know.
>
> (p. 205)

Donne forged for his known readership of sophisticated women
a special idiom founded on an assumption of their familiarity
with his own writing. The witty poet plays with his witty woman
reader.

In these verse letters Donne addresses the literate, thinking
woman through a shared culture of reading, writing, and scholarly activity: the puzzling out of difficult texts, the distinguish-
ing of the authentic from the false, of the original from the copy.
Instead of the Countess of Salisbury's reading the obscure letter
from her poet, the poet reads the difficult but illuminating text
of the lady: 'For as your fellow Angells, so you doe / Illustrate
them who come to study you' (p. 203), ending on a note struck
by Berowne in *Love's Labour's Lost*, when he recognises women's
eyes as the true seat of learning; Donne muses:

Yet may I see you thus, as now I doe;
I shall by that, all goodnesse have discern'd,
And though I burne my librarie, be learn'd.

(p. 204)

The communication between poet and woman reader exists in a
written universe, reified in the paper and ink which passes between the two, almost sacramentally, as Donne had declared in
a letter to Sir Thomas Lucy which recalls the terms of the poem,
'The Extasie': 'I make account that this writing of letters, when
it is with any seriousness, is a kind of extasie, and a departure
and secession and suspension of the soul, w^ch doth then communicate it self to two bodies.'[48]

Donne forged a language for women which depended on their
familiarity with his way of writing. His verse letters are not ego-
tistical effusions, but a correspondence between writer and reader.
They enter a private and secret world[49] where they negotiate
with the female reader almost on sexual terms, in a manner which
recalls Montaigne's trafficking with the ladies in private. When
he sends a verse letter to Magdalen Herbert the missive becomes
a disreputable, and (literally) ragged suitor, suing for favour to
a warm maternal figure: 'Who knowes thy destiny? when thou
hast done, / Perchance her Cabinet may harbour thee' (pp. 191–2).
The letter is the nearest to intimate of any of Donne's verse letters.
Did Mrs Herbert, admired for 'her inclination, and conuersation,
naturally cheerfull, and merry, and louing facetiousnesse, and
sharpness of wit',[50] laugh at his insouciance, or condemn him
for masculine presumption?

The question of sincerity which later readers find so problematic
in Donne's letters to his female patrons exercises the poet himself
in almost everything he writes. In a verse letter entitled 'On New-
yeares day' Donne meditates on the criticism that his praise of
Lucy Russell will not be credited in future times: 'So, my verse
built of your just praise, might want / Reason and likelihood, the
firmest base.' (p. 176) The lines recall Shakespeare's *Sonnet 17*:

Who will believe my verse in time to come
If it were fill'd with your most high deserts?

Donne may have remembered, as he wrote his own lines, Eleazar
Edgar's entry in the Stationer's Register for 3 Jan 1599/1600:

'Amours of J.D. with certen other sonnetes by W.S.', a failed venture which must go down in printing history as the most tantalising of losses.[51] Does he imagine that Lucy Russell reading his lines, will recognise the Shakespearean antecedent, as the Countess of Huntingdon might recognise Sidney's female reader scorning Petrarchan effusions? The unfinished verse letter to Lucy Russell *'Begun in France but never perfected'*, ends describing itself: readers who would never have the chance to read the original (Lucy Russell herself) would find in his verses 'Copies' of her (pp. 198–9). In another letter Donne diminishes his own status as a writer:

> Care not then, Madame, 'how low your praysers lye;
> In labourers balads oft more piety
> God findes, then in *Te Deums* melodie
>
> (p. 193).

The tedium of the *Te Deum* is a shared joke between reader and writer who both know that the Inns of Court poet couldn't write a ballad if he tried. The jest both spikes and spices the compliment. Even the poet's self-abasement – 'how low your praysers lye' – becomes an ironic recognition that the praiser might be accused of a different form of lowness: lying to a lady for gain. Donne's audacity deflects charges of mendacity.

Donne's verse letters conjure up a literary culture conditioned by the satisfactions or dissatisfactions of women readers because the poet is conscious of extreme social and financial disparity between himself and his female patrons. The almost painful sense of role reversal, of a man forced into a dependency usually construed as female, accompanies a verse letter to Lucy Russell in which the poet sees his course as a choice between 'Simony' and 'thanklessenesse':

> In this, my debt I seem'd loath to confesse,
> In that, I seem'd to shunne beholdingnesse.
> But 'tis not soe; *nothings*, as I am, may
> Pay all they have, and yet have all to pay.
>
> (p. 172)

A letter 'To the Countesse of Huntingdon' enlarges on the distance between the writer and the reader: 'To some ye are reveal'd, as in a friend, / And as a vertuous Prince farre off, to mee' (p. 178).

The poet is a subject owing tribute to the ruler, a tribute supplied by his verse. The topos of Prince and subject again suggests the reversal of male and female. As he writes these lines Donne accuses himself of sycophancy, despising his verse as a 'poyson'd fountaine still'. He challenges his woman reader: 'If you can thinke these flatteries, they are.' Donne claims youthful foreknowledge of the Countess's ascent to virtue: 'I was your Prophet in your yonger dayes, /And now your Chaplaine, God in you to praise' (p. 179). In acquiring the status of prophecy his flattery is purified and given a new sacred authority.[52]

In 'A *Letter to the Lady* Carey, *and Mrs.* Essex Riche, *From* Amyens', the fear of flattery is dispersed by the same appropriation of religious authority. Like Richardson's Pamela – and Donne's Protestant language in these letters seems especially addressed to the new women readers of the vernacular Bible – these ladies wound with their virtue, not with 'prophane and sensuall Darts'. But even this poem ends with some anxiety:

> May therefore this be enough to testifie
> My true devotion, free from flattery;
> He that beleeves himselfe, doth never lie.
>
> (p. 201)

The author of *Pseudo-martyr*, with its virulent attack on self-deception, could perhaps hardly rest comfortable even in the disclaimer of that last line.

Were the female recipients of Donne's verse letters in love with him? They could hardly have failed to feel flattered not by the extravagant compliments which he offers them, but by his confidence that the complexities of his situation, the sophistication of his thought, and the contortions which both create in his language, will be understood and pitied by the women to whom he addresses himself. Who else would have flattered them in that way in that period? Certainly the reaction of all male readers since has been simple incredulity that the poet could have thought any woman capable of comprehension.

## REBELS

Virginia Woolf's literary criticism disclaims authority. The opening sentence of the second volume of the *Common Reader* declares

that the reader can never re-enter an earlier time: 'That this "becoming an Elizabethan", this reading sixteenth-century writing
as currently and certainly as we read our own is an illusion, is
no doubt true' (p. 3). In the essay 'On Not Knowing Greek' in
the first *Common Reader* she attacks the (male) arrogance which
assumes that the reader who knows Greek can reconstruct Greek
culture. Anna Jameson, one of the earliest women to write on
Shakespeare's heroines, included a chapter on Donne and Anne
More in *The Loves of the Poets* (1829), confronting in her Preface
the problem of critical authority: 'It seemed to me that there was
far more propriety and much less egotism in simply expressing,
in the first person, what I thought and felt, than in asserting
absolutely that a thing *is so*, or *is said to be so*. Every one has a
right to have an opinion, and deliver it with modesty; but no
one has a right to clothe such opinions in general assertions and
in terms which seem to intimate that they are or ought to be
universal.'[53] For Woolf, as for Jameson, the general belonged to
a world of male cultural imperialism. Donne's particular, individual 'I' speaks to women in a new way.

Donne's rebellion is in part religious, in part related to language, and in part related to the reader. Donne had high expectations of his readers in his prose works as in his poetry. In 'An
Advertisement to the *Reader*' which he composed for *Pseudo-martyr*
he explains why he has addressed the reader at the end of the
book rather than at the beginning, 'because I thought not that
any man might well and properly be called a Reader, till he
were come to the end of the Booke'. The tone is dictatorial, but
it is the tyranny of one man to another, not of a man to a woman.
The reader is not just to read but to write: 'For his owne good
therefore (in which I am also interested) I must first intreat him,
that he will be pleased, before hee reade, to amend with his
pen, some of the most important errors, which are hereafter noted
to haue passed in the printing.'[54] The effect of this warning is to
undermine the authority of the printed text. The author's meaning can only be properly delivered through the intervention of
the reader.

That text itself also undermines authority, not least the established authority of the Catholic Church in which Donne was
brought up. He approaches his subject through Protestantism,
and therefore also through a woman's route, the vernacular, and
the translated Bible, protesting like an unruly adolescent against

the masters of his youth. The female metaphor is complicated however by the feminine metaphors of Catholicism[55] so that Donne's rebellion is also a breach with the mother church, at the same time as it is a breach, like Coverdale's translation of Galatians III, with the law of the 'schoolmaster'. In his attack on martyrdom Donne writes as a layman, an amateur in the theological world, as are also the women of the Protestant reformation, Catherine Parr, and all Foxe's ordinary female martyrs refusing to obey civil as well as religious authority. Amongst Foxe's Protestants is the Queen herself, slandered in the Index, where 'they haue onely expunged an Epistle of *Iunius* to her, in which there was no words concerning Religion, but onely a gratulation of her Peace and of her Learning'. In the second volume they have continued their insults by expunging the dedicatory epistle (p. 46). The textual corruption afflicts Donne as much as the misprinting of his own text. Through removing an authority, or changing what is printed, the text is vitiated.

Donne apologises in the Preface to *Pseudo-martyr* for failures of scholarship which he attributes disarmingly to '*my naturall impatience not to digge painefully in deepe, and stony, and sullen learnings: My Indulgence to my freedome and libertie, as in all other indifferent things, so in my studies also, not to betroth or enthral myselfe, to any one science, which should possesse or denominate me*' (B 2). In *Holy Sonnet* XIV he embraces a metaphor of enthralment: 'Except you'enthrall me, never shall be free' (p. 299), but in this Preface he shrugs off any chains, and protests that he wants his readers also to rest easy (despite the corrections they must make in his faultily printed text). He is aware that he exposes himself to his enemies for 'whatsoever such degrees of laziness, of liberty, of irresolution, can produce' (B 2). The spirit of Montaigne governs his choice of terms: laziness, liberty, irresolution. But two of them, laziness and irresolution, move Donne peaceably into the woman's world of amateurish and careless endeavour which Woolf evokes in the Preface to *The Common Reader* First Series: 'Hasty, inaccurate, superficial'. In both writers laziness and irresolution are the conditions of a liberty to read and write as they like, without the permission of authorities.

Authority structures are under attack at many places in *Pseudo-martyr*, which at one point (p. 83) interestingly anticipates Milton's argument in *The Tenure of Kings and Magistrates*, that there were no magistrates before the Fall. Also in the spirit of Montaigne,

as of Harington, Sidney, and his own great-grandfather Sir Thomas
More, Donne attacks superstition in the guise of Purgatory, as a
'*Comique-Tragicall* doctrine', like '*some Tragedie of hell, to make an
olde woman weepe or tremble*' (p. 108). 'Come, I think hell's a fable',
declares Marlowe's Faustus.[56] Corrupt texts, corrupt stories, the
erasure of truth in the erasing of words, or false claiming of
authorities, all these are the stuff of Donne's rebellion against
Catholic authority, as opposed to civil and secular authority.
Docherty, in an extreme deconstruction of Donne as stable text,
which aligns Donne again with Montaigne, speaks of 'the text
always spinning eccentrically away from any authority',[57] an
appealing judgement if applied to such works as *Pseudo-martyr*,
*Biathanatos*, and *Ignatius His Conclave*, all texts composed by a
man exiled from authority structures and free to write as he likes:
a woman? Certainly some of the time. *Pseudo-martyr* may strike
one as primarily a text for a male reader. But it comes out of a
personal and religious history (as Bunyan's *Grace Abounding* also
does) which looks more like a woman's than a man's.

Biathanatos*, Donne's tract on suicide, also attacks the authority of text, both Donne's own and the texts which he studies. At
the same time Donne chastises readers who might have the presumption to judge his text. If he as writer is suspect, they as
readers are more so. Readers fall into four categories:

> (Spunges, which attract all without distinguishing; Houre-glasses,
> which receive and powre out as fast; Bagges, which retaine
> onely the dregges of the Spices, and let the Wine escape; And
> Sives, which retaine the best onely.) If I finde some of the last
> sort, I doubte not but they may bee hereby enlightened.[58]

The process of reading is a fall from innocence which will have
a corrective effect on the reader's pride in his own intellect: 'And
as the eyes of *Eve*, were opened by the taste of the Apple, though
it bee said before that shee saw the beauty of the tree, So the
digesting of this may, though not present faire objects, yet bring
them to see the nakednesse and deformity of their owne reasons.' In the margin of this beguiling passage Donne has written: 'What reader I wish', so that already the dialogic, and indeed
ludic space has been created in which reader and writer spar.
The reader appears to be male, but is forced to consider himself
as female, learning, as Eve learnt, the hard way to truth.

Donne's attack on authority and its decrees is even more evident in *Biathanatos* than in *Pseudo-martyr*. If the Protestant religion gives the highest authority to conscience, the argument about suicide must be resolved by private conscience alone. In the Church of England, where there is no tradition of confession, 'may I not accuse and condemne my selfe to my selfe, and inflict what penance I will for punishing the past, and avoiding like occasion of sinne?' (*Biathanatos*, pp. 104–5). It is not surprising that Donne felt it best not to publish this work, considering how far it goes in its attack on civil law:

> For though in cases where there is a proper Court, I am bound to it; yet, as Kings which are both Soveraignes, may therefore justly decide a cause by Warre, because there can bee no competent Judge between them; So in secret cases betweene the Spirit of God and my conscience, of which there is not certainly constituted any exteriour Judge, we are our selves sufficient to doe all the Offices; and then delivered from all bondage, and restored to our naturall libertie, we are in the same condition as Princes are. (p. 107)

Here is the principle of natural law which led Montaigne to approve suicide. Donne invokes his great-grandfather Sir Thomas More in *Utopia*, that suicide is acceptable for 'men afflicted with incurable diseases' (p. 74). The poet himself admits to considering suicide: 'Mee thinks I have the keyes of my prison in mine owne hand, and no remedy presents it selfe so soone to my heart, as mine own sword. Often Meditation of this hath wonne me to a charitable interpretation of their action who dy so' (p. 18). In 1941 Virginia Woolf also claimed the keys to her own prison.

Extracts from *Biathanatos* were printed in the Nonesuch Donne, published in 1929 when Virginia Woolf was beginning to think about her tercentenary essay on the poet.[59] Donne insists on suicide as an act of personal liberty: the individual's right to decide his fate[60] – and it is never clear whether *her* fate is implied in the pronoun. He protests against the official tinkering with the texts which allegedly prohibit suicide, as if the concept of the liberty of an author is also subtly bound up with the right to commit suicide:

> In the order of the Divine books, the next place is produced out of *Job* [*Militia est vita homini super terram.*] for, though our

translation give it thus, [*Is there not an appointed time to man upon earth?*] yet the Latine Text is thus cited to this purpose by some not addicted to the Vulgat Edition, because it seems in Latine better to afford an argument against *Self-homicide*. (p. 160)

The reader ought to be as free to unlock the sacred text as to quench his own sacred fire if he so wishes. This conviction places Donne, despite his Catholic upbringing, as centrally in the school of Protestant biblical scholarship and of translation of the Bible as Bunyan himself was later to be.

However, Donne undermines his own textual authority. At the beginning of *Biathanatos*, in a section entitled 'Authors cited in this Booke' the writer announces that he has not checked his quotations, but 'trusted my owne old notes; which though I have no reason to suspect, yet I confess here my laziness; and that I did not refresh them with going to the Originall'. He excuses himself by explaining that even when he has lifted a quotation from a secondary source, he has always cited a Catholic author for a Catholic quotation and a Reformer for a Reformation one, 'so that I shall hardly be condemned of any false citation, except to make me Accessorie'. As author Donne abrogates authority, exposing his own frailties to the reader.

The undercutting of his own authority continued throughout his life in all his writings, not least in the reworking of images.[61] One of the most arresting examples is that of the compasses famous from 'A Valediction: forbidding mourning', where the lover is the compass's moving foot, and the woman (his wife?) the fixed point. In Expostulation 20 of *Devotions Upon Emergent Occasions*, which is followed immediately by a Prayer using the image of a marriage between man and woman for the marriage of God and the soul, Donne questions his own movement away from God in these terms:

As hee that would describe a *circle* in paper, if hee have brought that *circle* within one *inch* of *finishing*, yet if he remove his *compasse*, he cannot make it up a *perfit circle*, except he fall to worke againe, to finde out the same *center* so, though setting that *foot* of my *compasse* upon *thee*, I have gone so farre, as to the *consideration* of my selfe, yet if I depart from *thee* my *center*, all is *unperfit*. (pp. 123–4)

Just as in some of the letters he uses images to male correspondents which come from poems addressed to women, so here the image of relationship (and the subsequent Prayer offers confirmation that the marriage union is in his mind in this Expostulation) changes its centre of authority in 'A Valediction: forbidding mourning', from the woman – the 'fixed foot' – to the Godhead. The gender of the Godhead is called into question by the shift, with the consequent destabilising of the centre of authority.

At one point in the *Devotions* Donne has trouble with his pronouns, which in his theological works are so relentlessly male rather than *common*. In an Expostulation upon the subject of 'vapours', he claims that God is present to man in vapours, the dew of Heaven (God) meeting the spirit of man:

> And hee, in whom we *have*, and *are* all that we *are* or *have*, temporally, or spiritually, thy blessed *Son*, in the person of *Wisedome*, is called so to; *she is* (that is *he is*) *the vapour of the power of God*. (p. 71)

Wisdom, the Latin *sapientia*, feminine, becomes confused with the Son, which within the metaphor of vapours becomes punningly, the Sun, always masculine, and stridently so in Donne's poetry. But if God is wisdom, then Donne is too precise a thinker and a linguist to evade the feminine gender of the Latin word.

The same problem in different form arises in the metaphors of text in the *Devotions*, which recall similar metaphors in the verse letters to Donne's female patrons. Originals, copies, translations, are constantly in his mind. As a writer he is always conscious of himself as a secondary hand in the transmission of an original, something which relates him to the feminine imagery of Florio's dedication of the translation of Montaigne's *Essays*. Donne uses the metaphor of translation for the movement in the deity from rigour to clemency:

> Let me think no degree of this thy correction, *casuall*, or without signification; but yet when I have read it in that language, as it is a *correction*, let me translate it with another, and read it as a *mercy*; and which of these is the *Originall*, and which is the *Translation*, whether thy *Mercy*, or thy *Correction*, were thy primary and original intention in this sicknes, I cannot conclude, though death conclude me; for as it must necessarily

> appeare to be a *correction*, so I can have no greater argument
> of they *mercy*, then to die in *thee*, and by that death, to be
> united to him, who died for me. (p. 41)

Here the idea of the *original* is connected to the idea of *correction*, and *mercy* becomes the *translation* of that original, as the New Testament translates the old law. The feminising of the Old Testament God in the New Testament Christ is implicit in this movement, as the translation of the text is implicit in the liberation which is promised to everyone, not just to the chosen people, whether the Jews, or the learned men who guard the Latin text from the scrutiny of the vulgar. The new Bible belongs to the common reader, male and female, the working men and women to whom Bishop Gardiner had in 1543 refused access to the Bible in the vernacular.

Virginia Woolf observed of Donne: 'To remain in one posture was against his nature. Perhaps it is against the nature of things also' (p. 29). Annabel Patterson has urged that 'if we could purge from the idea of an *oeuvre* the ideal of coherence, we might be able to look at the whole Donne and see him not as a monster of ambition but as a mass of contradictions, many of which were known to himself and warily or wittily expressed as self-division'.[62] Donne worshipped change, declaring in the *Devotions* that 'the *Heavens* are not less constant, because they move continually, because they move continually one and the same way. The *Earth* is not the more constant, because it lyes stil continually, because it changes, and melts in al parts thereof' (p. 5). A quarter of a century earlier he had defended women against charges of inconstancy in the Paradox, 'A Defence of Womens Inconstancy': 'That Women are *Inconstant*, I with any man confess, but that *Inconstancy* is a bad quality, I against any man will maintain.'[63] For Donne, as for Montaigne, change is a condition of life, love, faith, writing:

> I scarce beleeve my love to be so pure
>   As I had thought it was,
>   Because it doth endure
> Vicissitude, and season, as the grasse;
> Me thinkes I lyed all winter, when I swore,
> My love was infinite, if spring make 'it more.

The perception of change is also a criticism of the male poet: 'Love's not so pure, and abstract, as they use / To say, which have no Mistresse but their Muse' ('Love's growth', pp. 30–1). On 8 December 1929 Woolf contemplated with ecstasy writing her new book of criticism, beginning with the Elizabethans, and remembering the excitement with which, at the age of fifteen, she first read Hakluyt:

> I was then writing a long picturesque essay upon the Christian religion, I think; called Religio Laici, I believe, proving that man has need of a God; but the God was described in process of change; & I also wrote a history of Women; & a history of my own family—all very longwinded & E[lizabe]than in style. (*Diary*, 3. 271)

In 1931 her essay on Donne was to grow from this soil, in which the celebration of change, disjunction, inconsistency and the particular nourished her new project for a history of women.[64]

Despite the celebrated masculine persuasiveness of Donne's writing, Woolf recognised in it a movement into her own world of disintegrated authority. He, like her, knew what it was like to watch others at the centre of an intellectual and social world from which he was excluded, not by his sex, but by a deliberate revolt against the *mores* of his time. Donne wrote from a position which partook of a woman's, as Montaigne also did. Ironically, *The Common Reader* volumes were perceived by their author, in supreme inconsistency, as a bid for insider status, even as they celebrated, in however sidelong a manner, a new tradition of outsiders: 'So very likely this time next year I shall be one of those people who are, so father said, in the little circle of London Society which represents the Apostles, I think, on a larger scale. Or does this no longer exist? To know everyone worth knowing. I can just see what he meant; just imagine being in that position—*if women can be*' (*Diary*, 2. 319, my italics). Donne shared her equivocal attitude to the world he both courted and despised. The irony, elusiveness and needling, rebellious energy of her words make Donne her natural ally and accomplice.

# 4

# Letters as Resistance:
# Dorothy Osborne,
# Madame de Sévigné and Virginia Woolf

## WRITING FOR PLEASURE

Virginia Woolf was not very gratified when her friends assured her in September 1920, in the course of her writing of *Jacob's Room*, that her main claim to immortality would be not as a novelist but as a letter-writer. It is evident from the context that she was being compared with the seventeenth-century French letter-writer, Madame de Sévigné (*Diary*, 2. 63–4). She read the compliment, no doubt correctly, as a put-down. Her friends' subtext stated that her claims to *real* writing (novels) were nothing much in the long run, but her letters – that supremely feminine form which would remove her from competition with Strachey and other male members of the Bloomsbury group – would ensure her immortality (of a kind). Not mainstream, not literary, not male. She accused herself ruefully of vanity in disliking this sidelining in the literary stakes, as Strachey boldly compared the Bloomsbury group to Johnson's set. Virginia Woolf in this literary scene seems cast as Mrs Thrale. No one would now risk the folly of admiring Virginia Woolf primarily for her letter-writing skills, but nevertheless her letters bear an integral relation to some of the most radical aspects of her non-fictional writing. The form of the letter always guaranteed her a special freedom, and when she read women letter-writers in the early modern period she registered a tradition of free writing and thinking whose legacy she had herself inherited.

What was the nature of that freedom? In the first place, it was the natural consequence of the privacy of letters, that it was possible for the letter-writer to refashion her world to her own mould for an audience of one. Virginia Woolf recognised that power when she responded in 1908 to a request from Clive Bell that she criticise his letter-writing style: 'I often think that we are most unlike in the values we attach to things; you will take seriously what is frivolous to me and vice versa' (*Letters*, 1. 362). In *A Room of One's Own* twenty years later, she meditated again on the different values of male and female worlds:

> Since a novel has this correspondence to real life, its values are to some extent those of real life. But it is obvious that the values of women differ very often from the values which have been made by the other sex; naturally, this is so. Yet it is the masculine values that prevail. Speaking crudely, football and sport are 'important'; the worship of fashion, the buying of clothes 'trivial'. And these values are inevitably transferred from life to fiction. This is an important book, the critic assumes, because it deals with war. This is an insignificant book because it deals with the feelings of women in a drawing-room. (*RO*, p, 74)

The early letter to Bell marks out the territory of that radical revision of culture along the female line which Woolf charted twenty years later not for a private audience of one, but for young women at two Cambridge colleges, and subsequently, in print, for many millions more. Margaret Ferguson has analysed the resistance to patriarchy contained in women's publishing of their writings in the early modern period, but that resistance was equally present in the unpublished letters of Dorothy Osborne, Lady Brilliana Harley, and (in France) of Madame de Sévigné. When Virginia Woolf read Osborne and de Sévigné she perceived an independence of spirit which created alternative values to those of the male world.[1]

Those alternative values were inseparable from writing style. Montaigne said that he would have written letters instead of essays if he had had a friend to whom to write. The provisional nature of the letter and its natural circularity of form he recaptured in his essays. Virginia Woolf said in her essay on Dorothy Osborne that letters were often essays in disguise because letter-writing was 'an art that a woman could practise without unsexing herself' (*CR II*, pp. 60–1). In part she meant that the letter did not impose on women the linear form of a logical argument which printed works, even arguably essays, required. She was aware of practising writing in her letters, as she did also in her diary, explaining to Violet Dickinson:

> This is a specimen of my narrative style, which is far from
> good, seeing I am forever knotting it and twisting it in con-
> formity with the coils in my own brain, and a narrative should
> be as straight and flexible as the line you stretch between pear
> trees, with your linen on drying. (*Letters*, 1. 300)

The form of the letter defied a classic structure. But also, of course,
because it was not printed, it allowed women in the early modern period to relish the pleasure of writing without the pains
associated with female authorship. Dorothy Osborne expressed
scorn for the Duchess of Newcastle: 'Sure the poore woman is a
litle distracted, she could never bee soe rediculous else as to
venture at writeing book's and in verse too. If I should not sleep
this fortnight I should not come to that.'[2] She did read it, however, and claimed that 'there are many soberer People in Bed-
lam, i'le swear her friends are much to blame to let her goe
abroade' (p. 79). Woolf commented on Dorothy Osborne's sleight
of hand in relation to her own letter-writing: 'the Lady Newcastle writing books a sign of her madness wh. D will never
come to: yet she was doing it as she wrote' (MHP/B.3c). Women
who wrote letters could disclaim authorship in the eyes of the
male world, and with it, authority over the reader, while in fact
practising both. They could also experience the subversive pleasure
of composition.

In 'The Pastons and Chaucer' (the essay which opens the first
*Common Reader*), the Paston women do not write for the pleasure of the pen: 'There is no writing for writing's sake; no use of
the pen to convey pleasure or amusement or any of the million
shades of endearment and intimacy which have filled so many
English letters since' (*CR I*, pp. 21–2). Far from being a mode of
feminine expression, the letters of Agnes and Margaret Paston
demonstrate a complete submerging of the feminine in business
concerns: 'The prattle of children, the lore of the nursery or
schoolroom, did not find its way into these elaborate communications. For the most part her [Margaret Paston's] letters are the
letters of an honest bailiff to his master, explaining, asking advice, giving news, rendering accounts' (*CR I*, p. 7). They are utilitarian documents. 'But Mrs Paston did not talk about herself'
(p. 6). The single sentence occupies a paragraph of its own. Just
as, in Woolf's view, the joy of reading Chaucer came to John
Paston once he had leisure to sit and dream instead of pursuing

his business, so the enjoyment of writing grows from a sense of self developed at leisure. Mrs Paston did not write about herself because she had no free time in which to discover the pleasure of writing which gives the writer a mental universe to explore and govern.

That pleasure Woolf found in different forms in both Dorothy Osborne and Madame de Sévigné, the former read for the second *Common Reader*, the latter for the 'Common History' which was to be its sequel. She would have found it also in the earlier letter-writer Lady Brilliana Harley, corresponding in 1638 with her fourteen-year-old son at Oxford. All three women relish access to the word as a means of resisting roles forced on them in society. Letters allow them a private theatre in which to create alternative voices for themselves. They are all to some extent conscious of both aspects of letter-writing: the delight in the word, and the new arena it provides for the flexing of unused muscles. Yes, even women letter-writers, allegedly sodden with sensibility, have sinews, which are evident in their awareness that the use of language involves choices which challenge male hierarchies.

Virginia Woolf fervently admired Dorothy Osborne's English, which she felt embodied conscious artistic aims. Dorothy Osborne wants to write as she talks, declaring in a passage which Woolf annotated in her Reading Notes:[3]

All Letters mee thinks should bee free and Easy as ones discourse, not studdyed, as an Oration, nor made up of hard words like a Charme. Tis an admirable thing to see how some People will labour to finde out term's that may Obscure a plaine sence, like a gentleman I knew, whoe would never say the weather grew cold, but that Winter began to salute us. I have noe patience for such Coxcomb's and cannot blame an old Uncle of mine that threw the Standish at his mans head because he writt a letter for him where instead of sayeing (as his Master bid him) that hee would have writ himself but that hee had the Goute in his hand; hee sayed that the Goute in his hand would not permitt him to put pen to paper. The ffellow thought hee had mended it Mightily and that putting pen to paper was much better then plaine writeing. (p. 131)

The tone is light, but the attack on pretensions to false eloquence is trenchant. Plain writing has its own anti-Ciceronian history in the early modern period, but an increasingly significant part of that history is redrawn along gender lines. Women do not want to write like male orators, and in making that choice they stake out an alternative entry into language. Dorothy's old uncle was probably Francis Osborne, whose *Advice to a Son* was a second Bible to Pepys; Osborne advised the letter-writer: 'When business or Complement calls you to *write Letters,* Consider what is fit to be said, were the Party present, and set down that.'[4] Letters are seen as part of an oral culture, a conscious choice by women of their own tradition.

For Woolf Madame de Sévigné's letters are also part of that alternative tradition of speech as opposed to writing: 'It is natural to use the present tense, because we live in her presence. We are very little conscious of a disturbing medium between us—that she is living, after all, by means of written words. But now and then with the sound of her voice in our ears and its rhythm rising and falling within us, we become aware, with some sudden phrase, about spring, about a country neighbour, something struck off in a flash, that we are, of course, being addressed by one of the great mistresses of the art of speech' (p. 39). Edward Fitzgerald, (whose letters, written in the mid-nineteenth century, Woolf admired), forms a link between Woolf's perception of the naturalness of the French writer, and the traditions of 'Anon' which were foremost in Woolf's mind as she read Madame de Sévigné in the last months of her life. In *A Room of One's Own* she had written that 'Anon' was 'often a woman. It was a woman, Edward Fitzgerald, I think, suggested who made ballads and the folk-songs, crooning them to her children, beguiling her spinning with them, or the length of a winter's night' (*RO*, p. 51). Fitzgerald called Madame de Sévigné the 'Queen of all Letter writers',[5] and compiled a *Dictionary* of the characters in the letters, which Woolf used and annotated.

Virginia Woolf insisted, against critical tradition, that there was nothing artless about Madame de Sévigné's letters.[6] Every sentence registered the writer's flexing of her powers over language. Woolf believes that Madame de Sévigné's ability to write with consummate art when she appears to take no pains to do so, comes from the company she keeps both in life and in books: 'La Rochefoucauld's wisdom, Madame de La Fayette's conversation, by hearing now a play by Racine, by reading Montaigne, Rabelais, or Pascal, perhaps by sermons, perhaps by some of those songs that Coulanges was always singing' (p. 39). Madame de Sévigné never thought of publication.[7] Nevertheless she wrote to her daughter, Madame de Grignan: 'Good heavens, my love, how lovely your letters are. There are passages in them worth printing: one of these days you will find that one of your friends has betrayed you.'[8] Was this ingenuous, a hint, or some subconscious sense that perhaps a friend would one day print *her* letters? It was a hint taken, if so, and one must perhaps forgive Madame de Grignan her legendary coldness for the virtue of having faithfully preserved her mother's voluminous correspondence. Madame de Sévigné never thought of a public readership, but every sentence is a demonstration of her control of her world.

The Frenchwoman's love of writing bewitched Woolf at a time when her own work was constrained by the onset of war and the narrowing of her life to the village scene at Rodmell consequent on the bombing of London. She read Madame de Sévigné to keep alive her own sense of the pleasures of the pen regardless of print and a wide readership. In that pleasure remained power, even if the public readership was no more. The letters that she received at this time had dwindled to mere business communications: 'Letters fret me. Never one thats disinterested.' She refreshed her spirit with 'Madame de Sevigne—who may inspire me, as good writing does, to write to Ethel [Smyth]—so no more' (5. 164). Reading Madame de Sévigné brought relief from the endless letters to be absorbed for the Fry biography, and became part of an ordered existence: 'I was just getting into the old, very old rhythm of regular reading, first this book then that; Roger all the morning; walk from 2 to 4; bowls 5 to 6.30: then Madame de Sevigné' (*Diary*, 5. 173). She wrote to Jacques-Emile Blanche, who had asked her for a copy of the second *Common Reader*:

> Having finished Chateaubriand, I am now reading 15 volumes of Madame de Sévigné. Has anyone written a life of her—a real life? But I must not begin upon Madame de Sévigné or you would have a whole new volume of the common Reader, solely devoted to her, upon your hands! (*Letters*, 6. 282).

In January 1939 she wrote to Ethel Smyth: 'My eyes swim with reading. Can't relish Sévigné or Chaucer' (*Letters*, 6. 309). Like Sainte-Beuve and Edward Fitzgerald, Woolf used Sévigné for consolation. The consolation came from the revitalising reminder that writing involves pleasures which provide alternatives to the acknowledged rewards and gratifications of the public male world, and that women historically have seized on those pleasures when they were denied other forms of recognition.

Woolf's pleasure in Madame de Sévigné's letters was inseparable from her resistance to the encroaching of war. Her Reading Notes on Madame de Sévigné are headed: '"Civilization; or, Mme de Sevigné. Written during the crisis of Sept 1938"'.[8] They contain an entry: 'The growl of war in the distance—guns heard very far off. . . . Grignan speaks of India. the heart the only thing she cares about' (Berg, XVI). The final paragraph of her posthumously published essay on Madame de Sévigné poignantly evokes a peacetime vision:

> Here is the garden that Europe has been digging for many centuries; into which so many generations have poured their blood; here it is at last fertilised, bearing flowers. And the flowers are not those rare and solitary blossoms—great men, with their poems, and their conquests. The flowers in this garden are a whole society of full grown men and women from whom want and struggle have been removed; growing together in harmony, each contributing something that the other lacks. . . . The voices mingle; they are all talking together in the garden in 1678. But what was happening outside?[10]

Paradoxically, that encroaching movement spurs the letter-writer to create a space from which to resist intrusion. The woman's creative pleasure in the pen is pitted against the male pursuit of destructive weaponry, for Woolf, as also for Madame de Sévigné. Patriarchy and hierarchy threatened for both women to destroy the garden in which the pen might create not only pleasure, but the pleasure of resistance.

Madame de Sévigné symbolised for Virginia Woolf her resistance not only to war, but to a male-dominated literary world:

> I am reading Sevigné: how recuperative last week; gone stale a little with that mannered & sterile Bussy [Comte de Bussy, Sévigné's cousin] now. Even through the centuries his acid dandified somehow supercilious well what?—cant find the word— this manner of his, this character penetrates; & moreover

reminds me of someone I dislike. Is it Logan [Pearsall Smith]?
Theres a ceremony in him that reminds me of Tom [Eliot].
There's a parched artificial cruelty &—oh the word! the word!
(*Diary*, 5. 320)

In the margin she wrote 'supercilious'. Madame de Sévigné's clear-
eyed mockery of her world ignited Woolf's sardonic fires. She
perhaps saw the Frenchwoman as the ideal subject for a common reader because her letters were written in the easy, vital
and informal style in which Woolf had always wanted to write
literary criticism. Woolf described her new 'Common History'
as burrowing into literature as into a great cheese, or wandering
into a maze: 'I'm going to write a book of discovery, reading as
one pulls a string out; & must follow my trail through Sevigne
Michelet Somerset Maugham &c. That's the idea; encouraged by
that vast marsupial Margery Strachey, who implored me to do
criticism: as indeed I've long wanted' (*Diary*, 5. 205). She still
courted new forms of critical writing: 'Suppose I used the diary
form? Would this make one free to go from book to book—or
wd it be too personal? . . . So to Sevigne &c. But I must let it
simmer' (*Diary*, 5. 210). Her ideal was to remain free of formal
constraint: 'I'm reading Sevigné, professionally for that quick
amalgamation of books that I intend. In future, I'm to write quick,
intense, short books, & never be tied down. This is the way to
keep off the settling down & refrigeration of old age. And to
flout all preconceived theories—For more & more I doubt if enough
is known to sketch even probable lines, all too emphatic and
conventional' (*Diary*, 5. 214). Madame de Sévigné flouted the
pretensions of her world in a style combustible in its lightness.

In her iconoclastic mood Woolf demolishes the inherited concept of the 'literary', as opposed to the unliterary, a distinction
carrying always in her thought charges of constraint and domination by educated men over uneducated women. One of her
earliest reviews, in 1905, had been of *The Letters of Jane Welsh
Carlyle*, an essay which, despite her enormous admiration for
the letters (which she classed, with Edward Fitzgerald's, as the
greatest ever written) she found difficult to write because 'letters
are not literature' (*Letters*, 1. 198). But by 1940 her career as a
literary critic had collapsed that distinction by which letters occupy outer darkness in the male category of 'literature'. She increasingly associated the 'literary' with 'insiders', university

professors such as F.L. Lucas, whom she declared cut up English literature with a pen-knife, demonstrating professionalism by insisting on dividing books into the literary and the unliterary. If letters were outsiders in the literary hierarchy, by 1940 they had joined the reputable club which she had proposed in *Three Guineas* for women and working men.

The question of where letter-writing fitted into literary activity always exercised her. She wrote to Clive Bell in 1907:

> Well then, how am I to write a letter? But perhaps you have observed that this is a favourite device with letter writers, they are always in haste, or in discomfort, or in a temper, so that you only get the dregs of their genius, and you can speculate what a letter it would have been—seeing there are six careful sheets already—had he had time & temper, or so on. And I put 'he' because a woman, dear Creature, is always naked of artifice; and that is why she generally lives so well, and writes so badly. (*Letters*, 1. 289).

Later Bell accused her letters of 'literariness' and she retorted: 'I deserve your taunt and I am stung by it. But why do I always feel self-conscious when I write to you? I wish you would think that out and tell me' (*Letters*, 1. 418). For Woolf the category of the unliterary always had the power to castigate the literary.[11] She wrote to Vanessa: 'I had my period 2 days ago and spent one morning reading old letters. Needless to say yours beat the literary gents hollow' (*Letters*, 2. 198). She wanted in her literary criticism to recapture some of the unliterary character of the private letter.

In January 1935 when she was beginning work on the novel which would become *The Years* Woolf noted: 'This is rather the style of Here & Now: my random rapid letter writing style' (*Diary*, 4. 199). Sketches for the new critical work which she contemplated in the couple of years before her death were called 'Notes for Reading at Random'.[12] Both ideas summon up her original sketch, in the Preface to her first book of essays, of the woman as common reader. In the letters she practised being a 'common writer': writing at random. She was planning a new fantasy 'The Jessamy Brides': 'Everything is to be tumbled in pall mall. It is to be written as I write letters at the top of my speed' (*Diary*, 3. 131). The provisional nature of the form fitted her wish to find some critical method which was loose and free and would suit her way of reading. Madame de Sévigné would be her ideal common reader because the Frenchwoman knew that artlessness was not lack of art but resistance to the world which determines the definition of art.

In her essay on Madame de Sévigné Woolf blurs the distinction between fiction and non-fiction, the literary and the non-literary form. Madame de Sévigné becomes momentarily a figure in a book, in the same way that the Frenchwoman regarded many of the people in her letters as copied from books she had read, or suitable for inclusion in future works by famous writers. Asking her daughter for the originals of Terence's works as she didn't like the translations, Madame de Sévigné wrote: 'My son will translate the satire against foolish love affairs for me and ought to write one himself, or at least to profit by this one.'[13] Her world is a theatrical spectacle. Of her interchanges with her son about his rejection by the courtesan Ninan she wrote: 'He said the maddest things in the world and so did I; it was a scene worthy of Molière.'[14] Of a match broken off: 'What a beautiful dream, what a beautiful subject for a romance or a tragedy.'[15] In this respect she resembles Woolf, whom Catharine Stimpson sees as 'a performer, an actress, and the letters are bravura, burnishing fragments of performance art. She creates a series of private theaters for an audience of one, each with its own script and scenery, lights and costumes' (p. 169). This is perhaps more true of Madame de Sévigné, because her experience was of plays rather than novels, whereas Woolf's letters convey a powerful sense of the reader. Woolf wrote that 'it was when the playhouses were shut presumably that the reader was born. The curious faculty of making houses and countries visible, and men and women and their emotions, from marks on a printed page was undeveloped . . . so long as the play was dominant.'[16] At the time that Aphra Behn in England was braving hostility as a female professional playwright, Madame de Sévigné created in her letters her own private dramas. If her audience is limited to one, her *Dramatis Personae* are many and varied. She relishes the fact that letters allow her to make free with the male world precisely because the audience they address laughs in a drawing-room instead of in an auditorium.

Madame de Sévigné wrote for love, ostensibly for love of her daughter, but equally for love of *writing*: an amateur. Her letters undercut professionalism as vigorously as Woolf's do. Virginia wrote to Clive Bell in 1909: 'I should like to turn Oxford into a Cathedral city and people it with Deans and widow ladies. The profession of learning should be carried on in a manufacturing town. Perhaps in your 18th century they managed things better, I detest the modern way of it. I detest pale scholars with their questioning about life, and the message of the classics, and the bearing of Greek thought upon modern problems' (*Letters*, 1. 386). The letter provides her with a unique space for articulating to a captive audience the message which was to dominate *A Room of One's Own*, and later, *Three Guineas*, of the resistance of women and of working men to the élite masculine world established in the two ancient universities. The subculture form marks out the ground on which Woolf can explore her resistance not only to conventional literary forms, but also to the masculine foundations of writing and thinking.

## PREACHING, PASSION AND PRIVACY

In the seventeenth century women's lives were dominated by religion and the family, whose demands dictated the boundaries of feeling and action. But in the letters of Lady Brilliana Harley, Dorothy Osborne and Madame de Sévigné, those boundaries are repeatedly transgressed, making the letter the repository of pioneer energy. The three writers differ in how they relate to religion and the family, yet their letters share a consciousness that the pen, wielded in private, is a prime instrument of both evasion and invasion, escape and intrusion.

As literacy advanced in the seventeenth century, women and working men acquired access to a medium of manipulation – the written word – hitherto closed to them. Patricia Meyer Spacks has argued that in Jane Austen's early experimental epistolary novel, *Lady Susan*, the novelist explores the subversive and revolutionary possibilities of the letter for women: 'Writing becomes a form of agency for their wishes.' The concerns of the novel are 'the problem of female power, the problem of feeling, the possibility for women of writing as action'. The letters in the novel 'experimented with quiet modes of undermining'.[17] This undermining could be traced in real letters by women, not just fictional ones. The letter spelled power over the reader, as Samuel

Richardson realised before he composed either *Pamela* or *Clarissa*, starting his writing career with a modest manual on letter-writing, *Familiar Letters on Important Occasions* (1741). Richardson was an admirer of Madame de Sévigné[18] and could hardly have failed to notice the way in which her epistolary narratives exercise dominion over the characters they describe and the reader they address. Sainte-Beuve's essay on Madame de Sévigné ends conjuring up a fictional reader who will read Madame de Sévigné's letters, as one would read *Clarissa*, on a rainy fortnight in the country.[19] Sainte-Beuve may have sensed other connections between de Sévigné and Richardson, besides the demands they make on the reader. In a male-dominated world Madame de Sévigné shares Clarissa Harlowe's independence of spirit.[20] Sainte-Beuve wrote of Sévigné that although she was brought up within sight of Port-Royal, this did not make her less responsive to Montaigne or less willing to quote the famous inscription on the gate of the Abbey of Thelema in Rabelais's *Gargantua and Pantagruel*: '*Fais ce que voudras*'. She knew that gender hierarchies, like social hierarchies, could be undermined within the private power structures of the personal letter. When Richardson composed his *Familiar Letters* he offered to the newly literate tools to enable them to assert themselves (and the modern word associations of 'assertiveness' is singularly appropriate for the kind of letters Richardson composes) in domestic and working environments.

Richardson's *Familiar Letters*[21] address themselves in the main to the social category of working men and women to which Pamela, the serving-girl heroine of his own later novel, belongs. His model letters encompass problems of both employment and family. Command of language and of forcible expressions enable the writer to stake out a territory of resistance, insisting on a contract between writer and reader. Seventeenth-century letters provided a vital forging ground for the novel because they renegotiated that contract.[22] Woolf believed that both Osborne and Madame de Sévigné would have been novelists in a later century. The dual relationship which Woolf had argued in 'The Patron and the Crocus' (*CR I*) was so vital to writing (writer and reader are twins, either of whom will die without the other) is enshrined in the letter as a form: 'A good letter-writer so takes the colour of the reader at the other end, that from reading the one we can imagine the other,' Woolf wrote of Dorothy Osborne's letters.[23] But equally letters allow the writer to fashion her own image in defiance of the marginalization which the unliterary form of the letter suggests.

Women do not in the early modern period have public voices in religion except within a very few of the dissenting sects. Yet radical Protestantism – both in its early manifestations and in Puritan thought – allowed women a new status of spiritual authority and new access to sacred writings, as indeed had been feared by Church authorities when the Bible was translated into English. Lady Brilliana Harley's letters, which Woolf had not apparently read, form an interesting complement to those of Dorothy Osborne and Madame de Sévigné. Harley writes to her son Edward with as passionate an attachment as Madame de Sévigné's to her daughter, even if it is expressed with more restraint. What is surprising is the degree of authority which Harley's letters claim, an authority grounded in religious conviction. The church may not have allowed her to preach, but her letters provide an outlet for convictions which in a man would undoubtedly have led to the pulpit. She wrote to Ned on his arrival at Oxford:

> You are now in a place of more varietyes then when you weare at home; thearefore take heede it take not vp your thoughtes so much as to neglect the constant saruis you owe to your God. When I liued abroode, I tasted something of those willes: thearefore I may the more experimentally giue you warneing.[24]

In this letter Harley (a devout Lutheran who uses a period of sickness to translate Calvin's *Life of Luther* into English) invokes Luther's privileging of experience and feeling over intellect and reason. That inversion, so significant for Bunyan, marks a movement towards the feminising of religious tradition.

Despite differences in class and education, Lady Brilliana Harley often anticipates Bunyan's spirit. It is odd to hear her use the language of Christian's defiance of Apollyon in *The Pilgrim's Progress*, written forty years later: 'Be confident, he is the best Master, and will giue the best waiges' (p. 16). Bunyan said that he owed his conversion to women, and Lady Brilliana Harley is one of the many women who seem to be the heirs of Anne Askew and her fellow martyrs in Foxe's record. She wrote to her son:

And my dearest, beleeue this from mee, that theare is no sweetnes in any thinge in this life to be compared to the sweetnes in the saruis of our God, and this I thanke God, I cane say, not only to agree with thos that say so, but experimentally; I haue had health and frinds and company in variety, and theare was a time, that what could I have saide I wanted; yet in all that theare was a trubell, and that which gaue me peace, was sarueing of my God, and not the saruis of the world. And I haue had a time of siknes, and weakenes, and the loose of frinds, and as I may say, the glideing away of all thos things I tooke most comfort in, in this life. (p. 34).

The world did not require martyrdom of her as it might have done a hundred years earlier, but nor did it allow her an outlet for her talents, such as would have been available to a man as well educated in theology and as gifted in spiritual exhortation as her letters show her to be. Instead, literacy allows her, as it would allow Bunyan, to break out of her silence through the writing of letters.

Madame de Sévigné, from a very different religious tradition, rebels in her own way. Her attitude to religion is brisk; after a religious dispute she wrote to her daughter: 'In the end this argument effectively woke me up: without it I would have died of boredom.'[25] She detested religious excess, declaring to Monsieur de Pomponne that she had seen his aunt at mass 'who was engulfed in religious sentiment; she attended mass in a state of ecstasy'; she commented tartly: 'I believe that the middle way between such extremes is always the best.'[26] In other aspects of her life she was not so addicted either to rationalism, or to the middle way, as Woolf perceived when she analysed Madame de Sévigné's passion for her daughter.

Madame de Sévigné knew that her feelings for her daughter were far beyond what was conventional in her own society for the relation between parent and child. She wrote to Madame de Grignan: 'The tenderness I feel for you, my dear child, runs in my blood-stream and is mingled with the marrow of my bones; it is a part of my being, I feel it as I speak it.'[27] She lives in longing for her daughter's letters: 'I only want for myself one page of writing, because your health matters to me more than anything else, including my own happiness, which can only be secured when you are once again well.'[28] She is conscious of a transference of religious feeling from the Deity to her daughter:

> If you think of me, my poor dear, rest assured that I think continually of you: it is what religious devotees call a constant meditation; what one ought to practise towards God, if one did one's duty. Nothing affords me any distraction; I am always with you; I see a carriage which always rolls forward but will never reach me; I am for ever on the great highway;. it is as if I am sometimes afraid it will overturn.[29]

The overturned carriage overturns the mysticism of the preceding image, which had momentarily invoked Donne's view of letter-writing as a mystic communication between souls.[30] In an increasingly secular world letters fill an emotional void created by the loss of religious fervour.

Although Madame de Sévigné's *Letters* are always spoken of as though they had no precedent, her devotion to her daughter finds a mirror image in Lady Brilliana Harley's letters, written between 1638 and 1643, to her son. For both women motherhood is a mystical condition of union with the child, which evokes a quasi-religious language. Harley wrote to Edward: 'You are my well-beloved child; thearefore I care not but tell you I mise you. . . . If you would have any thinge let me knowe it. Be not forgetful to rwit to me' (p. 8). She declared: 'My life is bounde with yours, and I hope I shall neuer have caus to recall or repent of my loue, with which I loue you' (p. 21). She wants him to share her feelings: 'My deare Ned, long to see me, as I doo, to see you' (p. 94). At one point she calls him her 'Joseph', just as Julia Duckworth Stephen had later called Adrian Stephen her 'Benjamin'. Letters allow both women to articulate a passion previously unrecorded. The letter becomes a document of female power, of women mapping out new territories for themselves.

Virginia Woolf's posthumous essay on Madame de Sévigné is initially unsympathetic to her feeling for her daughter. Woolf adopts a disparaging male critical voice, condemning the Frenchwoman's passion as 'twisted and morbid',[31] and highlighting the coldness of Madame de Grignan's response and the embarrassment her mother's effusions apparently caused her:

Sometimes, therefore, Madame de Sévigné weeps. The daughter does not love her. That is a thought so bitter, and a fear so perpetual and so profound, that life loses its savour; she has recourse to sages, to poets to console her; and reflects with sadness upon the vanity of life; and how death will come. Then, too, she is agitated beyond what is right or reasonable, because a letter has not reached her. Then she knows that she has been absurd; and realizes that she is boring her friends with this obsession. What is worse, she has bored her daughter. And then when the bitter drop has fallen, up bubbles quicker and quicker the ebullition of that robust vitality, of that irrepressible quick enjoyment, that natural relish for life, as if she instinctively repaired her failure by fluttering all her feathers; by making every facet glitter. (p. 38)

The tone of the paragraph quickens and warms as Woolf proceeds. Did it occur to her that Madame de Sévigné's passion for her daughter bore a resemblance to her own passion for her sister Vanessa, which on occasion caused equal discomfort? The comparison is worth making not just for the congruence of feeling the letters demonstrate, but for their control over the reader. While seeming to supplicate, both letter-writers in fact command. When Madame de Sévigné waits for her daughter's letters, she draws Madame de Grignan into the magnetic circle of a relationship not just of mother and daughter, but of writer and reader: 'I am completely convinced that letters will come for me; I have no doubt that you have written; but I am still waiting for them and they don't appear: I have to comfort and amuse myself by writing to you.'[32] Her anxiety, her demand to be read, creates its own centre of power to which the reader must submit.

The same dominance is evident in Woolf's letters to Vanessa Bell, which, in their hunger for a response, become formidably importunate. In 1908 she demanded: 'Write an immense long letter. I pine if they don't come' (*Letters*, 1. 358). A week earlier she had written: 'Shall you kiss me tomorrow? Yes, Yes, Yes. Ah, I cannot bear being without you. I was thinking today of my greatest happiness, a walk along a cliff by the sea, and you at the end of it' (*Letters*, 1. 355). She demands: 'Do you really love me? How often a day do you think of me?' (*Letters*, 2. 157). On another occasion: 'I now begin another letter, partly that should I die tonight you may know that my last thoughts were of you.

Not that you care—but think of all the gossip you'd miss—yes, that touches the one sensitive spot' (*Letters*, 2. 213). The unreciprocated passion, the extravagant language, the burning raw need for love, reincarnate Madame de Sévigné imploring her daughter to write to her.

Woolf's letters to Vanessa Bell combat the emotional sidelining which Virginia experienced once Vanessa was married and had a baby; Woolf gloatingly sketches a private past world of communication which excludes present intruders:

> At this season we should be walking together; I am in just the mood to discuss winter plans. Leaves are falling, and there is a soft gusty wind, not too cold though; I should make you stay out till dinner time, and I have found the perfect evening walk, with such a view for the home coming, which was wont to be the best time. We had got excited then, and were saying what we really thought, of our gifts and futures; and sometimes you said such delicious things, and I walked like a peacock, all aglow. I wonder if I ever said such things to you. Did you ever feel neglected? Well, your daughter will know more one day than I ever shall.

The needle of jealousy at the end is born out by the next sentence: 'By the way, I have imagined precisely what it is like to have a child. I woke up, and understood, as in a revelation, the precise nature of the pain' (*Letters*, 1. 348). As Woolf contemplates being displaced by Vanessa Bell's (so far imaginary) daughter, she displaces the daughter by imagining producing her. She reported to Violet Dickinson in 1907: 'Nessa comes tomorrow—what one calls Nessa; but it means husband and baby, and of sister there is less than there used to be' (*Letters*, 1. 307). She wrote to her sister in 1911, when she was herself already flirting with Vanessa's husband, Clive Bell: 'This is the first of the new series of letters, which is written for you only; and Clive shall have letters for himself only, and so we shall all profit, by the gain in passion' (*Letters*, 1. 468). The sense of exclusion is palpable, but it is also an attempt to divide, dominate and exclude one of the two recipients, thus forcing them to make a space for the writer of the letter. She lamented suggestively to Vanessa's husband: 'When Nessa is bumbling about the world, and making each thorn blossom, what room is there for me?' (*Letters*, 1. 330). The delicate fencing of the pen dominates the reader.

For Harley, de Sévigné and Woolf letters are manifestos of female power. Despite the fact that they are testimonies of loneliness, and of women's isolation in their own societies, all these women relish the solitude which allows them to write, even as they suffer from the isolation which creates that opportunity. The very privacy of the letter ensures the freedom of the writer. Woolf mused in August 1939, just three weeks before the outbreak of war: 'I have been thinking about Censors. How visionary figures admonish us. That's clear in an MS I'm reading. If I say this So & So will think me sentimental. If that...will think me Bourgeois. All books now seem to me to be surrounded by a circle of invisible censors. Hence their selfconsciousness, their restlessness. It wd. be worth while trying to discover what they are at the moment' (*Diary*, 5. 229). She had exhorted her cousin Emma Vaughan in 1899: 'Do write me a letter full of *thoughts*: I like *thoughts* in a letter—not *facts* only. By the way, did Nessa tell you of her long letter from Madge—she said that—but I remember you think it wrong to repeat other people's letters, so I certainly will not say any more about it. Only there were some *facts* in this letter of great interest' (*Letters*, 1. 28–9). Censorship of all kinds fascinated her.

For Virginia Woolf censorship had been associated with letters in a piquant manner in 1909 when she and her friends tried the experiment of writing a novel through a correspondence between imagined characters. Under the pseudonym of Vane Hatherly Lytton Strachey hinted at Virginia's flirtation with her brother-in-law Clive Bell. Virginia responded: 'So you've noticed it then? How clever you are, and how unkind! For don't you think that these "extraordinary conclusions" you like so much may be rather uncomfortable for me and perhaps (though I really won't admit it) a little uncomfortable for Clarissa [Vanessa]?' (*Letters*, 1. 382). Her own resistance to self-censorship consists mainly in flouting conventions of prudery. She wrote to Jacques Raverat that Lydia Lopokova was in trouble with the house staff at Charleston for burning her sanitary towels on an open fire. In equally coarse vein she accosted Duncan Grant:

I wish I could stop writing this letter—it is like an extremely long visit to the W.C. when, do what you will, fresh coils appear, and duty seems to urge you to break off, and then another inch protrudes, which must be the last; and it *isn't* the last—and so on, until—.... Do tell Nessa this one flaming

invention of mine—I make my own sanitary towels, and save
at least 2/6 a month (*Letters*, 2. 146).

She mocks wartime saving while flamboyantly indulging in
Bloomsbury free speech. Woolf always believed that letters fos-
ter a lack of inhibition, writing to Emma Vaughan: 'I have a
vague idea that your caution is thawed when you take a pen in
your hand. Surely it is very different to write secrets than to
speak them' (*Letters*, 1. 23). Her own caution was not much in
evidence in either writing or speaking.

Seventeenth-century letter-writers would have had no doubt
at all that it was safer to speak secrets than to write them down.[33]
Dorothy Osborne's letters to William Temple perhaps survive
because their personal nature made it safe for them to be kept,
where none of Temple's to her have survived. He obviously in-
structed her to burn his letters, for she wrote in 1653: 'You must
pardon mee I could not burn your other letter for my life. I was
soe pleased to see I had soe much to reade, & soe sorry I had
don soe soone, that I resolved to begin them again and had like
to have lost my dinner by it' (p. 82). On another occasion she
was enraged with the carrier for bringing a letter from Temple
with the seal broken and fell out with him mightily: 'Hee takes
it soe heavily that I think I must bee freinds with him againe
but pray hereafter seale your letters soe as the difficulty of opening
them may dishearten any body from attempting it' (p. 86). In
her reading of the letters of Lady Ann Bacon (which she reminded
herself to compare with Madame de Sévigné's letters), Woolf noted
Lady Ann's use of quotations in Latin and Greek.[34] Those quotations are not mere flights of learning; they are used for censorable remarks, to prevent their being read by servants or other
interceptors. When Lady Ann complains that Archbishop Whitgift
is destroying the Church she writes in Greek.

Dorothy Osborne's letters to Temple contain no politically
dangerous material, as do those of her contemporary, Lady
Brilliana Harley, to her son Edward. Harley admonishes Ned
that she would write more but for fear of being intercepted. She
warns him in 1638: 'When you rwite by the carrier, rwite nothing but what any may see, for many times the letters miscarry'
(*Nove.* 17, 1638, p. 11). During the siege of Brompton Castle she
wrote several letters which had to be read with the aid of a key
of cut paper held over the letter, which then consisted of the

parts which could be read through the cuts: 'You must pin that end of the paper, that has the cros made in incke, vpon the littell cros on the end of this letter; when you would write to me, make vse of it, and giue the other to your sister Brill' (*Mar: the first, 1642*, p. 192). It was safer to write to the seventeen-year-old youth than to his father: 'Tell your father what I haue writen; he may eassyly gees at the reson why I did not wright to him' (*Mar: 3, 1642*, p. 194).

Equally interesting is a kind of personal censorship: 'Your father dous not knowe I send. Thearefore take no notis of it, to him, nor to any' (*Decem. 14*, 1638). This is followed by a postscript to underscore the same point: 'Nobody in the howes knowes I send to you' (p. 17), creating a curious effect of relished intimacy in the secrecy of the whole enterprise, almost as though Harley were writing to a lover rather than to a son. She passes on a great deal of information about her husband's role in the army:

> On munday last, theare came a letter from the lord leftenants, with commande from the kinge to prees 200 men for soulders, and that they should be at theare randevous the first of Aprill; theare randevous is Assbe, as I take it, neare Yorke; neare Yorke the towne is, if that be not the name. If you weare with me, I could tell you more of my minde. (*Mar. 29*, 1639, p. 37).

A week later she writes: 'I haue told you if you remember of a paper that some statemen make use of, when they would not haue knowne what they rwite of. Rwite me word wheather you understand what I meane' (*April 5*, 1639, p. 40). Her fascination with politics shows her using the letter as a form of journalism, in the same way that Madame de Sévigné's letters might have made her a fortune in a later age as a court gossip columnist. Letters provide a testimony of women's determination to be involved in male activity; their censorable contents defy the isolation which their very existence proclaims.[35]

The privacy of letters ensures the freedom of women writers to resist the dominant modes of their own society, whether they be manifested in the constraints created by religious authority, in the conventions surrounding the expression of emotion, or in the secret censors which condition writing itself. Letters are sites for exemption. When Woolf wrote hers, she recognised that in the seventeenth century her female forebears in the art of letter-

writing had fashioned for themselves a formidable instrument
not just for the pursuit of pleasure but for the exercise of power.

## RESISTING THE FAMILY: DOROTHY OSBORNE

Lady Ann Bacon had written fiercely to her sons that they were
to remember that they had no father, and that it would have
been better for both of them if they had 'regarded your kind
and no simple mother's advice from time to time'.[36] They may
not have had a father, but they certainly had a Volumnia of a
mother. Few women in the early modern period could have stated
their authority in such explicitly male tones, especially to sons
who were themselves in the public eye. But the claiming of authority within the letter is not unusual in the early modern period, especially when it takes the form of resisting the dominance
of men within the family. Increased freedom of the Press in the
Civil War, which made it more possible for women to publish
their writings, may have encouraged women to write even if
they disapproved of the notion of publishing. The increasing gap
between patriarchal notions of women as all deference and obe-
dience, and the much more varied reality, became as strikingly
obvious during the Civil War years[37] as it was to be nearly three
hundred years later during and after the First World War.

Dorothy Osborne's letters to William Temple (written over a
period of two years between 1652 and 1654) are part of the legacy
of the Civil War; her romance with Temple began during the
course of that conflict. Her royalist family disapproved of her
love for Temple as much as his Parliamentarian one disapproved
of her. Resistance is part of the lovers' language. Temple's father
has to be propitiated, and Dorothy's family has to be dissuaded
from matching her with other suitors. Dorothy writes to William:
'I shall not blush to tell you, that you have made the whole
world besydes soe indifferent to mee, that if I cannot bee yours
They may dispose mee how they please.' She continues by offering
Temple advice on how to handle his father's opposition: 'What
his disposition may bee I know not, but 'tis that of many Parents
to Judge there Childrens dislikes, to bee an humor of aproveing
nothing that is Chosen for them, which many times makes them
take up another of denyeing theire Children all they Chuse for
themselv's' (p. 63). The letters constituted an act of rebellion not

only against the opposition of Temple's father to the match, but against her own brother and other members of the family who try to marry her off to wealthy suitors: 'I had noe quarrell to his Person, or his fortune but was in love with neither, and much out of love with a thing called marriage' (p. 42). Unpalatable matches, however, are not the only constraint on her freedom.

The role of daughter was for Dorothy Osborne an arduous one, as she was required to attend her sick father twenty-four hours a day, and Temple's letters to her served as a lifeline:

> You ought in Charity to write as much as you can for in Earnest my life heer since my Fathers sicknesse, is soe sad, that to another humor then mine it would bee unsuportable, but I have bin soe used to misfortun's that I cannot bee much surprised with them, though perhaps I am as sencible of them as another. (pp. 76–7)

She was accustomed to self-denial: 'I doe not know that ever I desyred any thing (Earnestly) in my life but 'twas denyed mee, and I am many times afrayed to wish a thing meerly least my fortunes should take occasion to use me ill' (p. 51). The Civil War only finds one explicit reference in her letters, but her resistance to her way of life grows from the awareness, which that time of political and social upheaval has given her, of other worlds in which personal liberty might wear a new face.

Dorothy Osborne's letters resist a familial authority, mainly, but not entirely, exercised by men. But they also create another kind of resistance of a more wide-reaching nature, in proposing a new kind of relation between men and women. In the mid-seventeenth century arranged marriage was still the norm, although the consent of the parties involved was considered more significant than it had been: witness Osborne's own success in stopping the progress of an unwelcome suit. The Puritans had urged in their marriage reforms that forced marriage should be abandoned. Nevertheless Dorothy Osborne describes a world in which inclination plays a small part in marriage arrangements, for both men and women. Her letters are significant documents of cultural history, because they rethink the terms of a relationship between a man and a woman.

A more equal relationship appears possible because the woman is better educated than she would have been fifty years earlier.

The Osbornes were not aristocrats, despite their country property. Dorothy is a match for William mentally, and the letters
are often about books they have both read. In the late sixteenth
century the wife of Robert Sidney, Barbara Gamage, seems, despite her many virtues and the happiness of her marriage, to
have been barely literate.[38] Dorothy Osborne is capable of taking issue with William Temple on various matters, including his
own behaviour and moods. She writes:

> I know not whither my letter were kinde or not, but i'le sweare
> yours was not, and am sure mine was meant to bee soe. It is
> not kinde of you to desyre an increase of my freindship; that
> is to doubt it is not as great already as it can bee, then which
> you cannot doe mee a greater injury, 'tis my misfortune in-
> deed that it lyes not in my power to give you better Testimo-
> ny's on't then words, otherwise I should soone convince you,
> that 'tis the best quality I have, and that when I owne a
> freindship, I meane soe perfect a one, as time can neither lessen
> nor increase. (p. 50)

Virginia Woolf described the emotion in this passage in her Reading Notes as 'fervour' (MHP/B3c). But the recurrence of the word
'friendship' is equally notable.

Dorothy Osborne often sounds like Jane Austen in her scepticism about passion. When she speaks of rejecting her unwelcome suitors, she explains to Temple:

> It was nothing that I expected made me refuse these, but some-
> thing that I feared, and seriously I finde I want Courage to
> marry where I doe not like. . . . Let them truste to it that think
> good, for my Parte I am cleerly of opinion (and shall dye int)
> that as the more one sees, and know's, a person that one likes,
> one has still the more kindenesse for them, soe on the other
> side one is but the more weary of and the more averse to an
> unpleasant humor for haveing it perpetualy by one, and though
> I easily beleeve that to marry one for whome wee have al-
> ready some affection, will infinitely Encrease that kindenesse
> yet I shall never bee perswaded that Marriage has a Charme
> to raise love out of nothing, much lesse out of dislike. (p. 46)

She despises romantic passion. Yet the letters, under their veil of restraint, are passionate: 'Noe, in Earnest my very dream's are yours, and I have gott such a habitt of thinking of You, that any other thought intrudes and grow's uneasy to mee' (p. 59). She asks: 'Can there bee a more Romance Story then ours would make if the conclusion should prove happy' (p. 164), and draws a picture of the married life she would like:

> Doe you remember Arme and the little house there[?] shall we goe thither[?] that's next to being out of the worlde[.] there wee might live like Baucis and Philemon, grow old together in our lltle Cottage and for our Charrity to some shipwrakt stranger obtaine the blessing of dyeing both at the same time. How idly I talk tis because the Storry pleases mee, none in Ovide soe much. (p. 164)

She continues: 'I remember I cryed when I read it, mee thought they were the perfectest Characters of a con[ten]ted marriage where Piety and Love were all their wealth and in theire poverty feasted the Gods where rich men shutt them out' (p. 165). This vision of marriage lifts Dorothy Osborne into another world from that which both she and Temple inhabit, and the letters create that vision as an ideal fiction hardly to be hoped for. But the written record plays its part in realising the vision, for the lovers did marry, and despite many disasters, appear to have been happy.

The letters cease, as Woolf points out, when the marriage begins. What would one not give, she ends her essay, 'for the letters that Dorothy did not write' (*CR II*, p. 66). The letters she did write both resist her own time and society in the vision of marriage which she proposes, but also create an agency through which a new kind of marriage might come into being. The equal interchange fostered in letters written by women – not formal, not trained, not subject to letter-writing conventions – creates a new contract between writer and reader which becomes the instrument of changed relations between men and women in society itself.

Just as Madame de Sévigné's letters to her daughters suggest a new dimension for the mother–daughter relationship, so letters could pioneer other new relations between women. The Duchess of Newcastle sensed this possibility when she composed her fictional correspondence, *Sociable Letters of Margaret Cavendish,*

*Duchess of Newcastle,* to an imaginary female friend. The Duchess, whose isolation Woolf describes in the first volume of *The Common Reader,* scorns the women she knows, preferring to invent a perfect correspondent, just as in one of her works she invented a new world over which she might reign:

> But womens Minds or Souls are like Shops of small-wares, wherein some have pretty toyes, but nothing of any great value. I imagine you will chide me for this opinion, and I should deserve to be chidden, if all Women were like to you; but you are but one, and I speak of Women, not of One woman; and thus I am neither injurious to You, nor partial to our Sex.[39]

Her contempt for women's triviality goads her search for an alternative. She criticises the normal vicissitudes of female friendships as frivolous: 'Women for the most part take delight to make Friendships, and then to fall out, and be Friends again, and so to and fro, which is as much Pastime and Recreation to them, as going abroad and staying at home.' She sounds dissatisfied with the ordinary run of women friends, and probably played her share in the falling-out. The fiction is more satisfying: 'But I wish all Friends were as constant Friends as your Ladiship and I, who are inseparably united, for as long as I live I shall be' (p. 43). As Virginia Woolf remarked in *A Room of One's Own,* 'if Chloë likes Olivia and Mary Carmichael knows how to express it she will light a torch in that vast chamber where nobody has yet been' (pp. 83–4).

If Margaret Cavendish's *Sociable Letters* look forward to Samuel Richardson they also reflect a movement in the writing of non-fictional letters where women look to each other for support, and in that respect undermine patriarchal culture. Virginia Woolf often used her letters to women to subvert the male world, complaining to her sister on Christmas Day 1909: 'Then there came Lytton and James [Strachey] and Frankie Birrell, Duncan Grant, Keynes, Norton, and [Horace] Cole. They sat round mostly silent, and I wished for any woman—and you would have been a miracle' (*Letters,* 1. 415). She had found that same system of support against the male world in the friendship between Jane Welsh Carlyle and Geraldine Jewsbury, which she celebrated in the essay 'Geraldine and Jane' in the second *Common Reader.* Geraldine wrote to her friend that Thomas Carlyle '"is much too grand for everyday

life. A sphinx does not fit in comfortably to our parlour life arrangements"' (*CR II*, p. 191). The capacity to resist adulation of
the great man to whom Jane Welsh Carlyle always referred to
as 'Man of Genius' highlights the function of letters as agents
through which the pretensions of the male world may be reduced to pulp. Woolf sees Mrs Carlyle as another Jane Austen,
using her pen to puncture the 'pretentiousness or pomposity' of
those around her, as Madame de Sévigné had done in the seventeenth century. Subversion begins at home.

## LETTERS, GREAT MEN AND CRITICISM

Woolf declared of Jane Carlyle that 'while her husband sat upstairs in the sound-proof room deciphering the motives and characters of the actors in some long-forgotten drama, Mrs Carlyle
was practising the same art over her teacups' (*Essays*, 1. 55). Woolf
had mixed feelings about practising any art over tea-cups, castigating herself for too much urbanity and discretion in her *Common Reader* essays. But she did admire any attack by the amateur
on the pretensions of the professional. The personal letter provides the physical and mental space for such aggression. When
Woolf picked out Edward Fitzgerald's letters as particularly congenial, their iconoclasm must have struck an answering note in
her own consciousness.

Edward Fitzgerald wrote in the mid-nineteenth century, before literary criticism had become institutionalised and academic,
something he recognised when he made comparisons between
himself and his friend Spedding, who spent his life working on
his monumental *Letters and Life of Francis Bacon* (1861). Fitzgerald's
letters suggest to Woolf a common reader who resembles herself, and provide a testimony of the kind of reading – and writing about reading – which she admired. After some extremely
discerning comments on Wordsworth, Byron, Shelley and
Tennyson, Fitzgerald declares: 'But I dislike this kind of criticism, especially in a letter. I don't know any one who has thought
out any thing so little as I have. I don't see to any end, and
should keep silent till I have got a little more, and that little
better arranged' (I. 31). The self-deprecation is more in the line
of Woolf's haphazard woman reader than of Johnson's discerning common reader, although Fitzgerald's genuine modesty does

not prevent his expressing outspoken views on everything he reads. The letter, like Montaigne's *Essays*, is a 'trial' form, whose ephemeral nature guarantees its experimental character. It is also a form in which writers, male and female, can swim against the tide of fashion, unhampered by tradition. Privacy creates audacity.

In Fitzgerald's letters literary criticism is often a cutting-down-to-size of great men: 'Then, old "Daddy Wordsworth," as he was sometimes called, I am afraid, from my Christening, he is now, I suppose, passing under the Eclipse consequent on the Glory which followed his obscure Rise. I remember fifty years ago at our Cambridge, when the Battle was fighting for him by the Few against the Many of us who only laughed at 'Louisa in the Shade' &. His Brother was then Master of Trinity College; like all Wordsworths (unless the drowned Sailor) pompous and priggish. He used to drawl out the Chapel responses so that we called him the "Mēēserable Sinner" and his brother the "Mēēserable Poet"' (I. 381). 'Daddy' in Fitzgerald's letters always connotes Wordsworth; he was even more derisive about Carlyle, with whom he was on good terms, but like many others (Jane Carlyle included) chafed under the Great Man's yoke, declaring, after a bout of flu:

> This state of head had not been improved by trying to get through a new book much in fashion—Carlyle's French Revolution—written in a German style. An Englishman writes of French Revolutions in a German style. People say the book is very deep: but it appears to me that the meaning *seems* deep from lying under mystical language. (I. 42).

He was equally scathing about *Heroes and Hero-worship*, expostulating to Frederic Tennyson: 'No new books (except a perfectly insane one of Carlyle, who is becoming very obnoxious now that he is become popular)' (I. 69). He enquires of another friend: 'Have you read poor Carlyle's raving book about heroes? Of course you have, or I would ask you to buy my copy. I don't like to live with it in the house. It smoulders. He ought to be laughed at a little. But it is pleasant to retire to the Tale of a Tub, Tristram Shandy, and Horace Walpole, after being tossed on his canvas waves. This is blasphemy. Dibdin Pitt of the Coburg [popular theatre] could enact one of his heroes' (I. 71). Irreverence was equally the hallmark of his comments on Carlyle's new project on Cromwell: 'I am afraid Carlyle will make a mad mess of

Cromwell and his Times: what a poor figure Fairfax will cut! I am very tired of these heroics; and I can worship no man who has but a square inch of brains more than myself. I think there is but one Hero: and that is the Maker of Heroes' (I. 110). His help with the Cromwell project he declared to have been misused: 'Carlyle has made a bungle of the whole business; and is fairly twitted by the Athenaeum for talking so loud about his veneration for Cromwell &c., and yet not stirring himself to travel a hundred miles to see and save such memorials as he talks of' (I. 183). Fitzgerald, often conjuring up the spirit of Lewis Carroll in his mockery of his world, anticipates Virginia Woolf in demolition mode.

Combined with the undercutting of great men in Fitzgerald's letters is an undercutting of high culture. He found Wesley's Journal fascinating and wrote of Lowell's critical essays, *My Study Windows* (annotated by Woolf in her Reading Notes): 'Voilà par exemple un Livre dont Monsr Lowell pourrait faire une jolie critique, s'il en voudrait, mais il s'occupe de plus grandes chose, du Calderon, du Cervantes. I always wish to run on in bad French: but my friends would not care to read it' (I. 427). The language of Madame de Sévigné, the subculture form, the non-literary, the lives of the obscure, all feed into the world of Virginia Woolf's woman reader. Fitzgerald (famous for his translation of *The Rubáiyát of Omar Khayyám* from Persian into English) translated Aeschylus – freely adapting it to a modern idiom – specifically for women readers.

Fitzgerald's spirit haunts many of Woolf's letters, as when she describes to Violet Dickinson in August 1907 an encounter with Henry James:

Henry James fixed me with his staring blank eye—it is like a childs marble—and said 'My dear Virginia, they tell me—they tell me—they tell me—that you—as indeed being your fathers daughter nay your grandfathers grandchild—the descendant I may say of a century—of a century—of quill pens and ink—ink—ink pots, yes, yes, yes, they tell me—ahm m m—that you, that you, that you *write* in short.' This went on in the public street, while we all waited, as farmers wait for the hen to lay an egg—do they?—nervous, polite, and now on this foot now on that. I felt like a condemned person, who sees the knife drop and stick and drop again. Never did any woman hate 'writing' as much as I do. But when I am old and famous I shall discourse like Henry James. (*Letters*, 1. 306).

Her love of sending up the pomposities of 'public' men was matched by her love of demolishing Oxford and Cambridge and the pretensions of their members. She wrote to Lytton Strachey: 'How difficult it is to write to you! It's all Cambridge—that detestable place; and the ap-s-les are so unreal, and their loves are so unreal, and yet I suppose it's all going on still—swarming in the sun—and perhaps not as bad as I imagine. But when I think of it, I vomit—that's all—a green vomit, which gets into the ink and blisters the paper' (*Letters*, 1. 498).

Criticism needed, in Woolf's view, to capture the territory of the letter, reproducing its irreverencies and informalities, its provisional insights and kinetic energy. She would have found in the correspondence between Flaubert and George Sand, which she so admired, Flaubert's attack on contemporary criticism and his hope for a different kind of criticism in the future:

> You speak of criticism in your last letter to me, telling me that it will soon disappear. I think, on the contrary, that it is, at most, only at its dawning. They [the critics] are on a different tack from before, but nothing more. At the time of La Harpe, they were grammarians; at the time of Sainte-Beuve and of Taine, they are historians. When will they be artists, only artists, but really artists? Where do you know a criticism? Who is there who is anxious about the work in itself, in an intense way? They analyze very keenly the setting in which it was written, and the causes that produced it; but the *unconscious* poetic expression? Where it comes from? its composition, its style? the point of view of the author? Never.
>
> That criticism would require great imagination and great sympathy. I mean a faculty of enthusiasm that is always ready, and then *taste*, a rare quality, even among the best, so much so that one does not talk about it any longer.
>
> What irritates me every day, is to see a master-piece and a disgrace put on the same level. They exalt the little, and they lower the great, nothing is more imbecile nor more immoral.[40]

The personal letter was the forging-ground of critical ideas. There was, after all, no 'Old' criticism to precede the 'New' criticism of the 1930s.[41] Literary criticism in the main took place in letters between friends, and it is this spirit that Virginia Woolf wants to revive, or continue, in her own critical writing.

The sense of beating out new ideas fascinated Virginia Woolf when she first encountered the correspondence between Flaubert and George Sand. She wrote to her cousin Madge Vaughan: 'It seemed to me one might write volumes upon all the questions it brought up. I think no letters I have read interest me more, or seem more beautiful and more suggestive.' She declared,

> I think I understand his [Flaubert's] artistic creed better: I knew all his features and boundaries—but I sink into her and am engulphed! I wanted to endorse, and add to, your pencil marks; whole passages seemed to start up as though writ in old ink. They penetrate so far and sum up so much that is universal as well as individual, and they say things that almost can't be said'. (*Letters*, 1. 229)

She virtually echoes a letter of George Sand's in which Sand debates the question of impersonality in art with Flaubert, expostulating, as many have done more recently: 'Criticism is in a sad way; too much theory!' urging the writer: 'Don't be troubled by all that and keep straight on. Don't attempt a system, obey your inspiration' (p. 150). Woolf wrote in her *Diary* on 21 June 1936: 'Really reading Flaubert's letters I hear my own voice cry out Oh art! Patience. Find him consoling, admonishing' (*Diary*, 5. 25). Despite Woolf's claim that she understood Flaubert better, George Sand, in her refusal to accept a hierarchy of letters, her anger at Flaubert for his scorn of the ordinary person, and her insistence that life must intrude on art, often speaks with Woolf's voice.

Woolf shared Flaubert's dislike of any moral stance and conviction that the only thing that mattered was writing well. But Sand found the novelist's absorption in his art constricting and thought it produced a melancholy which more diversity would dissipate:

> The artist is an explorer whom nothing ought to stop, and who does neither good nor ill when turning to the right or to the left. His end justifies all.
> It is for him to know after a little experience what are the

conditions of his soul's health. As for me, I think that yours is
in a good condition of grace, since you love to write and to be
alone in spite of the rain.[42]

Of herself Sand declared: 'I have preferred to leave my mind
incomplete' (p. 11). She suggested to Flaubert that he would have
been less unhappy if he had had in his life 'the *inclusion of the
feminine sentiment* which you say you have defied.—I know that
the feminine is worth nothing; but, perhaps, in order to be happy,
one must have been unhappy' (p. 269). She accused him of arrogance, and of writing for an élite: 'I have already combated your
favorite heresy, which is that one writes for twenty intelligent
people and does not care a fig for the rest. It is not true, since
the lack of success irritates you and troubles you.' She exhorts
him to 'write for all those who have a thirst to read and who
can profit by good reading', and concludes: 'Whatever you do,
your tale is a conversation between you and the reader' (p. 356).
Letters create the conditions of conversation, which for Woolf
was a paradigm for how criticism should be written and read.
At the end of her life she was still trying to capture, as she read
Madame de Sévigné, the voice of a letter-writer, speaking easily
and informally to women readers about how to read a book.

When Virginia Woolf read the letters of Madame de Sévigné,
Jane Welsh Carlyle, Edward Fitzgerald, and Dorothy Osborne,
she saw behind her a tradition of resistance which had created,
through the reading of letters, a female common reader. Her own
letters continue that tradition, and bind together her critical and
creative writing so that perhaps, as her friends suggested, the
form which most perfectly suited her, was in fact the personal
letter. Letters stimulated her to look for ways of writing which
would challenge the critical world, as much as her novels challenged traditions of representation. Jane Marcus has written that
'her anger and hostility at the exclusiveness of male institutions
are all the more effective because "cabin'd and cribb'd" in limited and limiting letters. Like prison journals and letters, read
while we know the author is in jail, they serve their cause not
only by what they say but by the very form'.[43] The metaphor
conjures up the world of Bunyan's two great prison narratives,
*Grace Abounding* and *The Pilgrim's Progress*. Yet Woolf's letters
do not in fact read as prison documents, but as scintillating outbursts of freedom. That freedom she observed in seventeenth-

century letter-writers, and most particularly, in Madame de Sévigné, who wrote from the liberty of a world which might have seemed to imprison her in the letter form, but which she in fact imprisoned within her letters. With an art which she concealed behind apparent artlessness she subjugated her readers, as Virginia Woolf also did, every time she lifted her pen to write a letter.

# 5

# Diaries:
# Pepys and Woolf

## A PASSION FOR RECORDS

Why did Samuel Pepys begin, in January of 1660, to keep a journal, which he continued until the last day of May 1669, when he believed himself obliged to stop writing shorthand for fear of going blind? When he began the *Diary* he was nearly twenty-seven, and had been married to Elizabeth St Michel since 1655. Five months after the final entry his wife died. The *Diary*, which covers from its inception the fortunes of the restored monarchy, is also the unique history of a marriage. This balance is plain from Pepys's preliminary note at the beginning of the first volume, which comments on his health, his household, politics and his personal standing and fortunes. He writes the *Diary* in order to record the moment of change which will totally alter the world into which he had been born and bred.

The fascination of the *Diary* for the ordinary reader – man or woman – derives from its vivid intertwining of State affairs with personal ones. On 26 March 1658, almost two years before Pepys began his journal, he had been 'cut of the stone' (without anaesthetic): an experience which left him full of a sense of his own good fortune in surviving, which he registered in an annual feast of thankfulness. The *Diary* is in part Pepys's own private medical record, begun in the awareness that he has survived an experience which might have killed him, and concluding with the sorrowful recognition that he can only continue it at a cost to his sight:

And thus ends all that I doubt I shall ever be able to do with my own eyes in the keeping of my journall, I being not able to do it any longer, having done now so long as to undo my eyes almost every time that I take a pen in my hand; and therefore, whatever comes of it, I must forbear; and therefore resolve from this time forward to have it kept by my people in longhand, and must therefore be contented to set down no more then is fit for them and all the world to know; or if there be anything (which cannot be much, now my amours to Deb are past, and my eyes hindering me in almost all other pleasures), I must endeavour to keep a margin in my book open, to add here and there a note in short-hand with my own hand. And so I betake myself to that course which [is] almost as much as to see myself go into my grave – for which, and all the discomforts that will accompany my being blind, the good God prepare me.

S.P.

May. 31. 1669.[1]

Although he did not go blind, he never resumed the practice of keeping a daily journal. The *Diary* ends as it began, in private matters. The final entry locates its supreme value for its author in the privacy of the record, assured from its being kept in short-hand, a privacy which remained virtually unchallenged until the 21-year-old John Smith, undergraduate of Magdalene College, Cambridge, undertook the transcription which formed the basis for Richard Neville's edition in 1822.

Virginia Woolf saw in Pepys's final entry the *raison d'être* for the whole record:

Not only from the last sentence, but from every sentence, it is easy to see what lure it was that drew him to his diary. It was not a confessional, still less a mere record of things useful to remember, but the store house of his most private self, the echo of life's sweetest sounds, without which life itself would become thinner and more prosaic. When he went upstairs to his chamber it was to perform no mechanical exercise, but to hold intercourse with the secret companion who lives in everybody, whose presence is so real, whose comment is so valuable, whose faults and trespasses and vanities are so lovable that to lose him is 'almost to go into my grave'. (pp. 236–7)

The need for a secret companion and the necessity of privacy Woolf identified as modern needs, first registered in the writings of Montaigne, Donne and Sir Thomas Browne, whose musings in private contrast with the public declamations of the theatre.

They are the first writers who explore their own inner lives, communing with solitary readers as opposed to groups of listeners, whether in the theatre or in the chamber where works are read aloud.

The diary was historically in the seventeenth century a woman's form.[2] Pepys knew that it was very unusual to keep one, and told only one person of the existence of his own. Its secrecy is jealously guarded by the use of shorthand, and by a combination of faked foreign languages when he describes his sexual escapades.[3] He composed it with care, often taking notes which he wrote up later. He looked back at his records for verification of his position when defending the Navy in Parliament against charges of corruption. Who did he think would read it? Virginia Woolf thinks he wrote it for himself, as a secret companion, but others have speculated that, with Sheldon's shorthand cheek-by-jowl with it in Magdalene Library – a system of shorthand in common use in his own time – he must have entertained the idea that it would find readers.[4] Robert Louis Stevenson wrote in the *Cornhill Magazine* in 1891:

> Pepys was not such an ass, but he must have perceived, as he went on, the extraordinary nature of the work he was producing. He was a great reader, and he knew what other books were like. It must, at least, have crossed his mind that someone might ultimately decipher the manuscript, and he himself, with all his pains and pleasures, be resuscitated in some later day; and the thought, although discouraged, must have warmed his heart. He was not such an ass, besides, but he must have been conscious of the deadly explosives, the guncotton and the giant powder, he was hoarding in his drawer.[5]

It seems likely that Pepys was aware of the *Diary's* value as an historical document, and might have hoped that it would be useful to posterity for the minuteness of its first-hand account. That historical consciousness was nourished in the diarist by his admiration for Francis Osborne's *Advice to a Son*, which he bought in January 1661.

Osborne's book begins with a section, 'Of Studies', which reflects on the nature of records. The author enjoins his son to make sure that his information comes from reliable sources: 'Be conversant in the *Speeches*, *Declarations* and *Transactions* occasioned by the *late Wars*: out of which more rational and *useful knowledge* may be sucked, then is ordinarily to be found in the mouldy Records of Antiquity.'[6] Lack of reliable information impeded the Civil War: 'When I consider, with what Contradiction *reports* arrived at us, during our late civil Wars: I can give the less encouragement to the reading of *History*' (pp. 10–11). History, in Osborne's view, is too often fiction. Even Caesar, whom he admires for his 'neat language', composes speeches too elegant to have been delivered; might he not also have embroidered his account of his soldiers' fighting ability? Osborne is sceptical on the same grounds about the authenticity·of the '*Orations*' of '*Thucydides, Livy, Tacitus* and most other Historians' (p. 11). Ancient records are always self-censored: '*There is as little reason to believe, Men know certainly all they* write, *as to think they* write *all they* Imagine: and as this cannot be admitted without danger, so the other, though it may in shame be denied, is altogether as true' (pp. 11–12). Montaigne believed that 'the only good histories are those that have been written by the persons themselves who held command in the affairs whereof they write, or who participated in the conduct of them, or, at least, who have had the conduct of others of the same nature' ('Of Books', II. 357). Pepys had the wit to see that he himself was such a man, and that his record would be a new kind of document of priceless value to later readers.

If Pepys began the record with Osborne's counsels in his mind and thought of his project as a utilitarian one, other aspects of it immediately engrossed him. Virginia Woolf sees his *Diary* as a confidant to whom he communicates a secret self at odds with his world. Although she queries its confessional nature, Pepys is explicit about the confessional aspects of the journal, which he uses to admonish and discipline himself in good Puritan form. For Woolf he is, like Montaigne, 'modern':

If ever we feel ourselves in the presence of a man so modern that we should not be surprised to meet him in the street and should know him and speak to him at once, it is when we read this diary, written more than two hundred and fifty years ago.[7]

She read Pepys's *Diary* in an expurgated version, the four-volume edition of the diaries by Lord Braybrooke.[8] This excises most of Pepys's sexual affairs, although not the one with his wife's serving-girl and companion, Deb Willett. Had Woolf had access to the unexpurgated Pepys, as she had to the unexpurgated edition of Rousseau's *Confessions* (1896), she might have felt even more affinity with the diarist. But she communicates with him even in his truncated form: 'He is modern in his consciousness of the past. . . . Standing midway in our history, he looks consciously and intelligently both backwards, and forwards.' Moreover, 'the very fact that he kept a diary seems to make him one of ourselves' (*Essays*, 3. 235). Her own *Diary*, multi-volume, handwritten, and of ambiguous literary status, can be read as an ongoing dialogue with Pepys's journal.

Virginia Woolf's love of records, and perception of the paucity of records relating to women, had led her to consider becoming an historian. As a lecturer at Morley College she was depressed by the lack of information about daily living which would have fleshed out the bones of history and made it interesting to her working-women pupils. In *A Room of One's Own* she was to urge the pursuit of records which would speak to the everyday lives of women in the past and allow a different kind of history to be written. The diaries written by her grandmother, which she encountered at Caroline Emelia Stephen's Cambridge house, fascinated her, with their detailed accounts of the childhood sayings and activities of her father and his siblings. Woolf lamented that Pernel Strachey's diaries would probably be consigned to the fire when she was about to die. Her own early fiction of Joan Martyn invents exactly such a diary as she wished had existed when she tried to prepare her classes on medieval history, and Rosamund, the historian in the story, writes an alternative kind of history from perusing such records.

Virginia Woolf often asked herself why she wrote her *Diary* and who would read it. She liked to read old volumes:

> What is the purpose of them? L. taking up a volume the other day said Lord save him if I died first & he had to read through these. My handwriting deteriorates. And do I say anything interesting? I can always waste an idle hour reading them; & then, oh yes, I shall write my memoirs out of them, one of these days. (*Diary*, 3. 125)

She often envisaged an older self communing with the younger one it found on the page: 'Old V. of 1940 will see something in

it too. She will be a woman who can see, old V.: everything—
more than I can I think' (*Diary*, 2. 319–20). She played with the
possibility of the *Diary*'s being printed, musing in 1938: '[I] have
half a mind one of these days to explain what my intention is in
writing these continual diaries. Not publication. Revision? a
memoir of my own life? Perhaps. Only other things crop up'
(*Diary*, 5. 162). She also played with idea of Leonard Woolf's
perhaps printing some of it while believing that much of it would
be unprintable. Clive Bell, who suffers a good deal from the
diarist's frankness, later claimed that much of it was fiction, and
that Leonard Woolf thought so too.[9] But Woolf saw it as a secret
companion requiring truth: 'As I cannot write if anyone is in the
room, as L. sits here when we light the fire, this book remains
shut. A natural slimming process' (*Diary*, 5. 338). She tries to be
frank with herself in the *Diary*, castigating herself if she feels
the record is fudged.

Part of the delight of Pepys's *Diary* has often seemed to readers to reside in its artlessness, and certainly Virginia Woolf thought
of her *Diary* as unliterary. The diary *per se* was not a literary
form, and neither her *Diary* nor Pepys's have either of them received much serious literary attention because this prejudice still
in part persists, despite the reclaiming of the form by feminist
scholars. Coleridge disparaged Pepys for the unliterary aspects
of the *Diary*, its calculated self-love and self-interest and lack of
idealism: 'What a cold and torpid Saturn, with what a sinister
and leaden shine, spotty as the moon, does it appear.'[10] Robert
Louis Stevenson, while relishing the vitality of Pepys's writing,
considered it unsophisticated: 'Though the manner of his utterance may be childishly awkward, the matter has been transformed
and assimilated by his unfeigned interest and delight' (p. 11).
When Virginia Woolf, like Flaubert, spurned the concept of separating style from subject-matter, believing that any subject, however
trivial, could be graced by the telling nature of the writing, she
had a forerunner in the man whose book Pepys used as his Bible,
Francis Osborne, who counselled the 'coming' man on his writing style. Osborne's niece Dorothy had observed his strictures
against pretension in her letters to her lover, William Temple.
Osborne declares:

*Books stately writ* debase your stile; the like may be truly ob-
jected to *weak Preachers*, and *ignorant Company*. Pens improving,

like children's legs, proportionately to their *Exercise* (so as I have
seen some stand amazed at the Length of their own reach, when
they came to be extended by Employment;) This appeared in the
late King *Charles*, who, after his more imperious destiny, had
placed him under the Tutorage of unavoidable necessity, attained
a *Pen* more Majesticall, than the *Crown* he lost. (pp. 15–16)

Practice creates a strong style. But equally the pen must not be
eclectic in its choice of subject:

> The way to *Elegancy of stile*, is to employ your pen upon every
> Errand; and the more trivial and dry it is, the more brains
> must be allowed for sauce: Thus by checking all ordinary In-
> vention, your Reason will attain to such an habit, as not to
> dare to present you but with what is excellent: and if void of
> Affectation, it matters not how mean the subject is, There be-
> ing the same Exactness observed, by good Architects, in the
> structure of the Kitchen, as the Parlour. (p. 16)

The last sentence recalls Montaigne's disparaging of Cicero's literary grandeur and preference for a kitchen-maid's style. No
subject is too trivial for Pepys, yet his accounts even of parlour
and kitchen are transformed by the precision and vitality of the
writing.

This admirable creed, that any subject is of interest if described
in the liveliest way, encourages women writers whose lives look
both trivial and ephemeral, as Woolf observed in *A Room of One's
Own*. Pepys's *Diary* associates itself with women's writing through
its informality and particularity, which forge a new record which
crosses and dissolves the boundaries between public and private. Virginia Woolf's *Diary* is not a record of historical and
political facts, but in it she nevertheless negotiates, as Pepys does,
conflicting professional and personal roles. Her *Diary* contains
in its account of mental and physical illness, of family life, of
books read and written, most of the information about daily living which she felt was lacking when she tried to teach history
to the working women at Morley College. Its private and often
exclusively female preoccupations are also, strangely enough, some
of the major preoccupations of the private as opposed to the
public voice of Pepys, communing secretly with himself within
the hospitable pages of his *Diary*.

Virginia Woolf, despite her loathing for the material realism of Bennett and Galsworthy, believed that writing became bloodless without some perceived relation to the everyday. In the *Diary* the unliterary could be captured before it became art (*Diary*, 3. 102). She claims that she used her own *Diary* to practise the art of writing: 'Habit is the desirable thing in writing' (*Diary*, 4. 318). She noted in 1924: 'It strikes me that in this book I *practise* writing; do my scales; yes & work at certain effects. I daresay I practised Jacob here,—& Mrs D. & shall invent my next book here; for here I write merely in the spirit—great fun it is too.' (*Diary*, 2. 319–20). She believed Dorothy Wordsworth used her journal for the same purpose: 'curious metaphor – crows like water – as if teaching herself to write' (Berg, XX). In April 1906 Madge Vaughan sent her a manuscript to read and she wrote back: 'It strikes me that you might make a really good book out of that Diary. Suppose you went on day by day, writing out soberly and exactly, what you think, feel, see, hear and talk about, as you have done that one day, all things growing naturally out of each other as they do—wouldn't the result be something very true and remarkable?' (*Letters*, 1. 220). The originality and novelty of such a record of a woman's daily life would create a new kind of fiction. In 1940, as she contemplated her new 'Common History', Virginia Woolf was still thinking of the *Diary* as a place where she could experiment with alternative ways of writing criticism.

Pepys had no time for fiction, both literally and figuratively, although chronologically he is within a stone's throw of Defoe, whose *Journal of the Plague Year* is a novel disguised as a journal. Christopher Hill begins his essay on Pepys with comparisons with *Robinson Crusoe*, whose adventures are initially chronicled in journal form.[11] There are respects in which the new world in which Pepys finds himself is a desert island which the *Diary* enables him to colonise for himself. The fact that writing the *Diary* becomes a compelling necessity for him in the midst of a life of intense practical concern, suggests that Pepys's Puritan upbringing channelled the energies into business concerns which in a different environment would have made him a novelist. But Pepys is too busy for fiction. He destroys, despite his surprised admiration of it, the romance that he wrote while he was at Cambridge. He kept a 'book of stories' (V. 103), which, however, never found their way into the library, so that perhaps

he tore them amongst other worthless papers. Certainly he retains a sense that fiction is time-wasting and consequently more
or less immoral. His literary creativity is the victim of a Puritan
view of the imagination as inherently sinful, but, like many women,
he evades the prohibition of his conscience, and of his world, at
the public writing of fiction, by keeping a private diary.

Virginia Woolf was reading Pepys for the first time when she
began her first surviving *Diary* – the '1897 Diary'[12] – containing
the marriage of her half-sister Stella Duckworth to Jack Hills.
Spring of 1897 was full of frenetic wedding preparations, and
for the fifteen-year-old Virginia, whose first serious nervous breakdown – following the death of her mother in 1895 – was still
fresh in everyone's consciousness, it foreboded further loss in
Stella's marriage and death, only three months later, from peri-
tonitis. On 29 March Virginia wrote in the 1897 *Diary*: 'Father
ordered himself a whole new suit for the wedding. . . . Gave back
Sterling and got Pepys diary' (*PA*, p. 62). Virginia and Vanessa
were to be bridesmaids: 'We had our linings tried on – I was
forced to wear certain underclothing for the first time in my life'
(p. 64). The wearing of stays is part of a rite of passage occasioned by an older sister's wedding, providing the cue for her
own official entrance into puberty. She 'finished 1st vol. of Pepys'
(p. 65), amidst pre-wedding fever:

> The drawing rooms are still topsy turvy and will not recover
> till everything is over – 'the beginning of the end' Aunt Minna
> cheerfully calls this. Indeed it is in danger of becoming very
> dismal – After dinner father read the Ancient Mariner which
> was rather a failure – almost ending in the middle furiously.
> My dear Pepys is the only calm thing in the house – (pp. 65–6)

Pepys provided a salutary antidote, perhaps, to Coleridge's insistent Wedding Guest, mischievously conjured up by Leslie
Stephen for a family occasion apparently dreaded by everyone.
By 7 April Virginia had 'finished . . . the 2nd volume of Pepys'
(p. 67). The day after the wedding she noted: 'Trying hard to
finish Pepys before Wednesday, so I may have a new book', and
rejoiced in a new luxury: 'Georgie had the fire lighted in his
room, and I sat there and read which was very nice. Finished
3rd vol. Pepys.' On the 13th:

I wrote to Stella, sitting in Georgie's room which is most comfortable and quiet. . . . Packing for Brighton began –
I got the 4th & last vol. of Pepys, which has to be finished by tomorrow. . . .
To bed very furious and tantrumical. (*PA*, p. 69)

Pepys's *Diary* and her own, the one read and the one written, function equally to alleviate disorder and disorientation.
Twenty-one years later in 1918 Pepys also came to the rescue when she thought that the *Times Literary Supplement* was not going to send her any more books to review: 'I may say I'm "rejected by the Times". To rub this sore point sorer, L[eonard] has 2 books from the Nation' (*Diary*, 1. 127). Two days later she recorded with relief: 'My dismissal is revoked. A large book on Pepys arrived, which I spent the evening reading' (*Diary*, 1. 128).[13] The review is Woolf's only published work on Pepys, but she continued to read the *Diary* throughout her life. In 1923 she published a review of Sir Thomas Browne's *Religio Medici*, which begins with one of her favourite subjects, the passion for reading: 'For the desire to read, like all the other desires which distract our unhappy souls, is capable of analysis. It may be for good books, for bad books, or for indifferent books. But it is always despotic in its demands, and when it appears, at whatever hour of day or night we must rise and slink off at its heels, only allowing ourselves to ask, as we desert the responsibilities and privileges of active life, one very important question – Why? Why, that is, this sudden passion for Pepys or Rimbaud?' (*Essays*, 3. 368–9). The passion for Pepys was linked both with momentous changes in her own life, and with her own writing of a diary, from the early 1897 journal to the final entries in her regular *Diary* before her death in 1941.
Virginia Woolf apparently contemplated including Pepys in the first volume of *The Common Reader*, when she noted that she had made 'a systematic beginning, I daresay the 80th'. In the margin she wrote four names, with dates:

Addison 1672–1719
Defoe 1659–1731
Pepys 1660
Evelyn 1660
(*Diary*, 2. 309)

Of these four, only Pepys did not appear in *The Common Reader*, perhaps because he would not have fitted its extremely careful structure. In the first *Common Reader* the Duchess of Newcastle follows Montaigne, because in some ways she is the realisation of the maverick feminine soul which watches Montaigne at work. She is also a reader, and this gives her kinship with that invisible figure in the Montaigne essay, Marie de Gournay. Evelyn follows the Duchess because he is her mirror-image. They are both, according to Woolf's judgement, common readers and common writers: not very gifted, fantastical, ignorant, creatures of their time, conceited and complacent, isolated from wider influences by their own narrowness as well as by circumstances. But how different is the treatment given to each by their own time and by posterity. The man, ordinary, dull, of crude sensibilities and mediocre writing ability, remains the author of a work known if not read; is respected in his time and given a hearing by later ages; allowed some license to be vain. The woman, ostracised and ridiculed in her own time, had, until recent feminist interest in her, fallen into such total obscurity, despite the far greater courage needed to take up her pen in the first place, that Woolf's essay was itself a landmark in the history of her reputation. The Duchess of Newcastle's conceit and fantastical qualities were counted as madness, where Evelyn's were humoured, even by a somewhat quizzical Pepys. Her coarseness was condemned where his moral crudity was glossed over. Virginia Woolf made the point in typically sidelong manner by juxtaposing the two essays at the centre of the first *Common Reader*. Pepys, altogether a more complex case, would have disturbed the symmetry of her arrangement of the essays.

The *Diary* was a document necessary to Pepys's self-confidence as he encountered roles in which he had a painful sensation of walking in the dark. Forty years earlier Lady Anne Clifford had written her *Diary* in order to create a special place over which her hand and her pen were mistress, even as her world denied her mastery – although in the end it gave up opposing her. This need for a refuge Virginia Woolf recognised when she reread Pepys for her 'Common History' in 1939–40. When the Great Fire destroyed London, Pepys's *Diary* bore witness to the capacity of human beings to cherish their symbols of civilisation, as Virginia Woolf registered in 'Anon': '"Hardly one lighter or boat in three that had the goods of a house in, but there was a pair of virginals in it." Music moved beneath the words'.[14] When Mecklenburgh Square was bombed Virginia Woolf was as relieved to find '24 vols of diary salved; a great mass for my memoirs' (22 October 1940, *Diary*, 5. 332), as Pepys was to recover his Journal: 'Thence to Bednall-green by coach, my brother with me, and saw all well there and fetched away my Journall-book to enter five days past' (VII. 282). The fire disrupted Pepys's life, but the absence of the *Diary* contributed to that disruption: 'I had forgot almost the day of the week' (VII. 277). He was distressed by the mislaying of his books: 'Up, and much troubled about my books; but cannot imagine where they should be' (VII. 291). The new presses, of which he was so proud, would ensure some measure of safety for them. The instability of the worlds both Pepys and Woolf inhabit creates a passion for records.

Pepys bought Florio's translation of Montaigne's *Essays* in 1668, but he retained in his library the Cotton translation of 1693 (IX. 120–1), preferred by Virginia Woolf. In the essay 'Of a Defect in Our Government' Montaigne meditates on the wisdom of keeping a journal:

My father in his domestic economy has this rule (which I know how to commend, but by no means to imitate), namely, that besides the day-book or memorial of household affairs, where the small accounts, payments, and disbursements, which do not require a secretary's hand, were entered, and which a stew ard always had in custody, he ordered him whom he employed to write for him, to keep a journal, and in it to set down all the remarkable occurrences, and daily memorials of the history of his house: very pleasant to look over, when time begins to wear things out of memory, and very useful sometimes to put us out of doubt when such a thing was begun, when ended; what visitors came, and when they went; our travels, absences, marriages, and deaths; the reception of good or ill news; the change of principal servants and the like. An ancient custom, which I think it would not be amiss for every one to revive in his own house; and I find I did very foolishly in neglecting it. (II. 62).

The records Montaigne describes resemble the mercantile accounts of the *quattrocento* Florentines described by Stephanie Jed, which involved secret family histories as well as business accounts.[15] Pepys's *Diary* marries Humanist and mercantile traditions in a secret script which allows him to combine with the record of political and social change a unique exploration of his relation to gender and class within the intimacy of his marriage.


## PEPYS: SOCIAL MOBILITY AND MARRIAGE

Born in 1633, Pepys hardly qualifies as a Renaissance figure. Yet the changes brought about by the Renaissance create the extraordinary breadth of his interests, in the classics, mathematics, maps, music, astronomy, medicine, philosophy, history, and the keeping of records. He was part of a new upwardly mobile generation which profited from Humanist education. His background was unpretentious, consisting of a father who was a tailor and a mother who took in washing, although a cousin was a lawyer, and there were family connections with Pepys's patron, Lord Sandwich. Pepys was conscious of cutting new ground in everything he did, and the *Diary* is a secular pilgrim's progresss, charting his negotiation of new worlds, both public and private.

The professional, social and domestic dilemmas recorded in Pepys's journal seem at first glance light years away from Virginia Woolf's *Diary*. Yet curiously, many of Pepys's concerns can be mirrored in the day-to-day preoccupations of her *Diary*. Woolf used the *Diary* to reconcile her roles of writer and printer, creating a new professional image for herself as woman writer which would be distinct from her father's sphere of Cambridge education and London literary life, symbolised by the London Library, 'a stale culture smoked place, which I detest' (*Diary*, 1. 25). It was a stale culture because it was a male culture. The *Diary* helped her to carve out a new place from which she, as a woman writer, could speak. Pepys, too, used the *Diary* as a tool with which to fashion his own surprised sense of himself as a professional public servant. For both writers the daily record created stability amidst flux.

The keeping of the *Diary* helps Pepys to understand his situation and conduct himself appropriately in a position of social mobility such as would have been inconceivable fifty years earlier for someone from his background. Education has made him what he is. But he also made good in a corrupt age through unusual standards of public honesty, and the *Diary* is as much a witness to his professional incorruptibility as it is to the personal fallibility which he ruthlessly records.

On his appointment as Secretary to Lord Sandwich Pepys is overcome with excitement:

All night troubled in my thoughts how to order my business upon this great change with me, that I could not sleep; and being overheated with drink, I made a promise the next morning to drink no strong drink this week, for I find that it makes me sweat in bed and puts me quite out of order. (I. 84).

Writing out his perturbation composes him so that he can take advantage of 'this great change'. The function of the *Diary* is both practical and mentally restorative, helping its author to negotiate his journey from insignificance to extraordinary esteem and prosperity.

As he writes, the new successful Pepys holds communion with his earlier self. Striking tallies in his new role as Navy Treasurer, he declares: 'Methinks it is so great testimony of the goodness of God to me; that I from a mean clerk there should come to strike tallies myself for that sum [17500*l*], and in the authority that I do now, is a very stupendous mercy to me' (VI. 100). When he throws a dinner for his friends he notes: 'I enjoyed myself in it with reflections upon the pleasure which I can at best expect, yet not to exceed this – eating in silver plates, and all things mighty rich and handsome about me' (VII. 388). The echo of Dogberry in *Much Ado About Nothing* – 'one that hath two gowns, and every thing handsome about him' is probably unconscious,[16] but Pepys's pleasure in his state invokes Dogberry's innocence as well as his words. The *Diary* provides Pepys with an index of his own social advancement. He registers his rise in the clothes he wears – 'I find that I must go handsomely, whatever it costs me; and the charge will be made up in the fruits it brings' (V. 302) – in the company he keeps, and in the ways in which he is treated both by his superiors and his subordinates.

This place at the heart of social mobility carries its own stresses. Pepys is not always prepared mentally, or even materially, for what he has to do, and for what is expected of him. He has a core of vulnerability and sensitivity which comes from being aware of often being a fish out of water. He does not feel comfortable at Hampton Court: 'I was not invited anywhither to dinner, though a stranger, which did also trouble me; but yet I must remember it is a Court, and endeed where most are strangers' (VI. 166). He is himself disturbed when the Court dines 'and all to dinner and sat down to the King saving myself, which though I could not in modesty expect, yet God forgive my pride, I was sorry I was there, that Sir W. Batten should say that he could sit down where I could not – though he had twenty times more reason then I. But this was my pride and folly' (VI. 170). He knows he couldn't expect the distinction but he woos the reader to love him for wanting it anyway.

What other men are to him as they become great, he sees himself become to his own friends and relations. He knows the discomfort of becoming easy in one set of circumstances at the cost of estranging himself from family and friends who are quick to sense his movement into a different class. When he goes home to Brampton there is a strong sense of parents overjoyed at the child who has made good but also moved beyond them, with Pepys registering the poignancy of such feelings: 'My father and mother overjoyed to see me – my mother ready to weep every time she looked upon me' (V. 298). His relation with his mother remains troubled throughout the course of the *Diary*. He blames himself for not showing her the respect that he ought; in part the problem arises from her garrulousness, which later in the *Diary* turns into senility: 'But Lord, to see how my mother found herself talk, upon every object to think of old stories' (VI. 112). His love for his father is evident in his delight at commissioning a picture of him: 'Here I find my father's picture begun; and so much to my content, that it joys my very heart to think that I should have his picture so well done – who, besides that he is my father, and a man that loves me and hath ever done so – is also at this day one of the most careful and innocent men in the world' (VII. 164). He declares in 1666 that had it not been for difficulties with his mother he would have liked his father to come and live with him. In one of the rare emotional entries in the *Diary* he notes: 'What with the going away of my father today and the loss of Mercer, I after dinner went up to my chamber and there could have cried to myself, had not people come to me about business' (VII. 176). The *Diary* is the comforter. Woolf writes: 'I want to lie down like a tired child & weep away this life of care—& my diary shall receive me on its downy pillow. Most children do not know what they cry for; nor do I altogether.'

The origin of her distress is the same as his: loneliness and the withdrawal of love, but where hers fits a construction of female emotion, Pepys's is totally at odds with his public *persona* of Navy Treasurer and shrewd business man, manifesting a female aspect of his nature which the *Diary* frequently highlights.

Pepys's Puritan upbringing ensures success in his progress to prosperity, but it also distances him from the prevailing morals and practices not only of the Restoration court, but of the Navy office itself, whose officials often outrage Pepys with their idleness and inefficiency. He retains an Elizabethan reverence towards monarchy, which is surprising considering his admiration for Cromwell and earlier devotion to the Roundhead cause. The King is worshipped by Pepys in the same terms that he would apply to his Creator, despite the fact that he observes the palpable human frailty beneath the crown, as Halifax did in his 'Character of Charles II': '*Charles Stuart* would be bribed against the *King.*'[17] The first occasion for Pepys's disillusionment occurs when he accompanies the king's footman in a boat while they are in Holland, 'with a dog that the King loved (which shit in the boat, which made us laugh and me to think that a King and all that belong to him are but just as others are)' (I. 158). Pepys talked in 1665 'of the ill-government of our Kingdom . . . the King himself minding nothing but his ease – and so we let things go wrack' (VI. 210). But his perception of the monarch's fallibility does not mitigate his conviction of what he owes to the king's service: in some ways it perhaps intensifies that allegiance, because the reality differs so glaringly from the ideal. This consciousness again isolates him from his contemporaries who often envy and fear his diligence and the success consequent on it.

Pepys always acknowledges the sources of his good fortune: 'So home and to dinner, where I confess, reflecting upon the ease and plenty that I live in, of money, goods, servants, honour, everything, I could not but with hearty thanks to Almighty God ejaculate my thanks to Him while I was at dinner, to myself' (VII. 215). A couple of weeks later he muses: 'And mighty proud I am (and ought to be thankful to God Almighty) that I am able to have a spare bed for my friends' (VII. 241). He is very sharp in the *Diary* with others who exult in their upward mobility: 'But Lord, to see how Povy overdoes everything in commending it doth make it nauseous to me, and was not (by reason of my large praise of his house) over-acceptable to my wife' (VI. 87). Pepys's *Diary* enables him to avoid such excesses, because it provides a private place for self-gratulatory sentiments, which are, however, softened by the author's unfeigned astonishment at his worldly progress. He watches himself marvelling at Vanity Fair, but the *Diary* performs an admonitory function which inhibits him from being corrupted by it.

His lack of ease in some of his new roles dominates the journal. The *Diary* shows a man and his wife setting up for the first time a household of which they neither of them have any childhood model. Samuel and Elizabeth Pepys are not used to servants; Pepys is an irascible and sometimes violent master, and his wife is mercurial, inclined to accuse her servants of lying and presumption, while simultaneously expecting them to be companions for her. When a servant leaves, Pepys is distressed to see her employed by his hated neighbour and colleague, Sir William Penn: 'By Sarahs going to live at Sir W. Penn's, all our affairs of my family are made known and discoursed of there, and theirs by my people' (IV. 7). The servants are assertive and certainly stay exceedingly short lengths of time in the Pepys household. Disciplining them prompts Pepys to painful self-examination: is he being too strict or too easy? When he dismisses a servant he and his wife sit sadly at their empty table and feel lonely. Pepys looks back to a different world (with which however he cannot have been familiar at first hand) when he writes of Mr Herbert that he is 'a very honest, plain, well-meaning man . . . and by his discourse and manner of life, the true Embleme of an old ordinary serving-man' (V. 241). This makes Herbert sound like Adam in *As You Like It*, suggesting a literary nostalgia for a world where everyone knew his or her place and was content; but the diarist is the child of a different world which he relishes even as he experiences its emotional discomfort.

Pepys married exceptionally young and very imprudently, and must have been aware of how much his 'father' Osborne would have disapproved of his behaviour. Like the secret family histories of the Florentine merchants in the Renaissance which often described the disciplining of wives and families, Pepys's *Diary* charts domestic battles, offering an antidote to easy remarks about seventeenth-century marriages. Pepys is hardly a 'new' man in the twentieth-century feminist sense, but the problems he and his wife experience are quickly recognised by the modern reader: tensions created by changes in class and fortune, the problems of running the household, the wife's loneliness, pressures of work, infidelity, in-laws, and conflicting expectations between the couple themselves. Elizabeth Pepys is a silent figure, but the urge to hear her speak in her own voice remains. In 1929 a book was published called *Mrs Pepys her book*, which details her life as presented in the diaries, as though in the wake of women's getting the vote, Elizabeth deserves to be seen separately from her husband: 'Mrs Pepys,' remarks the author, 'is a singularly lonely and defenceless figure, for we are forced to view her solely through the eyes of one whose judgments often erred by reason of his own defects of character.'[18] Elizabeth still doesn't get a first name in the title, however, any more than Virginia Woolf did in many of the reviews of her books. If the book was the offshoot of a 1920s feminism, its modern equivalent is Dale Spender's *The Diary of Elizabeth Pepys* in which Elizabeth is finally given a text of her own to rival her husband's, and is credited with giving him the idea for his own record.[19] Montaigne declared that 'the sharps, as well as the sweets of marriage, are kept secret by the wise; and amongst its other troublesome conditions this to a prating fellow, as I am, is one of the chief, that custom has rendered it indecent and prejudicial to communicate to any one all that a man knows and all that a man feels' ('Upon some Verses of Virgil', IV. 297–8). Pepys needs to write out his marriage, both its sweets and its sharps, and the *Diary* chronicles both the marriage and its author's sexuality.

Elizabeth and Samuel had in some ways an extraordinarily modern marriage, with recognisable vicissitudes. Pepys experiences difficulties with his role as husband, trying to enforce an authority which he believes to be his prerogative although his efforts often frustrate his wishes. Elizabeth Pepys's problems as wife of an aspiring and industrious civil servant not only appear from reading between the lines, but are registered by Pepys himself. They both suffer from their childlessness, and the *Diary* does not bear out a view that Pepys ceased to want offspring. Indeed, many of their marital difficulties would have been solved by a household of children. Pepys tries to run a marriage which is in significant ways out of line with those he sees around him. He operates a middle-class bourgeois domestic life, but he is distracted and confused by the upper-class culture into which his work thrusts him. His relations with his wife change perceptibly as he becomes more successful and his adjustments and ill-adjustments to his success are mirrored immediately in his marriage.

Pepys's married life and his infidelities are inseparable from his own negotiation of his rise in the world, of which Elizabeth Pepys is a symbol, but in which she is also his ally. In Pepys's upward progress, his wife is his most valuable and public piece of property, her clothes and bearing, her servants and her acceptability in society testifying to her husband's social and professional success, although he is often unwilling to pay the financial price for displaying her in this role. This consumer model of the wife is at war with a more creative model – which derives from his Humanist and Puritan upbringing – of Elizabeth as partner and confidante. In this latter role Elizabeth is often a pupil, with her husband a keen (though often impatient) instructor in arithmetic, the use of globes, astronomy and music. He is delighted by her progress, especially in her painting, promising to buy her a pearl necklace as a reward for achievement; but equally he is sometimes mortified by her lack of education:

> In the evening examining my wife's letter entended to my Lady and another Madamoiselle; they were so false-spelt that I was ashamed of them and took occasion to fall out about them with my wife, and so she writ none; at which, however, I was sorry, because it was in answer to a letter of Madamoiselle – about business. (IV. 29)

(One might comment that Pepys's own spelling of 'mademoiselle' is idiosyncratic). Elizabeth's accomplishments, which her husband fosters, are part of a competition with other men and their women: she paints better than Peg Penn who has the same master (VI. 210). Predictably, Pepys balks at the independence these pursuits create in his wife.

Their marriage reaches a singularly low ebb towards the end of 1664 with the arrival of a good musician from King's Chapel, the boy Tom Edwards, with whom Pepys can sing and make merry, together with the instrument-maker, Mr Hill. Tom takes the place which Elizabeth Pepys had for a while seemed to occupy, of being a partner in cherished leisure activities, although the marital relationship recovers for a time in Pepys's pride in his wife's drawing. But the reader receives a chilling impression of Elizabeth's trying to cultivate her own interests in an empty environment, where her husband's approval is mercurial, and his wish for their equal comradeship intermittent rather than continuous. When she becomes a better dancer than he is, Pepys fears she will become superior and move out of his sphere. His own insecurities are as disquieting to him as his perception of her dissatisfactions, and in both cases the *Diary* is, as Woolf pointed out, his confidant.

Pepys needs friends. People fascinate him, and intimacy is a condition he adores. Yet his position in the world forces him to be circumspect. Under these circumstances his wife is inevitably his best friend, and the *Diary* contains very tender observations about her. But the whole disposition of marriage in his society as a relationship in which he as man should exert authority, and in which she cannot be educated to be his equal, means that a powerful source of satisfaction is only partially available to him. To his credit, some of the time, despite the rulings of his world, it is available, and this makes his *Diary* an extraordinary record of a marital relation which, if it sounds old-fashioned in the professional middle-class scene of the late twentieth-century, would have many counterparts in the marriages of different social classes only slightly earlier in the century. In the end, the real friend is the *Diary* itself, where the partial friendship of the marriage is celebrated, and complemented by the more complete relationship which writing it all down allows to the solitary author. To that extent also, like Montaigne's *Essays*, and like *The Pilgrim's Progress*, Pepys's *Diary* is a record of loneliness, for which writing affords solace. In being so, it is a document which looks foward to the condition of many women writers including Virginia Woolf, who shares Pepys's sociable nature and his sense of being an outsider, however different the origins of that awareness.

In his professional rise Pepys is surrounded by men to whom he extends a wary cordiality, conscious, with Creed, Moore, Batten, Penn, Carteret, Coventry, even eventually with Lord Sandwich, that each person has self-interested motives for his behaviour. The diarist has many acquaintances but few real friends. His old schoolfriends, especially Jack Cole, remain dear to him, but the relationship is shot across with the realities of Pepys's phenomenal rise to political favour. Pepys needs his wife, despite his pursuit of other women; she is the only one whose absence makes him feel painfully alone. Herein lies another clue to the modernity and also, in a sense, to the success of the marriage, despite all its vicissitudes. Pepys does not have to pretend to Elizabeth, nor does he have to suspect her motives. Mr Coventry, whom he loves (a word seldom used in the *Diary* for women, and never for his wife, although he speaks of his passion for her), is nevertheless capable of making Pepys reflect that Coventry also can cool as he grows greater in the eyes of the world. At the time of Lord Sandwich's downfall Coventry becomes so deeply antagonistic to Sandwich and Carteret that Pepys is put to it to preserve relations with all three of them. The only man who is a true friend is Mr Hill, the viol player and singer, with whom the diarist has no business contact. His wife, by contrast, is his ally, but it is a relationship fraught with tension.

Pepys uses the *Diary* to write out his marital problems. It is almost as if the marriage is the record of it in the *Diary*. His infidelities are themselves as much an account of the marriage as they are of the liaisons involved. Elizabeth Pepys does not emerge from the *Diary* as simply a silent, obedient, domestic doormat, ill-treated within a patriarchal society. Pepys is taken aback on one occasion when he returns from a rendezvous with one of his mistresses, Mrs Martin: 'Here I did ce que je voudrais avec her most freely; and it having cost me 2s in wine and cake upon her, I away, sick of her impudence', to find his wife in assertive mood:

> So back again home, where, thinking to be merry, was vexed with my wife's having looked out a letter in Sir Ph. Sidny about jealousy for me to read, which she industriously and maliciously caused me to do; and the truth is, my conscience told me it was most proper for me, and therefore was touched at it; but took no notice of it, but read it out most frankly. But it stuck in my stomach. (VI. 2).

The passage from Sidney's *Arcadia* with which Elizabeth confronts Samuel, describes 'a jealous husband made a Pander to his own wife' (Latham, VI. 2, n. 3). She is capable of bringing her own husband to book in various other ways. Pepys is often much improved by the flaming rows he has with her. Her ability to stand up for herself is evident, from her calling him – after he has called her a 'beggar' – a 'prick-louse' because of his being a tailor's son (IV. 121 and n. 1). When she learns of his affair with Deb Willett, she wakes him in the night, and

brandishing 'tongs, red hot at the ends, made as if she did design to pinch me with them' (IX. 414).

Some of their worst disputes surround the vexed area of a
companion for Elizabeth, who writes her husband an eloquent
letter setting out her needs, which he found

> so picquant, and wrote in English and most of it true, of the
> retirednesse of her life and how unpleasant it was, that being
> writ in English and so in danger of being met with and read
> by others, I was vexed at it and desired her and then com-
> manded her to teare it – which she desired to be excused it; I
> forced it from her and tore it, and withal took her other bun-
> dle of papers from her and leapt out of the bed and in my
> shirt clapped them into the pockets of my breeches, that she
> might not get them from me; and having got on my stockings
> and breeches and gown, I pulled them out one by one and
> tore them all before her face, though it went against my heart
> to do it, she crying and desiring me not to do it. But such was
> my passion and trouble to see the letters of my love to her,
> and my Will, wherein I had given her all I have in the world
> when I went to sea with my Lord Sandwich, to be joyned with
> a paper of so much disgrace to me and dishonour if it should
> have been found by anybody. (IV. 9–10)

He then burns all these papers except a bond, their Marriage
licence and his first love-letter to her. When he returns home he
is ready to mock his own behaviour, but his joviality is misin-
terpreted by his wife: 'And to see my folly, as discontented as I
am, when my wife came I could not forbear smiling all dinner,
till she begun to speak bad words again; and then I begun to be
angry again, and so to my office.' The quarrel is patched up
with a new dress, 'which troubles me to part with so much money,
but however it sets my wife and I to friends again, though I and
she never were so heartily angry in our lives as today almost,
and I doubt the heart-burning will not soon be over. And the
truth is, I am sorry for the tearing of so many poor loving letters of mine from Sea and elsewhere to her' (IV. 10). Pepys has
to register, despite the structures of authority which his times
allow him, the realities of his wife's boredom, discontent and
lack of purposeful activity: 'I see I must keep somebody for company sake to my wife, for I am ashamed she should live as she

doth' (IV. 14). Ironically, the resolution of the problem, with the arrival of Deb Willett in the household, causes a real crisis in the marriage, which is only resolved by Deb's dismissal and the conclusion of the written account. The record of the *Diary* is in large part a record of the games Pepys played with his marriage.

The diarist's fencing with his conscience is not only of consuming interest to the reader, but also obviously to the writer himself. Pepys often espouses a double standard by which he condemns in other men what he condones in himself. Yet he recognises his own moral prevarications. He blames himself repeatedly for his jealousy, which he considers unfounded:

> It is a deadly folly and plague that I bring upon myself to be so jealous; and by giving myself such an occasion, more then my wife desired, of giving her another month's dancing – which however shall be ended as soon as I can possibly. [But I am ashamed to think what a course I did take by lying to see whether my wife did wear drawers today as she used to do, and other things to raise my suspicion of her; but I found no true cause of doing it]. (IV. 140)

He knows that his jealousy makes him ridiculous. Early in the *Diary* he declares that he ought not to blame her for wishing to stray, as he wishes to do so himself.

Pepys's sexual behaviour is at odds with his professions of principle. He is shocked when Creed appears to have attempted rape, but on at least one occasion his own conduct qualifies as rape: 'It being dark, did privately entrer en la maison de la femme de Bagwell, and there I had sa compagnie, though with a great deal of difficulty; néanmoins, enfin je avais ma volonté d'elle. And being sated therewith, I walked home to Redriffe, it being now near 9 a-clock' (VI. 40). The next day he complains of '(having a mighty pain in my forefinger of my left hand, from a strain that it received last night in struggling avec la femme que je mentioned yesterday)' (VI. 40). Only three months earlier he had written that Mrs Bagwell 'denied me; which I was glad to see and shall value her the better for it – and I hope I never tempt her to any evil more' (V. 313). Faint hope. He expects to make amorous advances to women, but he condemns them for complying, fearing that they are not so modest – and therefore of course not so desirable – as he thought.

Pepys's record of his own sexual behaviour is the best advertisement against a Puritan upbringing that one could imagine,
as it shows how strongly his sexuality is stimulated by a sense
of prohibition, which he invokes as often as he can. The writing
of the *Diary* itself is part of a structure of prohibitions, in both
the vows he takes and his record each year of reading them over
and remaking them. He makes an oath to write his journal before he goes to wine and women, so that the actual writing is
part of the process of self-discipline. Yet one also suspects that
the act of writing, with its secrecy and special codes, inflames
him to more prohibited actions so that he can have the pleasure
of writing them down.

## VIRGINIA WOOLF: NEW WOMAN

Virginia Woolf's *Diary* records changes in role on a scale comparable to those experienced by Pepys. As proprietor of the
Hogarth Press, journalist, novelist and married woman, she is
aware of being a very different creature from the young woman
brought up in Hyde Park Gate: different friends, different lifestyle, different perception of self. These new identities shape
themselves in the early diaries before she was married, but they
are continued throughout the later volumes. If the *Diary* is the
organ which reconciles the processes of writing and living (as
she urged women to do in 1931 when addressing the London /
National Society for Women's Service), the handwritten record
of a professional printer, it is also the space in which she negotiates social changes as great as any Pepys encountered, many
of which are related, as his were, to perceptions of gender role.

One such change can be demonstrated from her analysis of
her relation with Leonard's mother. It must have given Virginia
pause to be known professionally as Mrs Woolf, when her mother-
in-law typified the immersion in women's traditional roles from
which Woolf's writing liberated her. The 'Angel in the House'
whom the professional woman writer must murder bears some
resemblance not just to her own mother, Julia Stephen, but to
Leonard's. Of one of their many visits to her mother-in-law at
Worthing Virginia Woolf records:

This shaky ramshackle old lady of 76 wore us out. . . . What makes it difficult is that she divines states of feeling to some extent, & would say pointedly 'You must often think of your writing when you are not writing, Virginia', when through exhaustion I became silent. . . . To be attached to her as daughter would be so cruel a fate that I can think of nothing worse; & thousands of women might be dying of it in England today: this tyranny of mother over daughter, or father; their right to the due being as powerful as anything in the world. And then, they ask, why women dont write poetry. Short of killing Mrs W. nothing could be done. Day after day one's life would be crumpled up like a bill for 10 pen[ce] 3 farthings. Nothing has ever been said of this. (*Diary* 3. 195).

Virginia Woolf's harshness with her mother-in-law's attitudes to life is exacerbated by her fear of being submerged in that traditional 'feminine' lifestyle.

Woolf's *Diary* also delineates problems with servants which recall Pepys's uneasy negotiation of that relationship. Unlike Pepys, she came from a background peopled with family servants. When Virginia and her siblings moved to Bloomsbury the presence of trusted servants reconciled their doubting relatives to that disreputable neighbourhood. The Stephen family servants, Nellie and Lottie, are constant presences in Virginia Woolf's *Diary*, and the tensions involved in trying to make a new life with different social assumptions, while retaining two dependents born and bred in the old ways, form an ongoing saga as vivid as any Pepys recounts in his new-found function as master of a household. Virginia Woolf is deeply uncomfortable with her role of Victorian mistress[20] in her new life as free-wheeling professional woman, a dilemma which in some form or other many twentieth-century women would recognise.

Woolf is exasperated by the servants' demands on her even while she tries to understand the reasons for their intransigence: 'It strikes me that one is absurd to expect good temper or magnanimity from servants, considering what crowded small rooms they live in, with their work all about them' (*Diary*, 3. 257). She is only at peace when they are finally dismissed, and she settles down to life with that twentieth-century middle-class alternative, the daily help, although Nellie and Lottie's capacity to return to the fold after dismissal is almost inexhaustible. Even the preferred and liberating daily help comes with powerful nine-teenth-century strings attached; Woolf has to buy Annie, with her two-year-old child, a cottage to live in, so that she can 'do' for them forever (*Diary*, 3. 255). Nelly Boxall moulders on for the next five years, with considerable build-up to the final rift in the spring of 1934: 'I cannot describe how the Nelly situation weighs on my spirits. I am determined not to discuss it with L. either. She pressed me this morning. You show no confidence in me; you dont treat me like a maid. Oh dear—how tempted I was then to say Then go; but I bit my tongue. And then down here, trying to make it up. I couldn't imagine it would be so hard, & the worst to come' (4. 205). The *Diary*, rather than Leonard Woolf, is the confidant to whom the problem is described, as it was also for Pepys:

> I am a little proud of myself; for I have just read through the last pages, & pat myself on the back, & say that I kept to my resolution, through thick & thin, & am now back here with Nelly gone, Annie upstairs, & Mabel, declared by Ha. to be a treasure, coming to see me tomorrow. So this has been defi-nitely accomplished, after all these years. The sense of free-dom & calm—no more brooding; no more possessiveness; no more sense of being part of Nelly's world; & her planted there. Even if the cooking is less luxurious, that is all to the good. (*Diary*, 4. 206–7).

Thirty years on from the death of Leslie Stephen, the dismissal of the family servant marks the coming-of-age of that movement towards freedom which his daughters began when they moved to Bloomsbury. But the writing of the *Diary* helps Virginia Woolf to summon up enough strength to make that final break.

Virginia Woolf's marriage, although superficially as unlike Pepys's as might be conceived, shares with it a sense of being worked out on new terms which are spelled out in the *Diary*. It is not plain from that record that the relationship of Leonard and Virginia was a totally sexless one: various entries suggest otherwise. It certainly flourished on an ideal of freedom, mutual tolerance and equality which make it unusual for any union entered on as early as 1912. The working partnership which it involved – the shared venture of the Hogarth Press – also made it look like some of the marriages described by Pepys, where a

business was run jointly by man and wife. Virginia Woolf chronicles the emotional register of the relationship precisely, if
unostentatiously. She writes: 'I have a child's trust in Leonard'
(*Diary* 3. 29). They quarrel, but they also make up: 'My being
cross about my book on fiction; & Leonard silent; & a great quarrel
that hot night; & I coming up here to sit alone in the dark, & L.
following me; & sharp hard words; right & wrong on both sides;
peace making; sleep; content' (3. 154). His judgement of her books
has the power to lift her out of despair, as with his reaction to
*The Years* in 1936: 'He was in tears. He says it is "a most remarkable book"—he *likes* it better than the Waves.... The moment of relief was divine' (*Diary*, 5. 30). In 1937, the year of
their silver wedding, she wrote:

> No I didnt go to Paris. This is a note to make. Waking at 3 I
> decided I would spend the week end at Paris. Got so far as
> looking up trains, consulting Nessa about hotel. Then L. said
> he wd. rather not. Then I was overcome with happiness. Then
> we walked round the square love making—after 25 years cant
> bear to be separate. Then I walked round the Lake in Regents
> Park. Then...you see it is an enormous pleasure, being wanted:
> a wife. And our marriage so complete. (*Diary*, 5. 115)

Did she have any sense of the novelty of a woman's keeping a
record of her married life, even though the diary was supposed
to be a woman's form?

In recording his marriage, Pepys communicates to his *Diary*
something which Montaigne said a man could not communicate
to anyone, and in so doing crosses a gender boundary, writing
from a position more akin to a woman's than a man's. Yet Woolf
also crosses a boundary in writing about her marriage, because
she perceives it as happy. George Eliot said that of the happiest
lives there were no records, but Virginia Woolf's is a record of
such happiness, despite uncertain health, mental and physical:
'Fundamentally I am the happiest woman in all W.C.1. The happiest wife, the happiest writer, the most liked inhabitant, so I
say, in Tavistock Square. When I count up my blessings, they
must surely amount to more than my sorrows' (*Diary*, 3. 228).
Her *Diary*, like Pepys's *Diary*, celebrates happiness.

It is also for Woolf, as it was for Pepys, a place where the
diarist explores her sexuality, which requires the marriage to be

'open' in the late twentieth-century sense. She writes in May 1926 of her love affair with Vita Sackville-West:

> I am amused at my relations with her: left so ardent in January—& now what? Also I like her presence & her beauty. Am I in love with her? But what is love? Her being 'in love' (it must be comma'd thus) with me, excites & flatters; & interests. What is this 'love'? Oh & then she gratifies my eternal curiosity: who's she seen, whats she done—for I have no enormous opinion of her poetry. How could I—I who have such delight in mitigating the works even of my greatest friends. (*Diary*, 3. 87)

She called her relation with Vita 'a spirited, creditable affair, I think, innocent (spiritually) & all gain, I think; rather a bore for Leonard but not enough to worry him. The truth is one has room for a good many relationships' (3. 117). In 1935 she charts the demise of that affection:

> My friendship with Vita is over. Not with a quarrel, not with a bang, but as ripe fruit falls. No I shant be coming to London before I go to Greece, she said. And then I got into the car. But her voice saying 'Virginia?' outside the tower room was as enchanting as ever. Only then nothing happened. And she has grown very fat, very much the indolent county lady, run to seed, incurious now about books; has written no poetry; only kindles about dogs, flowers, & new buildings. S[issinghurs]t is to have a new wing; a new garden; a new wall. Well, its like cutting off a picture: there she hangs, in the fishmongers at Sevenoaks, all pink jersey & pearls; & thats an end of it. And there is no bitterness, & no disillusion, only a certain emptiness. In fact—if my hands werent so cold—I could here analyse my state of mind these past 4 months, & account for the human emptiness by the defection of Vita; Roger's death; & no-one springing up to take their place; & a certain general slackening of letters & fame, owing to my writing nothing. (*Diary*, 4. 287).

The *Diary* constructs a narrative in which new ways of negotiating relationships are explored. But it is also a territory of loneliness, as it had been when the fifteen-year-old Virginia first encountered

Pepys in the wake of disruption and loss consequent on the marriage of Stella Duckworth.

Virginia Woolf claimed that Pepys might not have written the *Diary* at all if his wife had been a more adequate confidante. But this was written when she was in her green and salad days as a diarist. As she became more engrossed in that practice herself, her perception of the complexity of Pepys's aims increased. In August 1929 she recorded her disillusionment at the apparent defection of Vita Sackville-West in favour of a new love:

> And why do I write this down? I have not even told Leonard; & whom do I tell when I tell a blank page? The truth is, I get nearer feelings in writing than in walking [*sic*]—I think: graze the bone; enjoy the expression; have them out of me; make them a little creditable to myself; I daresay suppress something, so that after all I'm doing what amounts to confiding. Why did Pepys write his diary after all? (3. 239).

Five days later there is a reconciliation, and she admits to having faked the record: 'Indeed I was more worried & angry & hurt & caustic about this affair than I let on, even to the blank page' (3. 241). She used the blank page, as Pepys did, to invent herself in an age which provided no models either in its gender roles or its social structures for the new person she wanted to be.

## PEPYS AND WOOLF: TEMPORAL AND SPIRITUAL ACCOUNTS

When Virginia Woolf said that some passages in Pepys's *Diary* were not fit for his wife's eye she recognised the confessional nature of some of the writing, but she also came to a clearer vision of the blank page as a method of accounting: physical, spiritual, material. Pepys's personal history required Puritanism. Throughout the ten-year period of the *Diary* he never completely abandoned religious practices. He continued to think in terms of the Puritan values which he breathed in through his education, and to wonder at the world which transgressed them. The *Diary* bears witness to his need to keep intact principles of accountability which make him the man he is. Although the concrete evidence of those principles is often highly secular, their origins are religious.

Pepys's *Diary* can be read within a number of traditions. In some ways it is a Puritan confessional of the kind which abounded in the period – of which Baxter's *Autobiography* and Bunyan's *Grace Abounding* are the most notable examples – the great difference being its privacy.[21] On 1 November 1660 Pepys records meeting an old schoolfellow who 'did remember that I was a great roundhead when I was a boy, and I was much afeard that he would have remembered the words that I said the day that the King was beheaded (that were I to preach upon him, my text should be: "The memory of the wicked shall rot") but I found afterward that he did go away from school before that time' (I. 280). Why he should write down what he hopes will not be remembered remains one of the most fascinating questions which surrounds all ten volumes of the work, noted by Robert Louis Stevenson when he commented on the strangeness of Pepys's plan to read a lewd French book (*L'Escolle des Filles*) which he subsequently bought, but intended to burn as soon as he had read it: 'Had he suppressed all mention of the book, or had he bought it, gloried in the act, and cheerfully recorded his glorification, in either case we should have made him out. But no, he is full of precautions to conceal the "disgrace" of the purchase, and yet speeds to chronicle the whole affair in pen and ink.'[22] The paradox comes in part from a deeply ingrained habit of Puritan self-examination. Pepys envisages as reader of his *Diary* a disapproving God, susceptible, however, to various forms of propitiation and manipulation.

Pepys is not nearly as secular as he seems to a modern reader. Not only does he testify to his interest in religious differences and ideas, but he also uses the *Diary* to reprove himself and reflect on his own behaviour, whether it be sleeping through a bad sermon or lusting after a woman. In the first two or three volumes his weaning from the strictest tenets of Puritanism is pronounced. He notes with surprise that 'we fell to dancing – the first time that ever I did in my life – which I did wonder to see myself do' (II. 61). He stays at home on a Sunday to take physic: 'And God forgive me, did spend it in reading of some little French romances' (II. 35). Later in the same year (1661) he writes: 'I home to my father (who could decerne that I had been drinking, which he did never see or hear of before)' (II. 148). Ten days later he confides to his *Diary* that he is 'troubled in mind that I cannot bring myself to mind my business, but to be so much in love with plays' (II. 156). The theatres, having been closed by the Puritans in 1642 (when Pepys was nine) opened with the Restoration, and Pepys never loses a fascination with the theatre created by the novelty and new freedom of being able to go to a play. Other aspects of Restoration court life pleased him less. Despite his philandering, he remains strict about professional prostitution, noting that they went to a 'pitiful ale-house' in Bartholomew Fair 'where we had a dirty slut or two come up that were whores; but my very heart went against them, so that I took no pleasure but a great deal of trouble at being there and getting there, for fear of being seen' (II. 166). The expense of whoring afflicts him almost as much as its debauchery (V. 219). He never loses his distaste of prostitution, although it does not dissuade him from private liaisons.

Drawing together his accounts at the end of August 1661 – both spiritual and monetary, as is his custom – Pepys reflects:

> At Court things are in very ill condition, there being so much aemulacion, poverty, and the vices of swearing, drinking, and whoring, that I know not what will be the end of it but confusion. And the Clergy so high, that all people that I meet with, do all protest against their practice. In short, I see no content or satisfaccion anywhere in any one sort of people. (II. 167).

This final sentence casts some light on Pepys's unexpressed motives for writing. He is caught at a moment in time which reveals to him the relativity of all the absolutes in which he has been raised. Those firm Puritan truths have been transformed, almost overnight, into dogmas and practices open to challenge. He is shocked in 1660 by Lord Sandwich's scepticism in matters of religion (I. 201). Observing a small congregation at vespers, he declares: 'I see that religion, be it what it will, is but a humour, and so the esteem of it passeth as other things do' (I. 257). The decline in Church piety is as strange to him as the conflicts which changes of faith create even in his own family, as when he argues with his mother in 1660: 'She and I talked very high about Religion, I in defence of the Religion I was born in' (I. 76). Later he writes tolerantly of a conversation with Philip Howard, Catholic Lord Almoner to the Queen, about their religious opinions: 'So away with the Almoner in his coach talking merrily about the differences in our religions' (VIII. 27). But Pepys never believed that his religion was purely a humour. He needed to keep a firm hold on the Puritan spiritual past into which he had been born, however completely it might appear to have vanished under the pressures of the Restoration present.

In Pepys's *Diary* monetary accounts can never be separated from a religious framework, because worldly prosperity is for him the sign of God's favour:

So home and fell hard to my monthly accounts – letting my family go to bed after prayers. I stayed up long, and find myself, as I think, fully worth 670*l*. So with good comfort to bed, finding that though it be but little, yet do I get ground every month. I pray God it may continue so with me. (IV. 88)

The family at prayers, and his own prayer to God to continue to increase his wealth, are part of a package of careful habits – of which regular financial accounting is one – which create that wealth. In bringing himself to book spiritually, Pepys casts up what he is worth financially, blames himself if he has spent too much and renews his vows about the theatre, women, drink and music: 'Fearful of being too much taken with musique, for fear of returning to my old dotage thereon and so neglect my business as I used to do' (IV. 48). Pepys's *Diary* evinces a man keenly sensitive to, and hungry for pleasure, but this instinct, as with Milton's passion for the beautiful, is often at war with his Puritan conscience. Throughout the *Diary* he watches himself 'even' his accounts. God, the master accountant, must be allowed proper credit, and, if the books have been cooked, forfeits must be paid.

The gaining of money is vital to Pepys as evidence of his value to himself, other people, and his Maker. During the almost ten-year period of the *Diary* he loses some of his Puritan fervour as he progresses within a secular society which affords him few models for that mode of thinking. *The Pilgrim's Progress* was not in his library, although both *Paradise Lost* and Milton's 1645 *Poems* were,[23] but its spirit is part of Pepys's heritage. The *Diary* demonstrates that as the material account improves, the spiritual one becomes impoverished. Pepys registers with uncanny accuracy the degeneration in his own behaviour: as he grows rich, he grows mean:

But it is a strange thing to observe, and fit for me to remember, that I am at no time so unwilling to part with money as

when I am concerned in the getting of it most (as I thank God,
of late I have got more in this month, *viz.* near 250*l*) than ever
I did in half a year before in my life, I think. (V. 276)

His miserliness is at its most striking with his wife. He cannot
bring himself to feel that what he earns belongs to her, and is in
a constant fret about her spending: 'Coming home tonight, I did
go to examine my wife's house-accounts; and finding things that
seemed somewhat doubtful, I was angry. . . . I fear she will forget by degrees the way of living cheap and under a sense of
want' (V. 283). By the end of the *Diary*, as he tries desperately
to make amends to Elizabeth for his infidelity with Deb Willett,
the material account is thriving but the spiritual one is in trouble.

With the love affair with Deb Willett, which was not begun
until a year after these entries, the *Diary* becomes inextricably
associated in Pepys's mind with prohibited pleasures, rather than
with the accounts which even and reprove those pleasures. The
increased pain in his eyes underwrites his awareness that he is
straining his sight in keeping a less than blameless record. As a
consequence he begins to need to abandon the *Diary*, just as he
abandons the affair with Deb: 'But my great pain is lest God
Almighty shall suffer me to find out this girl, whom endeed I
love, and with a bad amour; but I will pray God to give me
grace to forbear it' (IX. 519). The act of keeping the *Diary* separates itself in his conscience from purgative confessional accounting, and instead becomes allied to the guilty and clandestine
pleasures of evil imaginings. He may himself have had some
inkling of the psychological complexities of his need to record
what he does, and have sensed, from his own capacity for exceptional self-awareness, that 'confessional literature is likely to
wear the most masks of all'.[24] In 1661 he records that 'Mr.
Woodcocke preached at our church; a very good sermon upon
the Imaginacions of the thoughts of man's heart being only evil'
(II. 48). He recognises his own capacity for fantasy: 'We home
and I to bed – where (God forgive me) I did please myself by
strength of fancy with the young country *Segnora* that was at
dinner with us today' (II. 44). Pepys's imagination plays a vital
part in his sexual fantasies, of which the most beautiful is his
dream, at the height of the plague, of having Lady Castlemaine
in his arms, the innocence of which he touchingly avouches:

[I] was admitted to use all the dalliance I desired with her, and then dreamed that this could not be awake but that it was only a dream. But that since it was a dream and that I took so much real pleasure in it, what a happy thing it would be, if when we die in our graves (as Shakespeare resembles it), we could dream, and dream but such dreams as this – that then we should not need to be fearful of death as we are this plague-time. (VI. 191)

The mention of Shakespeare opens a different world which Pepys usually keeps ruthlessly at bay, distrusting, in true Puritan fashion, the realm of fiction. Yet it is possible that some of his sexual adventures took place more in his mind and on the pages of the *Diary* than in actuality.

Pepys, a man of exceptional public probity, with an instinct for self-scrutiny which he found uncomfortably intense, and which he both relieves and exacerbates by keeping the *Diary*, often recognises the masks he assumes. In this respect in the latter part of the *Diary* he touches the edges of the novel (anticipating Richardson) by stepping, as author, outside a narrative in which he, like Deb and his wife Elizabeth, plays an active part. It was perhaps no accident that when Woolf contemplated putting Pepys into the first *Common Reader* she was overcome by an urge to run into the house to fetch *Clarissa*.

Readers of Pepys's *Diary*, and especially women readers, must be struck by the failure of any literary work of the period to portray relations between the sexes with the subtlety of Pepys's account of his daily married life. Very little separates him from Richardson. The petty bourgeois world of the *Diary*, the struggles with Puritan conscience in a debauched society, the domestic form of the journal, all seem to anticipate Richardson's *Pamela*, as does the situation of the affair between master and servant. The social mobility of the world in which Pepys finds himself makes the arrival of Deb Willett a dangerous one precisely because Pepys registers the levelling between himself and his wife – who have risen from humble circumstances – and Deb, who is well-educated: 'She seems by her discourse to be grave beyond her bigness and age, and exceeding well-bred as to her deportment, having been a scholar in a school at Bow these seven or eight year' (VIII. 451). He reflects: 'She is very pretty, and so grave as I never saw little thing in my life. Endeed, I think her a little too good for my family, and so well-carriaged as I hardly ever saw – I wish my wife may use her well' (VIII. 456). In the event it is he himself who does not use her well. The account of his 'amours' reads as though Richardson's Mr. B had written up his courting of Pamela, except that Pepys is no aristocrat, but a man singularly exposed by being unused to having dependants in his household. Deb's presence is a beguiling sign of his material success, and his debauching of her marks his uneasy and only partial assimilation to the master class whose morals he always despised.

When Virginia Woolf writes her own *Diary*, Pepys remains just below the surface, as a model which she uses to question her own practices and to understand her own place in that tradition of diary-writing. Surprisingly, considering the distance between seventeenth-century Puritanism and Bloomsbury, Woolf's *Diary* reflects Pepys's concept of accountability. The Stephen heritage, with its background in the Clapham sect, was an intensely Puritan one. Woolf knew that the practice of keeping a diary was more in her father's family tradition than in her mother's, although it descended to her from Stephen women, not men. Within that female Stephen tradition, principles of accountability permeate her record as insistently as they govern Pepys's earlier one.

Virginia Woolf wrote in January 1923: 'I will try to make up my accounts on the spiritual side before attacking the temporal' (*Diary*, 2. 222). She was almost certainly reading Pepys during this period, while she mourned for Katherine Mansfield, castigating herself for her jealousy of her and wishing that she had been more aware of her physical suffering, an impulse dictated by her own recurrent physical illnesses. At the end of the month she reflected: 'In casting accounts, never forget to begin with the state of the body' (*Diary*, 2. 228). Pepys's *Diary* opens in 1660 with the state of the body, in his relief from recovering for his operation for the stone.

In the traditional afterlife of Virginia Woolf as genteel invalidish Bloomsbury lady – a portrait already painted during her lifetime – money plays very little part. But Virginia Woolf's *Diary* records, as Pepys's *Diary* does, her sense of her own progress, not just spiritually or creatively, but in material things. Money matters to her. She charts what she earns, both from reviewing and from her novels. It is part of her competition with Vanessa:

And L. & I were very extravagant, for the first time in our lives, buying desks, tables, sideboards, crockery for Rodmell. This gave me pleasure; & set my dander up against Nessa's almost overpowering supremacy. My elder son is coming tomorrow; yes, & he is the most promising young man in King's; & has been speaking at the Apostles dinner. All I can oppose that with is, And I made £2,000 out of Orlando & can bring Leonard here & buy a house if I want. To which she replies (in the same inaudible way) I am a failure as a painter compared with you, & cant do more than pay for my models. And so we go on; over the depths of our childhood. Do you re member going down to the town to fetch – which ancient memories Duncan cannot share. (*Diary*, 3. 232)

She relishes planning how to spend the money she has earned, and the success for a book is measured in material terms: 'The greenhouse began to be built yesterday. We are watering the earth with money. Next week my room will begin to rise' (*Diary*, 3. 257). Reviews are as significant to her as to any other publisher, because they affect sales.

Her material advancement is linked to technological advances as startling as any of the developments in knowledge recorded by Pepys. Electricity, cars, aeroplanes all have a place in Woolf's *Diary*: 'Then of course, being now so well off, with 2 frigidaires & *everything handsome*, I need not fritter & fribble about clothes, & having little sense of the duty of society left, shall hope to take my way about unhasting unresting' (*Diary*, 4. 25, my italics). Dogberry's phrase is there as it is in Pepys's *Diary*. Virginia Woolf itemises material prosperity with Pepysian satisfaction. Typical of Pepys also is the alleviation of materialism with the language of religion: 'Unhasting, unresting' are the words of the hymn, 'Immortal, invisible, God only wise'.

In her *Diary* Woolf often uses the language of the Puritan record, although adapting it to a different context. She notes that 'this is to be a chart of my progress' (2. 208), before recording her friends' approval of *Jacob's Room*. Progress is here an author's progress, perhaps with a wry memory of the book entitled *The Author's Progress* which (in the first flush of her professional journalism) she had reviewed with such loathing as a Grub Street hack's record. But it is also inevitably a pilgrim's progress, and when she noted of Spenser's *Faerie Queene* that 'all great books

are the story of the souls adventures – nothing else – a perpetual odyssey & divine comedy' (MHP/B2m), she might have
found in a corner of her mind the conviction that Pepys's *Diary*
and her own ranked as outsiders' odysseys in that Homeric
tradition.

Woolf begins 1923 weighing up her life and regretting her lack
of children:

> Let me have one confessional where I need not boast. Years &
> years ago, after the Lytton affair, I said to myself, walking up
> the hill at Beireuth, never pretend that the things you haven't
> got are not worth having; good advice I think. At least it often
> comes back to me. Never pretend that children, for instance,
> can be replaced by other things. (*Diary*, 2. 221)

One confessional where I need not boast. She speaks of her as-
sessment of herself as 'the sort of tap a chemist might give to
the jars in his shop, naming them shortly, because he knows
what is in them' (2. 222). In this entry her self-examination, and
her search for direction and meaning, and for an understanding
of responsibility and its relation to happiness, conjure up the
'minute scrutiny' of the Puritan diary.[25] She asks herself: 'Perhaps I have been too happy for my soul's good?' (*Diary*, 2. 222).
She recognises connections between her *Diary* and inherited Puritan instincts:

> I am not satisfied that this book is in a healthy way. . . . The
> truth is that I have an internal, automatic scale of values; which
> decides what I had better do with my time. It dictates 'This
> half hour must be spent on Russian' 'This must be given to
> Wordsworth.' or 'now I'd better darn my brown stockings.'
> How I come by this code of values I dont know. Perhaps its
> the legacy of puritan grandfathers. I suspect pleasure slightly.
> God knows. (*Diary*, 2. 94)

Her puritan grandfather, James Stephen, did in fact keep a diary.[26]
The suspicion of pleasure spills over into Woolf's own practice:
'I always have to confess, when I write diary in the morning. It
is only 11.30 to be honest, & I have left off Mrs Dalloway in
Bond Street; & really why is it? I should very much like to ac-
count for my depression' (*Diary*, 2. 190). The word 'account'

acquires meaning from the preceding 'confess'. In writing the *Diary*, Woolf confesses her depression, 'evens' (Pepys's word) the account of it, and anaesthetises it with the stolen pleasure of writing the *Diary* in the morning.

Guilt is often to the fore, either because she has neglected the *Diary*, or because she shouldn't be writing it at that moment: 'I have lost my writing board; an excuse for the anaemic state of this book. Indeed I only write now, in between letters, to say that Orlando was finished yesterday as the clock struck one' (3. 176). The record of a precise time is itself reminiscent of Pepys. They are going to France. The body is also tiresome.

> Since February I have been a little clouded with headache, had a touch of influenza; & so, with the lights down, & all energy turned to forcing my book along, have not written here. I dislike these months. Shall we try Rome next year? Control of life is what one should learn now: its economic management. I feel cautious, like a poor person, now I am 46. But I may be dead then, I think, & so take my French lessons now, instead of waiting. (*Diary*, 3. 177)

Control, economy, the husbanding of energy, reflections on mortality, the seizing of the moment, and the physical record, are all part of Pepys's vocabulary as a diarist.

Woolf's *Diary* provides a space in which the more recalcitrant problems of her novels can be contained, and thus controlled: 'I fill in this page, nefariously; at the end of a morning's work. I have begun the second part of Waves—I dont know, I dont know. I feel that I am only accumulating notes for a book—whether I shall ever face the labour of writing it, God knows' (*Diary*, 3. 268). At the end of the same entry she observed: 'Certainly it is true that if one writes a thing down one has done with it' (*Diary*, 3. 269), which again is the genuine confessional instinct, although the word 'nefariously' gives the *Diary* itself an almost guilty pleasure. Her penultimate entry before her suicide returns to the *Diary* as a mode of control:

> I insist upon spending this time to the best advantage. I will go down with my colours flying. This I see verges on introspection; but doesn't quite fall in. Suppose, I bought a ticket at the Museum; biked in daily & read history. Suppose I selected

one dominant figure in every age & wrote round & about. Occupation is essential. And now with some pleasure I find that its seven; & must cook dinner. Haddock & sausage meat. I think it is true that one gains a certain hold on sausage & haddock by writing them down. (5. 358).

The proper use of time, the sense of the discipline of daily occupations, and the control of life through writing about it, again strike the chord of Pepys's own practice as diarist.

Virginia Woolf did not apparently ask herself, as she asked for Dorothy Osborne, why Pepys was not a novelist. At the first dinner of the Pepys' Society in 1905 verses were recited in honour of the diarist:

> You ask me what was his intent?
>   In truth I can't conjecture;
> 'Tis plain enough he neither meant
>   A Sermon nor a Lecture.
>
> But there it is, the thing's a fact.
>   I find no other reason
> But that some scribbling itch attacked him
>   In and out of season.[27]

The 'scribbling itch' allies Pepys with Woolf, for whom the *Diary* was an outlet for her passion for words. Almost, she treated it as an addiction, as Pepys perhaps came to do, for although his eyes recovered, he did not resume the record after his wife's death in the summer of 1669.

For a woman one of the main pleasures of reading Pepys's *Diary* is that it seems to be written from a perspective constructed more from a woman's point of view than from a man's, showing a man in the process of moving into worlds of which he has no experience, trying to negotiate power structures which are entirely new to him. In this negotiation women both help him and are to some extent the victims of his desperate need to restore his shattered nerves. The language of the *Diary* is never a public male language. It always remains a new language, forged out of the vernacular, by a man who had to write to order to assure himself that he remained at the still point of the turning world. The new language – that unpretentious but precise vital language recommended by Francis Osborne – of the upwardly mobile writer and reader, belongs to the novel: to the Londoner, Defoe, and to the master printer, Samuel Richardson, whose shop was in Salisbury Court where Pepys was born. In literary terms that language belonged to women more than to men, and Pepys's *Diary*, written in a woman's form, from a position in the world which in its insecurities belongs historically to women and working men, speaks vividly to women readers, Virginia Woolf amongst them. The language of his *Diary* is the language of hers, sharp, unliterary, from oral rather than written traditions, spurning a high style. Both *Diaries*, the seventeenth-century man's and the twentieth-century woman's, liberate into writing new forms of thought and feeling.

When Virginia Woolf looks back at Pepys she sees a man poised between past and present, relishing the moment. Diaries, from her own early fiction of Joan Martyn, express a central aspect of her aesthetic: the seizing of the present moment. But Pepys's double stance, looking back, and looking forward, is also an emblem for her own project in her writing of literary criticism. For in *The Common Reader* volumes, both the two that were published, and the third which remained unfinished at her death, she searches the past in order to discover a tradition to which she and other women might belong, of common readers and common writers. In that tradition the diary marks a vital transition, a circular, non-literary form, practised in the main by women, whose most outstanding practitioner was a man curiously ill at ease in the public male-gendered role allotted to him in a changing society. The *Diary* enables Pepys to negotiate a new role which will, in just half a century, emerge in those works which mark in Woolf's first *Common Reader* the beginning of a tradition of women readers: the novels of Defoe, of which two, *A Journal of the Plague Year* and *Robinson Crusoe*, are cast in the form of a journal.

When Virginia Woolf writes her own journal, she uses Pepys's *Diary* as a sounding-board for observing her own writing practices. As she queries through her *Diary* the predominantly male literary traditions in evidence all around her, she creates, as Pepys also did, an alternative mode of writing and being which belongs to the female line.

# 6

# Bunyan and Virginia Woolf:
# A History and a Language of Their Own

## WOMEN AND THE VERNACULAR: BUNYAN, FOXE AND THE BIBLE

When in August 1924 Virginia Woolf considered Pepys for the new volume of *The Common Reader* she also noted in her Diary: 'It strikes me, I must now read Pilgrim's Progress' (*Diary*, 2. 309). Like Pepys, Bunyan does not appear in either volume of *The Common Reader*, but Woolf's critical enterprise is suffused with his spirit.[1] In the early 1930s she reread *The Pilgrim's Progress* as part of her programme of study for *The Pargiters*,[2] which fed into her polemical attack on the patriarchal establishment in *Three Guineas*. In November 1900 Thoby Stephen, then an undergraduate at Trinity College, Cambridge, had presented his sister Virginia with an elegant 1776 Folio edition (with copper plates) of Foxe's Protestant history.[3] As Virginia Woolf assembled notes in the late 1930s for her 'Common History' – the projected literary history which she never completed – she could have observed that Bunyan had discovered for himself from reading Foxe's *Book of Martyrs* a past which promised him a new language and a voice. Bunyan used Foxe as many working men who felt themselves to be born and bred outside mainstream culture were to use *The Pilgrim's Progress*: as an adjunct to the Bible, in which the reader might find some paradigm for personal history, some alternative cultural tradition. Woolf's thesis in *Three Guineas*, that women must recognise that they had been written out of mainstream culture alongside working men and other minority groups, produced a language and an impetus in that work which often echo Bunyan's writings. In view of the ease with which the twentieth-century woman reader can dismiss Bunyan as sexist,[4] it is worth exploring the extent to which the activity of writing led the author of *The Pilgrim's Progress*, a man with no inherited intellectual pedigree, into the same kind of negotiation with the

166

past that Woolf herself undertook, not primarily in her role as woman novelist, but in the more pioneering role of female literary critic and intellectual historian.

Woolf's work on her 'Common History' was a continuation of a plan of study conducted for *Three Guineas*, which took her into the unlikely but immensely productive area of early Church history. When (possibly in 1931) she reread and wrote notes on *The Pilgrim's Progress*, she seems to have become aware that Bunyan represented a key figure in the alternative tradition which she wanted to unearth. She may have left him out of the drafts of 'Anon' and replaced him with another 'hedgerow' preacher, Hugh Latimer, because Bunyan's late date made him so exceptionally awkward to the literary historian. Like Milton, he makes an odd Restoration figure. But Milton, with his phenomenal classical learning and Humanist inheritance, annexes easily to a concept of the late English high Renaissance. Bunyan, a man who constantly rejoiced in his ignorance of Latin and Greek, who received only a modicum of formal education and who scorned university learning, looks more like a figure from *Piers Plowman* than a prototype for Milton's innocently cultivated, orthodoxly Humanist Adam. Bunyan was the first man in his family to know how to read and write. Yet that notable advance from the condition of his father and forefathers registers slow but certain changes set in motion in the high culture of the early sixteenth century. Like Pepys, and like many women writers and readers, Bunyan's Renaissance postdates traditional divisions into literary and historical periods. Both of Bunyan's major works – *Grace Abounding to the Chief of Sinners* and *The Pilgrim's Progress* – could not have existed without the ferment of new ideas caused by the translation of the Bible into the vernacular by Tyndale and Coverdale.

Virginia Woolf believed that later readers must take responsibility for seeing connections between originally disparate entities. She was herself a virtuoso in this mode of reading and writing. If her self-definition as radical thinker was through a number of early writers, amongst whom Bunyan and the Protestant reformer Hugh Latimer were the most prominent, she seems to have been fully conscious that the redirection of culture which she wanted to trace, began and was fostered in the changing world which produced Bunyan. She sensed, as he did, that a vital undermining of the world of the Fathers took place when the Bible became available in the vernacular, and that the implications of that change reached far beyond the initial impetus of linguistic transformation.

Bunyan's search for a past with which he could identify his own particular condition was destined to be focused almost exclusively on the Bible in English and the one other book which he took with him to Bedford gaol on his arrest in 1660 for preaching without a license: Foxe's *Book of Martyrs*. From these two books and his own experiences as itinerant tinker and preacher, he created his two prison narratives: *Grace Abounding* (1666) and *The Pilgrim's Progress* Part I (1678). Foxe and the English Bible – arguably the two central volumes of the Protestant Reformation in England – provided him with a means of self-definition as an individual outside a dominant and repressive culture, and with a language and body of metaphors in which to recreate and express that condition.

Foxe's *Book of Martyrs* communicates a powerful sense of the heroism displayed by ordinary men and women without learning or influence. First printed in England in 1563, the *Book of Martyrs* offered its readers a reconstruction of the past which aimed to establish the true traditions of Protestant England for the new Protestant monarch, Elizabeth I.[5] By the early seventeenth century Foxe's creation of a Protestant history, in which the development of the vernacular itself played a central part, had served a purpose of providing popular material for new common readers, many of them women. Foxe's narrative offered Bunyan class identity. He knew that he belonged to the class of ordinary men and women who peopled Foxe's pages. It mattered to him to stay in that class because he thus had access to a past and a tradition of his own. Bunyan saw himself, when he submitted to an arrest he knew he could have avoided, as the direct descendant of the early Protestant martyrs celebrated in Foxe's record.[6] He could have read many descriptions in Foxe of the cramped conditions, hardship and squalor of prison life.[7] But he shared his bondage, as he also shared his origins and his calling, with men and women who would have been anonymous if they had not been made illustrious within Foxe's book. The class bias of *The Pilgrim's Progress*, in which the wicked are always gentlemen and ladies, Bunyan could have imbibed from Foxe's information that those who stood fast in the Marian persecutions were artisans like himself, while the gentry either went into exile or conformed.[8]

As a man born to no authority within his own culture[9] Bunyan found in the Protestant religion the explosive potential which had made the early Reformers such menacing figures to the establishment in their own time. The nature of that threat was contained in the other book which accompanied Bunyan to prison, the Bible in the vernacular. In *A Relation of my Imprisonment* Bunyan crosses swords with Justice Keelin (Sir John Kelynge) over his (Bunyan's) claim to have authority from the first Epistle to St Peter to preach the Word. Keelin remonstrates: 'As every man hath received a trade, so let him follow it. If any man have received a gift of tinkering, as thou has done, let him follow his tinkering. And so other men their trades. And the divine his calling, &c.'[10] When Thomas Smith – Reader in Rhetoric, lecturer at Christ's College, Cambridge, and Keeper of the University library – castigated Bunyan for his theological views, the scholar's distaste is transparently for the social presumption of 'a wandering preaching tinker'. Another Cambridge man, Henry Denne, retorted wryly: 'You seem to be angry with the tinker because he strives to mend souls as well as kettles and pans.'[11] In the remarkable account which Bunyan wrote of his wife's pleading with the Justice on his behalf, Elizabeth Bunyan exclaims: 'Because he is a Tinker, and a poor man; therefore he is despised, and cannot have justice' (*GA*, p. 128). Bunyan exemplified what the official opponents of the translated Bible had anticipated: the refusal of the ordinary reader to remain in his or her allotted station in life.

Historically, Bunyan belonged to the silent majority whom the early translators sought to empower with the Word in their own mother-tongue.[12] Foxe represents Tyndale, the first translator of the Bible into English, as a martyr for the English language,[13] a man who 'thought . . . if the Scripture were turned into the vulgar speech, that the poore people might also read and see the simple plaine Word of God'. Tyndale was determined to teach the reading of the Word, on the grounds that any intermediary authority could quench or distort its truth: 'He wisely casting in his mind perceived by experience, how that it was not possible to stablish the lay-people in any truth except the Scripture were so plainely laid before their eyes in their mother tongue, that they might see the process, order, and meaning of the text' (II. 363). Bunyan wrote in *I will Pray with the Spirit* [?1662] that 'understanding is to be taken for speaking in our mother-tongue;

and also experimentally'.[14] Tyndale was perfectly aware of the
socially inflammatory aspects of vernacular translation: 'Some
said . . . it would make the people to rebell and rise against the
king' (II. 364). When Bunyan was arrested at Samsell for preaching without a license, he records that the authorities anticipated
'some fearful business' but 'found us only with our Bibles in
our hands, ready to speak and hear the word of God'.[15]

Tyndale might have denied that he wished to undermine civil
authority, as Bunyan himself also did, but his translation per-
formed exactly the same function as *The Pilgrim's Progress* would
perform for the working men of the 1790s.[16] The people did not
take the Word in their own tongue with the quietness which
Cranmer desired. Interruptions of services, disputations, interpretations of texts, followed immediately on the translation of
the Holy Book. In 1543 the conservative bishops under Stephen
Gardiner passed an act 'forbidding the reading of the Bible by
women, artificers, apprentices and others of insufficient status'.[17]
Foxe describes a further proclamation following the death of Anne
Askew in 1546:

> First, That from henceforth no man, woman, or person, of what
> estate, condition, or degree soever *he or they* shall be, shall
> after the last day of August next ensuing, receive, have, take,
> or keep in *his or their* possession, the Text of the new Testa-
> ment of Tindals or Coverdales translation in English . . . nor . . .
> any manner of books printed or written in the English tongue.
> (II. 587)

The indeterminacy of the pronoun in this passage is striking.
This must be one of the earliest examples of a refusal to accept
that 'he' is an unmarked pronoun designating equally both sexes.
The metaphor of 'mother-tongue', the stress on the pronoun, the
long list of women martyrs in Foxe's record, all underline the
extent to which the translation of the Bible was undertaken in
the name of an attack on the world of the Fathers by men and
women outside the power structures of patriarchy. Their position as outsiders was reinforced by the Church through its use
of an official language, Latin, which was still almost exclusively
the territory of priests and educated men.

The terms in which Foxe casts his history of the Protestant
religion thus invite analysis along the lines of gender confronta-

tion. The arguments in favour of a vernacular Bible, the attacks on the Prelates, the privileging of feeling and experience over reason within religious discourse, and the identification of problems relating to language and expressiveness, were all part of a repudiation by many Protestant reformers of the Church as the organ of patriarchal state authority. Foxe, like many other sixteenth-century Protestants, distrusted and despised learned men as the inheritors of a corrupt ecclesiastical tradition. He revered the aristocratic learned women tutored by eminent Humanists as the new guardians of a central Protestant tradition. The many eulogies to learned women in this period – Catherine Parr, the Princess Elizabeth, Lady Jane Grey, Foxe's own praise of Jane, Countess of Westmoreland – can be construed as an attempt to establish an alternative authority, which the Protestant church required in its early days for its scholarly credentials. Under that alternative authority the Reformers hoped to enlist not the educated few, but the massed ranks of nameless men and women who would read the Bible in their own language.

One of the key texts for the Protestant reformers was the crucial third chapter of St Paul's Epistle to the Galatians. This text, with its fervent proclamation of an egalitarian principle, has subsequently provided the battle-cry for various kinds of radical political protest. Coverdale's translation reads:

> Before faith came, we were kepte and shut up under the lawe, unto the faith which shulde afterwarde be declared. Thus the lawe was our scolemaster unto Christ, that we might be made righteous by faith. But now that faith is come, we are nomore under the scolemaster. For ye all are the children of God by the faith in Christ Jesus.
>
> For as many of you as are baptysed, haue put on Christ. Here is nether Jewe ner Gent[il]e: here is nether bonde ner fre: here is nether man ner woman, for ye are all one in Christ Jesu. Yf ye be Christes, then are ye Abrahams sede and heyres acordynge to the promes.[18]

The 'scolemaster' meant to Coverdale and his contemporaries not only the rigidities of Scholasticism, but also the domination of the priesthood, whom the translators blamed for the ignorance of the people who had only ever heard the Bible in Latin instead of in their own tongue.

Bunyan was constantly subject to criticism as a man who did not know the Bible in the original Biblical tongues. In 1658 he had written scathingly in *A Few Sighs from Hell* (1658) of men who scorned poor Christians because 'they are not Gentlemen, because they cannot, with *Pontius Pilate*, speak Hebrew, Greek and Latine'.[19] He insisted on his own lack of education,[20] as when he writes in the Epistle to the Reader in the *Doctrine of the Law and Grace unfolded* (1685):

> Reader, if thou do find this Book empty of fantastical Expressions, and without light, vain, Whimsical Scholarlike terms, thou must understand, it is because I never went to School to *Aristotle* or *Plato*, but was brought up in my Father's House, in a very mean condition, among a Company of poor Countrymen. But if thou do find a parcel of plain, yet sound, true and home sayings, attribute that to the Lord Jesus, his Gifts and Abilities, which he hath bestowed upon such a poor Creature as I am, and have been. (A 4v)

Bunyan claimed that he stood for a different kind of learning. John Burton, author of the Dedicatory Epistle to *Some Gospel-truths Opened* (1656), declared that

> this man is not chosen out of an earthly, but out of the heavenly University, the Church of Christ. . . . He hath, through grace taken these three heavenly degrees, to wit, union with Christ, the anointing of the spirit, and the experience of the temptations of Satan, which doe more fit a man for that weighty work of preaching the Gospell, than all University Learning and degrees that can be had. (A 11v)

Bunyan's repudiation of established learning in Latin, and his constant search for a new model of writing and reading made Luther his natural ally.

Bunyan discovered Luther's Commentary on Galatians when he was eager to read 'some ancient Godly man's Experience, who had writ some hundred of years before I was born'. The impact which Luther's work had on him grows out of Bunyan's urgent need for a history in which to root his own experience:

> Well, after many such longings in my mind, the God in whose

hands are all our days and ways, did cast into my hand, one day, a book of *Martin Luther*, his comment on the *Galathians*, so old that it was ready to fall piece from piece, if I did but turn it over. Now I was pleased much that such an old book had fallen into my hand; the which, when I had but a little way perused, I found my condition in his experience, so largely and profoundly handled, as if his Book had been written out of my heart; this made me marvel: for this thought I, this man could not know anything of the state of Christians now, but must needs write and speak of the Experience of former days. (*GA*, p. 40)

Bunyan's own creativity is awakened by communion with a mind from a time long past; the old book almost disintegrates in his hands, but speaks to him in a voice which he recognises as his own.

This sense of revelation at the discovery of like minds in the past animated the whole project of translating the Bible into the vernacular. Parker's *Preface* to the Bishops' Bible (1568) grounds translation in an historical continuum, reminding his readers of the suppression of the Bible by the Roman emperors and of the exhortations of the 'olde fathers in the primative Church' to 'all persons, aswell men as women, to exercise them selves in the scriptures, which by Saint Hieroms aucthoritie be the scriptures of the people'.[21] Foxe likewise records John Lambert's account of Old English translations of the Bible: 'When the Saxons did inhabite the Land, the king at that time, which was a Saxon, did himselfe translate the Psalter into the Language that then was generally used' (II. 415). For Lambert the vernacular gospel of the sixteenth century stands at the end of a long and reputable tradition of translation.

In the pages of Foxe Bunyan found ample confirmation that the Protestant martyrs offered him a past and a tradition which would empower his own writing. The translated Bible opened up for him, as it had done for them, a world of feeling and experience[22] not controlled by the learned hierarchies of the Church. One could call it, historically, a woman's world, such as Virginia Woolf sought to recover in her projected literary history. For Bunyan it looked like a new place from which working men might speak.

In the *Book of Martyrs* Foxe deliberately sets forth the English Bible as a handbook through which men and women traditionally voiceless within their own society find a means of expression. In submitting to imprisonment Bunyan was not only denied literal freedom – and as an itinerant tinker he was used to a degree of physical liberty which must have made the cramped conditions of his life particularly galling – but also the freedom to preach. Enforced captivity was for him the peculiarly distressing state of enforced speechlessness. The Bible offered him, as it also offered Tyndale and his fellow martyrs, the parallel of the captivity of the Israelites in Egypt.[23] Bunyan would have found in Foxe's history ample witness of the ways in which the vernacular Bible, and particularly the Psalms, provided a language for the special suffering attendant on being silenced for speaking in the name of one's religion. Once the Bible had been translated the Psalms opened up for ordinary men and women a language in which to articulate being voiceless. In Part I of *The Pilgrim's Progress* Christian's terror of death expresses itself through Psalms 42 and 88:

> Then they addressed themselves to the Water; and entring, *Christian* began to sink, and crying out to his good friend *Hopeful*; he said, I sink in deep Waters, the Billows go over my head, all his Waves go over me, *Selah*.[24]

The Psalms provide Christian with a language for the extremity of feeling, a way out of his own sense of being overwhelmed. Bunyan in prison consoled his desolate state with the Bible. The texts which pepper his margins[25] in *The Pilgrim's Progress* show him using Biblical reference as a kind of shorthand communication[26] with the reader which annotates not only the text, but the process of its composition. Time and again Bunyan stresses the relief which access to language offers to the oppressed spirit.

Bunyan's marginal gloss in the first paragraph of *The Pilgrim's Progress* both of Psalm 38 (numbered 37 in the Coverdale translation, following the Vulgate) and of the Old Testament prophet, Habakkuk, focuses the reader's attention on the nature of Christian's burden. For the Psalmist of 38 (Coverdale 37), the burden is sin: 'For my wickednesses are gone over my heade, and are like a sore burthen, too hevy for me to beare.'[27] But Bunyan's gloss of Habakkuk 2.2 refers the reader to the opening verse of the Book which identifies the burden as an unheeded lament: 'O Lorde, how longe shal I crie, & thou wilt not heare?' (Coverdale).

The marginal gloss on this passage from Habakkuk in both the Bishops' Bible and the Geneva explains the burden as tyranny inflicted by the Chaldeans on the Jews. By contrast, the Coverdale translation omits this marginal explanation, offering instead two parallel texts: Psalm 21:2 and Job 19:2, which direct the reader back to the spiritual burden of the speaker's helpless pleading with an unresponsive Deity.

The burden for Coverdale lies in an expressive dilemma. God is deaf to the Psalmist's complaint. Psalm 39 (Coverdale 38) makes the point even more clearly: 'I helde my tonge, I was domme, I kept sylence, yee even from good wordes, but it was payne and grefe to me. My hert was hote withn me, & whyle I was thus musynge, the fyre kyndled: so that I spake with my tonge.' The Biblical texts chosen by Bunyan to illuminate his pilgrim's spiritual burden concentrate on the problems of finding a voice and a language.

Once liberated into language, the Psalmist of 39 (Coverdale 38) prays passionately for a response: 'Shewe not thy self as though thou sawest not my teares. For I am a straunger and *pilgrimme* with the as my forefathers were' (my italics).[28] The Coverdale translation is the only one to use the word 'pilgrimme.' The Great Bible, the Geneva and the Bishops' Bible all use the word 'sojourner'. Bunyan created from the Psalmist's anguished metaphor his own literal pilgrim, a man, like himself, unable to endure enforced silence any longer:

I dreamed, and behold I saw a Man clothed with Raggs standing in a certain place, with his face from his own House, a Book in his hand, and a great burden upon his Back. I looked, and saw him open the Book, and Read therein; and as he read, he wept and trembled: and not being able longer to contain, he brake out with a lamentable cry; saying, what shall I do?

The answer given by the Old Testament prophet is glossed in Bunyan's first paragraph: 'Wryte the vision planely upon thy tables, that who so commeth by, maye rede it' (Habakkuk 2.2).[29] For Bunyan, forbidden to preach, confined to prison, obliged to watch the persecution of the faithful, the voice of the prophet offers relief from the burden through access to language: write the vision.[30] Bunyan declared that in prison he learnt to dwell on the invisible.[31] When he read of Foxe's martyrs drawing strength from the English Bible, he himself became part of a continuous history of men and women imprisoned in the cause of their religion. He found both in the Protestant martyrs and in the Biblical Israelites to whom they likened themselves, an historic parallel to his own condition as a silenced preacher.

When Bunyan opened Luther on Galatians he felt as if here at last was a man like himself. In Part II of *The Pilgrim's Progress* Greatheart's narration of Mr Fearing causes Christiana to declare that she recognises herself: '*I see there was some semblance 'twixt this good man and I; only we differed in two things. His Troubles were so great, they brake out, but mine I kept within*' (p. 211). More than any of the figures in *The Pilgrim's Progress* Christiana describes Bunyan's own experience of reading. The only difference between Mr Fearing and Christiana at this point in the narrative lies in Christiana's assertion that Mr Fearing's troubles were so great that they broke out, where hers remained within. She has no access to a language of suffering.

In the *Book of Martyrs* Tyndale advises Frith to '*stand fast*, and commit your self to God, and be not overcome of mens persuasions' (II. 370, my italics). The phrase 'Stand fast' catapults the reader into Bunyan's world, where Stand-fast embodies many of Tyndale's characteristics: his passionate self-abasement, his love of the Word, his belief in the Covenant. Tyndale was arrested in Antwerp through the treachery of Henry Philips and Thomas Pointz (the British merchant at whose house he had been living for a year). Like Bunyan, he was easy prey: 'The officers . . . afterward . . . said to Pointz when they had laid him in prison, that they pitied to see his simplicity when they tooke him' (Foxe, II. 365). In Woolf's *Between the Acts*, Miss La Trobe's history of England is staged at Pointz Hall, perhaps reminding the reader of the man who in Foxe's alternative Protestant history, the *Book of Martyrs*, dies championing the vernacular for ordinary men and women.[32] It has been suggested that Bunyan gives Christiana's language to Stand-fast, thus usurping her role and giving the male hero the perfect realisation of the feminine.[33] But Bunyan's identifying of Stand-fast with Tyndale implies that he recognised in Christiana's speech the historic moment of his own writing. If he saw himself as heir to Tyndale – a man who stood fast, and was able to speak out in his troubles – so women, who had been so important in his own conversion,[34] would be the natural heirs of *The Pilgrim's Progress*, a book which authorises the search for a language and a voice. Bunyan was empowered to write because through Foxe and through the English Bible he discovered a history which belonged to him, in which the destinies of working men and women were inseparable from the language which they used: the vernacular of the translated Bible.


OUTSIDERS


For Virginia Woolf reading and writing about the literature of the past involved constructing for women a place in a male-dominated record. This is as true of the first volume of *The Common Reader* (1925) as it is of *A Room of One's Own* (1929), of the more polemical *Three Guineas* (1938), and of the projected ambitious 'Common History'. In all these works Woolf searched for a history which belonged to women, and in so doing discovered that that history was inseparable from the history of women's relation to language. As a sceptic, Virginia Woolf had no entry into Bunyan's confidence in language as the instrument of the Word of God. But she was convinced that control over language lay at the heart of one group's power to dominate another, and that women's oppression under patriarchy was rooted in their lack of a language of their own.[35] Woolf's use in *Three Guineas* of the metaphor of a promiscuous 'Mother English'[36] to attack patriarchal culture demonstrates her understanding of the way in which the history of the vernacular encapsulates the history of women's struggle for a past and a voice, and in so doing, links them inseparably with the condition of working men.[37]

Both *A Room of One's Own* and *Three Guineas* – Woolf's analysis of women's position in a culture hasting towards war – owe some of their urgency to modes of thinking and writing set in motion by Bunyan. Bunyan's works formed for Virginia Woolf, as for her whole generation, part of the household stuff of her inherited culture. Leslie Stephen's library, which provided her with the resources for her education, contained the 1862 three-volume edition of *The Whole Works of John Bunyan* edited by George Offor. Leonard and Virginia themselves owned a 1728 edition of *The Pilgrim's Progress*.[38] In an essay written by Virginia in August 1905 on 'The Value of Laughter' an illustration from Bunyan forms the only precise literary reference in the piece:

If we took time to think – to analyse this impression that the comic spirit registers – we should find, doubtless, that what is superficially comic is fundamentally tragic, and while the smile was on our lips the water would stand in our eyes. This – the words are Bunyan's – has been accepted as a definition of humour; but the laughter of comedy has no burden of tears. (*Essays*, 1. 59, 60 n2).

The naturalness of the literary allusion here suggests that she expected her readers to recognise it without having to name the source, which comes as an afterthought. Later in life she returned to Bunyan in a less instinctive and more political mood.

Woolf's rereading of Bunyan in the early 1930s may have been prompted by her admiration for *The Life of Joseph Wright*, published in 1932 by Elizabeth Wright (his wife). She used this biography for the Fifth Essay of *The Pargiters*, in which the upper-class professional world of the Malone family – Kitty Malone is daughter of the Master of an Oxford College – is contrasted with the very different household of the Brooks, modelled on the family of Joseph Wright. Wright's real respect for his working mother, as well as for his wife, reinforced Woolf's conviction that the oppression of women was intensified by the professional training of middle-class men.

The story of Joseph Wright (1855–1930), Professor of Comparative Philology at Oxford, is probably only one of many histories of remarkable Victorians who rose to eminence from humble backgrounds, but even now the degree of that progress startles the reader. Elizabeth Wright describes Joseph Wright's mother, a woman who at the the time of her marriage could neither read nor write, who taught herself to read at the age of forty-five. She owned three books: the New Testament, an English translation of Klopstock's *Messiah* and *The Pilgrim's Progress*.[39] The fifteen-year-old-Joseph – then a wool-sorter in the Baildon Bridge Mill, Windhill – was inspired, when listening in 1870 to newspaper accounts of the Franco-Prussian war, with an ambition to read. He set about teaching himself with two books: the Bible and *The Pilgrim's Progress*. Elizabeth wrote to him during their engagement that she told girls to whom she was teaching Old English poetry to 'read the psalms before sitting down to translate' so that they wouldn't serve her up 'with long pedantic words'. Joseph Wright wrote back: 'Now Lizzie dear, here is a point upon which we may possibly differ. I think the Pilgrim's Progress is a better model than the Psalms for the purpose you describe.'[40] Bunyan had taught him to read; Wright now claimed the author of *The Pilgrim's Progress* as a model for writing.

Woolf recorded her fascination with Elizabeth Wright's book in her Diary on Wednesday 13 July 1932; her most arresting comment comes at the centre of the entry: 'Their attitude to life much our own':

> Old Joseph Wright & Lizzie Wright are people I respect. Indeed I do hope the 2nd vol. will come this morning. He was a maker of dialect dixeries [sic]: he was a workhouse boy—his mother went charing. And he married Miss Lea a clergyman's daughter. And I've just read their love letters with respect. And he said 'Always please yourself—then one person's happy at any rate'. And she said 'make details part of a whole—get proportions right'—contemplating marriage with Joe. Odd how rare it is to meet people who say things that we ourselves could have said. Their attitude to life much our own. . . . Had his old working mother to Oxford. She thought All Souls would make a good Co-op. Had a fist & struck boys. His notion of learning. I sometimes would like to be learned myself. About sounds & dialects. . . . Joe taught himself to read at 14; taught mill boys in a bedroom for 2d a week. . . . Now this is a testimony to Joe & Lizzy that I've been thinking how I should have liked to see them—would now like to write to her. (*Diary,* 4. 115–16)

The modern reader can hardly at first glance establish the grounds of Woolf's sympathy with the Wrights. Whom does she mean by 'we'? Elizabeth Wright describes her husband's view of his self-made status:

> He always said that it was owing to his plebeian ancestry that he brought with him to the field of science and letters that prodigious vitality of brain which enabled him to accomplish the intellectual feats which marked his progress from this time onwards. His forbears had never spent their brain-power in the pursuit of book-learning. Joseph Wright could draw on unlimited capital behind him. (I. 37)

In her Reading Notes on Wright Woolf has circled this page in her margin, and written: 'J. said his plebeian ancestry certainly gave him vitality: his forebears illiterate' (Berg, XX). Virginia Woolf's Stephen heritage, with its line of male writers, could hardly have provided a more marked contrast. If Woolf's partial portrait of her father in Mr Ramsay in *To the Lighthouse* suggests his daughter's sense that the Stephen intellectual resources might in her own generation begin to be overdrawn, Woolf might also have observed that the bank account was in the male name. The 'we' of her community with Joseph and Elizabeth Wright consists not of her literary ancestors nor of her Bloomsbury friends, but of her Jewish husband, Leonard Woolf, and of herself as a woman.[41]

Virginia Woolf knew that the unlimited capital of the outsider belonged to women just as much as it belonged to Joseph Wright. Her own lack of formal education never ceased to rile her. She was amused by reviews and comments on *A Room of One's Own* which implied her intimate knowledge of school life: 'And I've only had the tip of my nose in one once, taking Nessa's child there' (*Letters*, 5. 96). She made a special note of Wright's conviction that because he had never been to school, 'unknowingly I developed an individuality wh. is unique in its kind'.[42] Joseph Wright's sense that lack of education built up immense reserves of creative and intellectual power only echoed what she had herself written in *A Room of One's Own*, that 'women have sat indoors all these millions of years, so that by this time the very walls are permeated by their creative force' (*RO*, p. 87). For Joseph Wright *The Pilgrim's Progress* opened the door to an intellectual world from which he was locked out by poverty. It is hardly surprising that Woolf chose this moment to reread Bunyan's work herself.

What then did she make of *The Pilgrim's Progress*, re-encountered in the wake of her sense of its significance for people whose attitude to life she felt she shared, who said things she would have said herself? The Reading Notes suggest one level on which *The Pilgrim's Progress* worked on her imagination. She copies out Valiant's farewell from Part II: 'My word I give to him that shall succeed me in my pilgrimage, and my courage and skill to him that can get it. My marks – scars I carry with me, to be a witness for me, that I have fought his battles, who now will be my Rewarder. . . . So he passed over, and the Trumpets sounded for him on the other side.' Woolf's omission, marked by her ellipsis, is even more significant than the words she quotes:

When the Day that he must go hence, was come, many accompanied him to the River side, into which, as he went, he said, 'Death, where is thy Sting?' And as he went down deeper, he said, 'Grave where is thy Victory?' (PP, pp. 259–60)

Woolf's entry in the Notebook needs to be read in conjunction with another comment on *The Pilgrim's Progress* in the same group of notes: 'The fiend whispers to Christian, who thinks that he is himself saying it—a sign of madmen—hearing voices. Was Bunyan ever mad?'[43] Both this note and the 'Valiant' quotation seem to underpin Woolf's *Diary* entry for Saturday 7 February 1931.

Here in the few minutes that remain, I must record, heaven be praised, the end of The Waves. I wrote the words O Death fifteen minutes ago, having reeled across the last ten pages with some moments of such intensity and intoxication that I seemed only to stumble after my own voice, or almost, after some sort of speaker (as when I was mad). I was almost afraid, remembering the voices that used to fly ahead. (*Diary*, 4. 10)

Woolf drew inspiration for the ending of *The Waves* from what the Romantics would have seen as the 'poetic Bunyan',[44] associating his religious vision with her own troubled creativity.

However, Bunyan's presence in her consciousness at this time exemplified a conflict in her own spirit which created delays even as she tried to finish the novel. She was on 20 January 1931 transported by the vision of 'an entire new book—a sequel to a Room of Ones Own—about the sexual life of women: to be called Professions for Women perhaps—Lord how exciting! This sprang out of my paper to be read on Wednesday to Pippa's society. Now for the Waves. Thank God—but I'm very much excited' (*Diary*, 4. 6).[45] Not surprisingly, the next *Diary* entry (for Friday 23 January), about the new project, despairs of concluding the novel: 'Too much excited, alas, to get on with The Waves. One goes on making up The Open Door, or whatever it is to be called. The didactive demonstrative style conflicts with the dramatic: I find it hard to get back inside Bernard again' (4. 6). The poetic and visionary faculty required to complete *The Waves* is at war at this stage in her writing with the 'didactive demonstrative style' necessary for her new work on the position of women.

Woolf had written at the end of 1930 that she would construct Bernard's final utterance in *The Waves* to 'show that the theme effort, effort, dominates: not the waves: & personality: & defiance' (*Diary*, 3. 339). This vision of defiant individuality recalls the Protestant martyrs of Foxe's narrative, who provide an ancestry for Bunyan's Pilgrim. Bunyan's contempt of the closed world of the learned, professional, prelatical and authoritarian, and his identification of the Protestant message as the solitary and strenuous assertion of the individual will – most striking in the encounter between Christian and Apollyon – connect, in Woolf's mind, the end of *The Waves* with the new polemical project of *Three Guineas*.

When Woolf read, during her work for *Three Guineas*, the Report of the Archbishop's Commission on the Ministry of Women (1935), one particular passage struck her with such force that it is annotated twice:

> We believe that the general mind of the Church is still in accord with the continuous tradition of a male priesthood. . . . 'Male and female created He them' is as much a fact determined by the creative will of God as 'in Christ there is neither male nor female' is a fact determined by His redemptive purpose.[46]

Woolf might have recalled, as she read the famous quotation from Galatians which had meant so much to the Protestant reformers, Joseph Wright's judgement on St Paul's view of women:

> The world may talk of the 'weaker sex' as much as it likes, the whole idea is based upon a false conception; it is based upon the body and not upon the mind, soul, and heart. I have always held woman far higher than man in God's creation. If it were otherwise I should never have been so intensely interested in the general welfare of womankind. St. Paul and the likes of him have much to answer for, and it is ever my most pious wish that they will reap their due reward. It is due to them, and them *alone*, that woman has been such a downtrodden creature in the past. It is only the present generation of women that is beginning to realize the abject state of woman in the past. (*Life*, I. 315)

In a long and excoriating footnote in *Three Guineas* about St Paul's views on chastity Woolf offers her readers some of her most radical thinking about sex: 'Even today it is probable that a woman has to fight a psychological battle of some severity with the ghost of St Paul, before she can have intercourse with a man other than her husband.' St Paul is for Woolf a type of dictator: 'He was of the virile or dominant type, so familiar at present in Germany, for whose gratification a subject race or sex is essential.'[47] Woolf would have found a precedent for her linking of race and sex in the minority report which concludes the Archbishop's official record, written by W.R. Matthews, the Dean of St Paul's:

> St. Paul, in his often-quoted saying that in Christ Jesus there is neither male nor female, asserts a doctrine which is fundamental for the Christian outlook—that of the supreme value of personality.... There is no more justification for discriminating against women than there would be for discriminating against Jews or men with red hair. (pp. 77–8)

Matthews' identification of 'the supreme value of personality' in Christianity recalls Woolf's invoking of the death of Valiant at the end of *The Pilgrim's Progress* Part II in her stress on effort, defiance and personality in Bernard's final speech in *The Waves*. Significantly for Woolf's argument in *Three Guineas*, Matthews identifies the cause of women with that of racial minorities.

It is easy to overlook Woolf's conviction in *Three Guineas* that the oppression of women and the persecution of minorities sprang from the same source. The unthinking racism of Woolf and her whole generation can be demonstrated from any number of entries in the *Diary*. But in *Three Guineas* she urged her readers to appreciate that the same tyranny which oppressed races, oppressed women:

> Now you are being shut out, you are being shut up, because you are Jews, because you are democrats, because of race, because of religion.... The whole iniquity of dictatorship, whether in Oxford or Cambridge, in Whitehall or Downing Street, against Jews or against women, in England, or in Germany, in Italy or in Spain is now apparent to you. (*TG*, p. 118)

She argues that the Commission's wish to keep women in their separate sphere is congruent with Nazism and Fascism.

For Woolf the official Church becomes aligned with all the other professions who wish to exclude women in order to maintain economic dominance over them. Her reading of Protestant history (and perhaps of Foxe himself – from Thoby's presentation copy) set before her the egalitarian ideals of both the early Christians and Foxe's Protestant martyrs: 'It would seem then that the founder of Christianity believed that neither training nor sex was needed for this profession. He chose his disciples from the working class from which he sprang himself' (*TG*, p. 140). Working men and women have moved into the same sphere in her mind as they occupy within the pages of Foxe's narrative.

As a woman Woolf constructs an ancestry for herself which draws on a woman's perceived lack of intellectual forebears, rather than on the Stephen male literary heritage. Woolf's Reading Notes locate Bunyan not in the 'print-culture' of men but within an oral tradition belonging to groups of women. She thinks of *The Pilgrim's Progress* as 'a story for old wives, full of superstitions and old lore. Compare him with dante – a poetic wisdom. hedgepreachers discourse' (Berg, XXIII). Bunyan, who wrote from a position of being silenced as a preacher, always retained a close connection in his writing with the spoken word, identified by Woolf as the world of 'Anon' which was effectively destroyed with the advent of the printing press. As *The Pilgrim's Progress* became established as a printed text, its printers tried systematically to regularise its language, standardising dialect usages, thus marking, as Roger Sharrock has pointed out, 'an important staging-post in the transition from an oral to a print culture'.[48] When Woolf identified Bunyan as a teller of old tales for old wives, she thought of him as a prototype of her own invented figure of 'Anon', who precedes the printing-press: 'When in 1477 Caxton printed the twenty one books of the Morte DArthur he fixed the voice of Anon for ever.'[49] The figure of 'Anon' dies when 'the authors name is attached to the book'. The change, so important in Woolf's mythology, is barely susceptible to recording: 'There was no English literature to show up the change in the mind. Anons song at the back door was as difficult for him to spell out as for us. & more painful. for [it] reminded him of his lack of intellectual ancestry' (p. 385). At the heart of Woolf's construction of the figure of 'Anon' and her/his significance in history lies the brooding on intellectual origins which made Joseph

Wright's sense that his lack of intellectual ancestry was a source of energy so compelling to her.

In *A Room of One's Own* Woolf – no doubt recalling her own madness, and her question of Bunyan's hearing voices: had he ever been mad? – hazards the guess that women who were condemned as witches or madwomen were in fact thwarted poets. In *Three Guineas* she associates this vision of 'Anon' as a woman singer outlawed from regular society with the role of women in the early Church. The only gift needed by Christ's followers was one open to women as well as to men – that of prophecy:

> Thus the profession of religion seems to have been originally much what the profession of literature is now. It was originally open to anyone who had received the gift of prophecy. No training was needed; the professional requirements were simple in the extreme – a voice and a market-place, a pen and paper. (*TG*, p. 141)

Woolf goes on to quote 'No coward soul is mine' from the poems of Emily Brontë. Her own important footnote to this passage describes the impact of the Song of Songs on poets and offers thanks that Shakespeare 'lived too late to be canonized by the Church', for had he been, his works would have been systematically parcelled out for consumption and 'he would have been as unreadable as the Bible. Yet those who have not been forced from childhood to hear it thus dismembered weekly assert that the Bible is a work of the greatest interest, much beauty, and deep meaning' (*TG*, p. 199). Woolf wrote to Ethel Smyth on 23 January 1935: 'I have 3 mins: before settling down to read the Bible. Why did you never tell me what a magnificent book it is! And the Testament? and the Psalms!' (*Letters*, 5. 366). For her the society of the early Christians, which embraced and allowed a voice to untrained men and women whose religious vision created its own eloquence irrespective of education and training, was the prototype of her own society of outsiders.

The woman in 'Professions for Women' who for ten shillings and sixpence might have written all the plays of Shakespeare becomes in *Three Guineas* the natural successor of the women who frequent the Acts of the Apostles: 'In three or four centuries, it appears, the prophet or prophetess whose message was voluntary and untaught became extinct; and their places were taken by the three orders of bishops, priests and deacons, who are invariably men, and invariably, as Whitaker points out, paid men, for when the Church became a profession its professors were paid' (*TG*, p. 141). 'Anon', the anonymous woman writer, is one with the anonymous prophetess of early Christianity: 'When the Church became a profession, required special knowledge of its prophets and paid them for imparting it, one sex remained inside; the other was excluded' (*TG*, p. 142). She had called her Quaker aunt, Caroline Emelia Stephen, a prophetess who had spent her life hearing voices. As Montaigne observed in his 'Apology for Raimond de Sebonde', madness and sainthood have often gone hand in hand (*Essays*, III. 104), but in Woolf's new history both form the creative subsoil from which women writers will emerge. In her own case she seems to have recognised that in some degree her aunt's Quaker vision provided a hinterland for her own creativity. In Foxe's history the translators of the Bible into the vernacular with one voice attack the priesthood for heirarchising access to the Scriptures through the use of Latin, a process which Woolf perceived to have automatically excluded the women prophetesses of the early Church.

When in *Three Guineas* Woolf tries to define '"culture and intellectual liberty"', the words Latin and Greek keep recurring. The 'paid-for' culture of men means education in the classics, extending in an unbroken line from Montaigne in the sixteenth-century to her own brothers and their friends in the twentieth. But she wants to address herself instead to a different group, 'to those whose culture is the unpaid-for culture, that which consists in being able to read and write in their own tongue' (*TG*, p. 104):

> Therefore let us define culture for our purposes as the disinterested pursuit of reading and writing the English language. And intellectual liberty may be defined for our purposes as the right to say or write what you think in your own words, and in your own way. (*TG*, pp. 104–5)

She orders women to dispense with the whole male-dominated apparatus of publishing, urging the purchase of a private printing press. This was for Woolf, as both printer and writer, a doctrine written in her own blood. She had declared on 15 April 1920: 'I took a vow I'd say what I thought, and say it in my own way' (*Diary*, 2: 30). In *Three Guineas* Woolf proposes an alternative to the literary criticism *written* by educated men in their official capacity as the guardians of culture: 'Are not the best critics private people, and is not the only criticism worth having *spoken* criticism?' (my italics). The question is addressed specifically to women, as inheritors of the vernacular: 'Those then are some of the active ways in which you, as a writer of your own tongue, can put your opinion into practice' (*TG*, p. 113). She criticises male scholarship for 'the vast deposit of notes at the bottom of Greek, Latin and even English texts' (*TG*, p. 200 n31). Intellectual freedom is inextricably linked in her mind with the use of the vernacular.

This belief leads Woolf in the projected literary history back into the Protestant reformers' world, where the use of the vernacular was equally politicised, and where intellectual ancestry consisted of classical learning rather than of a vernacular tradition. In the preliminary 'Notes for Reading at Random' Woolf repeatedly jots down comments on language: 'Bring in Latin'; 'The split into several languages for writers'; 'The difference between reading & seeing: acting: the word heard. Its solidity: its depths.' She meditates on 'The condition of the Eln [Elizabethan] writer who had no literary past; only read classics in translation.' In the final short section of Notes she raises a subject which surfaces in most of her printed Elizabethan essays: the place of the Bible in the development of prose writing: 'Influence of the bible on prose. The biblical style limited & emphatic'.[50] As she meditated on the history of the vernacular Woolf observed that a key figure in that narrative was the Reformer and Marian martyr, Hugh Latimer. Latimer forges for her a link between the translators of the Bible and the transitional moment of Bunyan's mode of writing.

Woolf was reading Latimer's *Sermons* in the late 1930s.[51] Latimer is a sympathetic figure, in Woolf's characterisation of him, an outsider both in relation to the court but also to the poor, as his education gives him an insight into the nature of superstition which they cannot share. She sees him, as she sees Bunyan, as a story-teller with 'a curious sympathy for the human', a man with a sense of humour who wants to educate the poor out of their ignorance: '"There be now none but great mens sons in college"' ('Anon', pp. 387–8). In her speech to the London/National Society for Women's Service (1931), in which she dwelt on the paucity of her own professional experiences, Woolf castigated Clare College, Cambridge, for spending six thousand pounds on an elegant history of the College, instead of on women's education:

> If the members of Clare college handed over the six thousand
> pounds that they have spent upon a book to Girton [*say*] some
> of the difficulties of imitation would be removed, and what is
> more I am sure that the lady of Clare would rise from her
> grave and say Gentlemen you have done [*me honour*] <my
> will>.[52]

Latimer speaks, as Woolf herself does, from a position outside privilege, but also outside poverty, from which he urges his society, as she urges hers four centuries later, to rethink its values and rewrite the language which expresses those values.

Woolf's ten pages of notes on Latimer's famous 'Plough' Sermon meticulously record the preacher's insistence on the vernacular in preference to Latin, his championing of the poor against the rich, his fervent belief in education and his loathing of false scholars.[53] As Woolf meditated in *Three Guineas* on the position of women as outsiders and on their special relation culturally to their own vernacular, she found in her reading of Latimer a man who, like herself, stands between disparate worlds. Latimer was educated but uncourtly, just as she herself was educated but a woman. He urged the vernacular on to a world of élite classicists and uneducated poor, just as she tried to shape for herself and other women writers an English language which would not be the language of Cambridge men.

In Bunyan, as in Latimer, Woolf might have perceived some marriage between the oral and the written. Access to a new language of spiritual life was for many Puritans and certainly for Bunyan, not simply the acquisition of a new spoken word, but entry into a medium they hardly perceived as distinct from speaking, that of the written word,[54] a movement from Woolf's figure of 'Anon', the hedgerow preacher, into a new apprehension of identity through writing.

In the 'Author's Apology for his Book' Bunyan not only holds his own dialogue with his potential readers, but also commends the method of dialogue: 'I find that men (as high as trees) will write / Dialogue-wise.' The dialogue method is presented explicitly as anti-authoritarian in a book which Bunyan's first wife brought him on his marriage, which very much influenced his own writing: Arthur Dent's *Plaine Mans Path-way to Heaven* (1601). Arthur Dent belongs as much as Bunyan does to the period of transition which Woolf tried to capture in her literary history, when 'Anon' gave way to the popular printed work and newly literate reader.[55] In the Epistle to the Reader Dent exhorts critics of his teaching to 'remember I am in a Dialogue, not a Sermon, I write to all of all sorts: I speake not to some fewe of one sort'. Woolf used the dialogue form in both of her polemical works. In *A Room of One's Own* she engages, as woman writer, in a dialogue with her women readers. *Three Guineas* is structured on a much more aggressive dialogue with the authors of the letters requesting money.[56] Woolf always wanted to use the dialogue form in her critical essays but could not see how it was to be done without becoming too personal. Dialogue, as has been seen in Donne's case, breaks down an authoritarian relation between writer and reader, allowing the reader to assume the role of writer, to enter the text as an essential part of its structure. This collaborative role lay at the heart of the project of translating the Bible into the vernacular. The reader was to participate in the text, to have access to it direct rather than through the mediation of a superior authority.[57]

Woolf declared of the composer Ethel Smyth: 'She is of the race of pioneers, of pathmakers. She has gone before and felled trees and blasted rocks and built bridges and thus made a way for those who come after her.' She herself feels, in comparison, 'rather like an idle and frivolous pleasure boat lolloping along in the wake of an ironclad'.[58] But Virginia Woolf had copied into her notebook Octavia Hill's image: 'The bridge is what we care for, and not our place in it.'[59] Woolf knew that she herself shared the vision of those who went before, building bridges for others to cross. The Messianic language which she uses for Ethel Smyth, deliberately invoking the figure of John the Baptist, forerunner of Christ, recalls the final exhortation of 'How It Strikes A Contemporary' – the essay which concludes the first volume of *The Common Reader* – to modern critics:

> Let them take a wider, a less personal view of modern literature, and look indeed upon the writers as if they were engaged upon some vast building, which in being built by common effort, the separate workmen may well remain anonymous. . . . Let

us buttonhole them as they leave, and recall to their memory
that gaunt aristocrat, Lady Hester Stanhope, who kept a milk-
white horse in her stable in readiness for the Messiah and was
for ever scanning the mountain tops, impatiently but with
confidence, for signs of his approach, and ask them to follow
her example; scan the horizon; see the past in relation to the
future; and so prepare the way for masterpieces to come. (*CR I*,
p. 241)

As she contemplated her third volume of *The Common Reader* in
the late thirties with the guns of another war already sounding
in her ears, she was herself following the advice she had given
the critic in a quieter and more hopeful time: see the past in
relation to the future, and so prepare the way for masterpieces
to come.

The Messianic language links Woolf to the sixteenth-century
Reformers, whom she was to study in her search for an alternative tradition, tracing the waning of 'Anon' – consequent on the
development of the printing press – and the birth of the modern
reader. Luther believed that 'the remarkable disclosure of the
Word of God would not have taken place had God not first prepared the way by the rediscovery of language, and sciences, as
by Baptist fore-runners'.[60] By the time of the Restoration the Puritan
who, like Bunyan, insisted on continuing to preach at the hedgerow
for an audience of ordinary men and women, was voluntarily
insisting on his role as outsider, denying himself and his children access to the public institutions of learning.[61] But in so doing,
he remained a symbol for that other group of outsiders whom
Woolf discovered in her research for *Three Guineas*, ordinary
women who by the end of the seventeenth century had found a
spokeswoman in Mary Astell. Astell, less confident than Bunyan,
felt that her 'Ignorance in the Sacred Languages ... makes me
incapable of expounding scriptures with the learned'.[62] She was
supported in her attempts to found a college for women by men
as well as women, but ultimately thwarted by the opposition of
churchmen,[63] the same educated professionals who dismissed
Bunyan as a tinker. Bunyan perceived himself as a man speaking, as he also does in *A Book for Boys and Girls* (1686), to and
for a new readership of newly literate people who will be empowered by what they read to break silence.

This newly literate group is not just 'yeomen, artisans and small tradesmen',[64] but newly articulate women readers who would also in some cases become, like Bunyan, a first generation of writers. Elaine Showalter has declared that 'gynocritics begins at the point when we free ourselves from the linear absolutes of male literary history, stop trying to fit women between the lines of the male tradition, and focus instead on the newly visible world of female culture'.[65] But male culture is not monolithic, as Bunyan discovered from reading Foxe's *Book of Martyrs*. As Virginia Woolf absorbed sixteenth and seventeenth-century writing in preparation for *Three Guineas* she perceived that women shared a history with working men. Newly visible culture emerges from a past, real if invisible, the recovery of which could, for Bunyan, transform his prison cell into a room of his own.

The central message which has lured men and women from disparate cultures to read Bunyan's creaking and often totally alien theology is nothing to do with the ostensible message of the book, any more than it is to do with its outmoded social structures and embarrassing prejudices. Bunyan stands at a crossroads between language and silence, a man on whom his world forced silence and captivity, who yet found within the Bible, within the pages of Foxe's *Book of Martyrs*, within the writings of Tyndale and Coverdale and Martin Luther, a history and a language. Virginia Woolf was one of the first women to realise that women readers might scan the writings of a patriarchal culture and be forgiven for thinking, like Christiana recognising her own condition in Mr Fearing's narrative: 'I thought nobody had been like me.' But 'nobody' within that sentence is virtually reified into 'somebody', accommodated to the figure of 'Anon' who in Woolf's history is already in the sixteenth century almost a silenced voice, bearing witness to a vanished past. Bunyan, constructing in his prison cell the tradition from which he could speak to a new readership, offers a prototype for Woolf herself. As reader and writer Woolf searched for a history and a language which women could recognise as their own.

# 7

## The Body and the Book

### BODY AND MIND

If Virginia Woolf's novels inhabit a relentlessly high culture environment, her literary criticism and non-fictional writings belong to a less rarified stratosphere, as her contemporaries recognised (sometimes to her annoyance). Yet her descent into a populist mode was in those writings a deliberate political act, in which she set herself to undermine the distinctions between pure thought and physical experience as thoroughly as her purchase of the Hogarth Press had undermined the notion that a book could exist independent of the material object which the reader holds in her hands. The body, always intrusive in Virginia Woolf's own life, was for her the route back into an ideal of wholeness which would allow women to re-enter a culture colonised by male authors after the introduction of print in the fifteenth century. If she creates her own mythology around this idea, she nevertheless found in some Renaissance writers attitudes to the body which spoke to the world she wanted to recreate in defiance of Victorian traditions of separatist high culture. The physicality of the body, and the material nature of the book, are for her the partners of reading and writing, which begin as physical acts. The ascendancy of body over mind she knew to be a revolutionary upturning of the wisdom of Western philosophy in which the spirit dominates the flesh. In her search for an alternative literary tradition for women Woolf attacked those inherited gender divisions in which men inhabit the world of the mind and women the territories of matter.

Virginia Woolf declared in *A Room of One's Own* that 'the book has somehow to be adapted to the body' (*RO*, p. 78). Women need books which bridge the high culture chasm between body and mind. In an essay 'On Being Ill' (1925) she identifies the way in which culture has dictated the rule of mind over matter: 'Literature does its best to maintain that its concern is with the

mind; that the body is a sheet of plain glass through which the
soul looks straight and clear, and, save for one or two passions
such as desire and greed, is null, and negligible and non-exist-
ent. On the contrary, the very opposite is true. All day, all night
the body intervenes.' After myriad physical experiences 'the body
smashes itself to smithereens, and the soul (it is said) escapes'.
But literature, voluble about the soul, is silent about the body:
'Of all this daily drama of the body there is no record. People
write always of the doings of the mind . . . how [it] has civilised
the universe. They show it ignoring the body in the philosopher's
turret.'[1] The body demands a 'new language . . . more primitive,
more sensual, more obscene', together with 'a new hierarchy of
the passions' (p. 16). New literary forms, new language and the
undermining of hierarchies, dominate Woolf's reading of sixteenth
and seventeenth-century writing.

Both Donne and Montaigne found in Rabelais an irreverence
towards the spirit and an exuberant celebration of the body which
nurtured the claims of both men that the body exerts its own
imperatives over the spirit. Montaigne, writing in the vernacular in his own new experimental form, the *essai*, insists on
privileging the body over the mind:

We must command the soul not to withdraw and entertain
itself apart, not to despise and abandon the body (neither can
she do it but by some apish counterfeit), but to unite herself
close to it, to embrace, cherish, assist, govern, and advise it,
and to bring it back and set it into the true way when it wanders;
in sum to espouse and be a husband to it, so that their effects
may not appear to be diverse and contrary but uniform and
concurring ('Of Presumption', III. 331).

The gender inversion here is as radical as the central argument:
the female soul becomes the guardian to the male body, invert-
ing the traditional cultural opposition of form versus matter, the
spiritual versus the physical, in which woman has always been
identified with matter and physicality. Typically, Montaigne's
parenthesis contains the hub of the argument, that it is impossible for the soul to abandon the body except through 'some apish
counterfeit'. In the essay 'Upon Some Verses of Virgil' which
Woolf annotated in her Reading Notes (Berg XXIII), and used
for 'The Pargiters' (the draft of her novel *The Years*), Montaigne

enquires why, if the body must be regulated by the mind, it should not also be the case that the mind must be regulated by the body. The two are, like writers and readers, inseparable partners: 'May we not say that there is nothing in us, during this earthly prison, that is purely either corporeal or spiritual?' (IV. 331). Even his essays are 'flesh and bone' (IV. 257). Montaigne knows that the reinstatement of the body within culture has vital consequences for the way women are treated. To claim that the body masters the spirit questions the male universe of value in which women are subject to men.

This process is evident in the work which Donne wrote when he suffered from prolonged illness, the *Devotions Upon Emergent Occasions* (1624). Donne speaks in his Dedication to Prince Charles of his 'humiliation', meaning both the spiritual humiliation of his debasement through illness, but also the literal 'lying low' which obliges him to write from his bed. He asks: 'Is there a verier child then I am now?',[2] and compares himself in his sickness to a woman in childbirth, dictated to by the body: 'A *woman* that is weake cannot put off her *ninth moneth* to a *tenth*, for her *deliverie*, and say shee will stay till shee bee *stronger*; nor a *Queene* cannot hasten it to a *seventh*, that shee may bee ready for some other pleasure' (p. 111). Donne is reluctantly and ruefully aware that the condition of sickness feminises him.

In the *Paradox* 'That the Gifts of the Body are better then those of the Minde', Donne imitates Montaigne: 'I Say again, the *body* makes the *minde*, not that it created it a *minde*, but *forms* it a *good* or a *bad minde* . . . then the *soul* it seems is enabled by our *Body*, not this by it.' He declares that 'this *perfection* then my *body* hath, that it can impart to my *minde* all his *pleasures*'. The body determines the satisfactions of the mind. The virtues usually associated with the mind – '*chastity, temperance,* and *fortitude*' – are more properly located in the body: '*Health* is the gift of the *body*, and *patience* in *sicknesse* the gift of the *minde*: then who will say that *patience* is as good a *happinesse*, as *health*, when wee must be extremely *miserable* to purchase this *happinesse*.'[3] Donne, like Montaigne – and later, Pepys – knew what he was talking about, as he suffered continual ill-health and could observe the similarities between his own plight and that of his wife, who was laid low by continual pregnancies. Donne's stepfather, furthermore, was a doctor and President of the Royal College of Physicians,[4] whose presence in the family may have stimulated his stepson's extraordinarily fertile anatomical imagination.[5] It is no accident that many of the writers who do undermine gender hierarchies in relation to mind and body in this period have some acquaintance with medicine. Rabelais, the anarchic spirit behind all of them, was himself a doctor.[6] In this respect too, the male world conjoins with the female, in that women were traditionally the guardians of family and community health.[7]

Of women's special relation to health Virginia Woolf had every reason to be conscious, as her mother wrote a book on the home-nursing of the sick. Woolf employed a woman doctor, Elinor Rendel. She recorded in her *Diary* for February 1931 that her final writing of Bernard's soliloquy in *The Waves* 'was ruined by Elly, who was to have come at 9.30 sharp but did not come till 11. And it is now 12.30, & we sat talking about the period & professional women, after the usual rites with the stethoscope, seeking vainly the cause of my temperature.... How strange & wilful these last exacerbations of The Waves are! I was to have finished it at Christmas' (*Diary*, 4. 9). The body intruded on her own pursuit of high culture through the writing of a novel which would tax the common reader. Woolf was intimate with the Vaughan family, whose daughter Janet became well known for her research into pernicious anaemia, and probably provided Virginia with the source material for the episode in *A Room of One's Own* in which Chloë and Olivia share their laboratory research. Woolf annotated in her Reading Notes Margaret Todd's biography of the medical pioneer, Sophia Jex-Blake.[8] Male opposition to women's attending anatomy classes in the late nineteenth century was as fierce as to female attendance at life drawing classes, which required nude models. Women's access to the body, although in the practice of daily living much greater than men's, challenged the cherished masculine shibboleths of chastity and propriety.[9]

Virginia Woolf's belief in the power of the body to undermine high culture dates from very early in her writing life. She wrote in her Diary for 1897: 'After dinner father read Tennyson. A hot bath for the first time these three weeks' (*PA*, p. 21). Like the fifteen-year-old Jane Austen of *Love and Freindship*, Woolf was already laughing at her world, and using the exigencies of the body to undermine its literary pretences. The body intruded on her own life not only through a succession of family deaths and illnesses, but through her madness, registered in eating disorders, suicide attempts, and the hideous regime of the rest cure which she was forced to endure.[10] Well might she argue that soul and body must coexist, and if one were master, it would always be the body: 'Never was anyone so tossed up & down by the body as I am, I think' (*Diary*, 3. 174). For her the body symbolised women's confrontation with masculine culture.

That confrontation is present from the inception of 'Bloomsbury' as an alternative to the oppressive Kensington home which for both Virginia and Vanessa epitomised the inherited social world of their Stephen inheritance. However delighted Virginia was finally to have access to her brother Thoby's Cambridge sphere, she was from the start in rebellion against its rarefied male 'literary' atmosphere. On 9 November 1905, at the first of the Thursday evenings at Gordon Square which marked the beginning of the original Bloomsbury group, Violet Dickinson's brother joined Thoby's Cambridge friends, who had just published privately a volume of their poems: 'The little poets were rather afraid of his evening dress, and huddled together in corners like moping owls' (*Letters*, 1. 210). Virginia sent a copy of the poems to her friend Nelly [Lady Robert] Cecil, and contrasted the melancholy effusions of the youthful poets – 'the eldest cant be over 25' – with 'a real poem in the Daily Chronicle this morning, which had a right to be melancholy. It was written by a charwoman, on a piece of paper in which sugar was wrapped, and she then went and hung herself'. She quotes in full the 'Charwoman's Lament':

> 'Here lies a poor woman who always was tired
> She lived in a house where help was not hired.
> Her last words on earth were "Dear friend I am going
> Where washing aint done, nor sweeping nor sewing;
> But everything there is exact to my wishes,
> For where they dont eat theres no washing of dishes.
> I'll be where loud anthems will always be ringing:
> But having no voice I'll be clear of the singing:
> Dont mourn for me now, dont mourn for me never;
> I'm going to do nothing for ever and ever."'
>
> (*Letters*, 1. 202–3)

The verse is in fact traditional. Even at this early stage in her own career as a writer, when she was just embarked on her first attempts at book-reviewing, Virginia Woolf uses the working woman's 'unliterary' doggerel rhyme to undermine the literary pretensions of the male academy. The charwoman is an example of the figure of 'Anon', sometimes man, sometimes woman, whom in 1940 Woolf would invoke as her own ancestor in a writing which hails from a female oral culture rather than from a male-owned print culture. The 'unliterary' is characterised by the incantatory couplet form, the colloquial language, the physical world evoked, and the working woman who chants. The verse provides a medium for the body not the mind, the voice not the pen, the ordinary woman rather than the classically educated man. The poem records a woman's world not susceptible to the written record of the male writer, such as Woolf describes a quarter of a century later in *A Room of One's Own*:

And if one asked her, longing to pin down the moment with date and season, But what were you doing on the fifth of April 1868, or the second of November 1875, she would look vague and say that she could remember nothing. For all the dinners are cooked; the plates and cups washed; the children sent to school and gone out into the world. Nothing remains of it all. All has vanished. No biography or history has a word to say about it. And the novels, without meaning to, inevitably lie. (*RO*, p. 89)

The body writes no books, and therefore, historically, women have written no books, because the body has been their domain.[11]

The dynamite fuse hidden in the light-hearted letter about the melancholy undergraduate poets is more exposed in Woolf's unpublished (and unfinished) review in 1906 of their volume, which makes explicit her sense of exclusion: 'There is much to be said surely for that respectable custom which allows the daughter to educate herself at home, while the son is educated by others abroad'. After enquiring into the causes of literary gloom from young men nursed in the loving bosom of the Cambridge *alma mater*, Woolf reflects acidly on the condescension with which the pickings from their meditations are offered to the common reader, 'carelessly, as though the Beast could hardly appreciate such fare, even when simplified & purified to suit his coarse but innocent palate, but ought perhaps to be allowed the chance of tasting it'.[12] In Bloomsbury this exclusive group of privileged men have invaded a new feminine territory in which their ascendancy is at last under threat. An owl, the symbol of wisdom, is challenged by a nightingale in the form of a charwoman, who has found the keys to her own prison. In 1905 the prison of Hyde Park Gate was for Virginia Woolf transformed into the heady freedom of a room of her own in Bloomsbury, where the body might mock the mind.

## BLOOMSBURY: FEMALE SPACE

To whom did the new territory of Bloomsbury belong? Virginia Woolf and her sister saw Bloomsbury as their own geographical escape from their parents' Kensington home at Hyde Park Gate. It spelled freedom from duty to the Victorian family, and the opportunity to launch their own professional lives, Virginia's as a writer, Vanessa's as a painter, as Virginia explained in a paper entitled 'Old Bloomsbury' which was delivered to the Memoir Club sometime in 1921 or 1922: 'Though Hyde Park Gate seems now so distant from Bloomsbury, its shadow falls across it. 46 Gordon Square could never have meant what it did had not 22 Hyde Park Gate preceded it.'[13] Hyde Park Gate was saturated with family history: 'It seemed as if the house and the family which had lived in it, thrown together as they were by so many deaths, so many emotions, so many traditions, must endure for ever. And suddenly in one night both vanished' (p. 161). The move took place in 1904.

The difference between Hyde Park Gate and Gordon Square was almost the difference between two centuries, the Kensington house furnished with William Morris wallpaper, the Bloomsbury one with plain light distemper; in it two women would pursue their avocations: 'We were going to paint; to write...everything was going to be new; everything was going to be different. Everything was on trial' (p. 163) – Montaigne's word: an 'essai'. Many friends and relations were alienated, including her stepbrother's wife, Margaret Duckworth, who wrote that she would not expect them to visit: 'Is that a snub? I think so—but we had to bring it upon us, and the sooner the better. And now we are free women!' (*Letters*, 1. 228). They were free because they had their own physical and mental space.

Virginia Woolf acknowledged that her version of Bloomsbury might not be the same as that of her listeners: 'Naturally I see Bloomsbury only from my own angle—not from yours' (p. 159).

That proved to be true in the afterlife of Bloomsbury as recollected not only by its own members, but by critics and historians. Clive Bell believed himself to be the originator of Bloomsbury, claiming that it grew out of the Reading Society which he held in his rooms on Saturday nights at Cambridge. Leonard Woolf thought Bloomsbury began with his own return from Ceylon in 1911.[14] Quentin Bell claims that Thoby Stephen started the Thursday evenings in his house at Gordon Square so that he could continue seeing his Cambridge friends. This last version links Bloomsbury to the Cambridge Apostles, the society to which Clive Bell did not belong. Frances Spalding in her biography of Vanessa Bell also identifies Bloomsbury with Thoby and Cambridge: 'Its roots went back to Cambridge where these friends first met, and the Thursday "at homes" became its seedbed. They brought Vanessa and Virginia into closer contact with Thoby's friends for, *though he may not have intended this*, his sisters were present from the start' (my italics).[15] It seems odd that Thoby might have considered his sisters' not being present in a house which belonged to them as much as to him, and for which Vanessa had chief financial responsibility, as one of her letters makes plain: 'If I was sometimes uneasy, being supposed to be in control of the family finances, yet on the whole all that seemed to matter was that at last we were free, had rooms of our own and space in which to be alone or to work or to see our friends.'[16] Yet her brother perhaps didn't intend her or Virginia to put in an appearance at 'his' Thursday evenings. Can this be fair to Thoby, let alone to his sisters, the two *ladies*, as Clive Bell calls them (p. 130)? These accounts all testify to a transformation of female space into male ground, because Bloomsbury became so culturally prestigious that it seems that it must have belonged to men, and furthermore, to men educated at Trinity College – 'Cambridge of course' (p. 129), as Clive Bell so beguilingly puts it in *Old Friends*.

Certainly Virginia Woolf saw the Gordon Square Thursday evenings as a chance to participate in university life: 'Vanessa and I got probably much the same pleasure that undergraduates get when they meet friends of their own for the first time', but her Bloomsbury grows out of a past very different from that 'shared Cambridge education'.[17] In Hyde Park Gate under the tutelage of George Duckworth she and Vanessa had been marriageable property, every action dictated and judged by its efficacy in the prospective marriage market:

All that tremendous encumbrance of appearance and behaviour
which George had piled upon our first years vanished
completely. One had no longer to endure that terrible inquisition
after a party—and be told, 'You looked lovely.' Or, 'You did
look plain.' Or, 'You must really learn to do your hair.' Or,
'Do try not to look so bored when you dance.' Or, 'You did
make a conquest', or, 'You *were* a failure.' All this seemed to
have no meaning or existence in the world of Bell, Strachey,
Hawtrey and Sydney-Turner. In that world the only comment
as we stretched ourselves after our guests had gone, was, 'I must
say you made your point rather well'; 'I think you were talking
rather through your hat.' It was an immense simplification.
(p. 169)

Bloomsbury offered intellectual liberty in place of social constraint.
However, the Stephen girls had known intellectual space in their
father's home. In a paper called 'Am I a Snob?' Virginia describes
being asked by the society hostess Sibyl Colefax to meet Paul
Valéry. She observes scathingly: 'Now as I have always met Paul
Valéry or his equivalent since I can remember, to be asked out
to tea to meet him by a Sibyl Colefax whom I did not know—I
had never met her—was no lure to me.'[18] What was different in
Bloomsbury was that the new mental territory belonged to women,
partly because, for once, the physical territory belonged equally
to the men and women who occupied it.

The contrast between conventional Kensington and freewheeling
Bohemian Bloomsbury is captured in the early untitled story
'[Phyllis and Rosamond]'. Phyllis reflects, driving from Kensington
to Bloomsbury, on the mental distance she simultaneously traverses:

The stucco fronts, the irreproachable rows of Belgravia and
South Kensington seemed to Phyllis the type of her lot; of a
life trained to grow in an ugly pattern to match the staid ugliness
of its fellows. But if one lived here in Bloomsbury, she began
to theorise waving with her hand as her cab passed through
the great tranquil squares, beneath the pale green of umbrageous
trees, one might grow up as one liked. There was room, and
freedom, and in the roar and splendour of the Strand she read
the live realities of the world from which her stucco and her
pillars protected her so completely.[19]

Virginia wrote to Madge Vaughan in April 1906: 'We have begun our Bohemian dissipations: tonight Thoby is reading a paper to the Friday Club upon the Decadence of Modern Art' (*Letters*, 1. 224–5). Such a meeting is described in '[Phyllis and Rosamond]', where the heroines encounter a writer, Sylvia Tristram, who asks Phyllis what she does:

> 'What do I do?' echoed Phyllis. 'O order dinner and arrange the flowers!'
> 'Yes, but what's your trade,' pursued Sylvia, who was determined not to be put off with phrases.
> 'That's my trade; I wish it wasn't! Really Miss Tristram, you must remember that most young ladies are slaves; and you mustn't insult me because you happen to be free.' (p. 27)

The story which charts a pilgrim's progress from Kensington to Bloomsbury is a fiction not just of spiritual freedom, but of physical freedom: the emancipation of slaves.

Peter Stallybrass and Allon White have argued that eighteenth-century coffee houses created a 'self consciously democratic' environment: 'The importance of the coffee-house was that it provided a radically new kind of social space, at once free from the "grotesque bodies" of the alehouse and yet (initially at least) democratically accessible to all kinds of men – though not, significantly, to women.'[20] Here an alternative cultural world could flourish. The public space of the coffee house with its democratic and liberal mixing, in a new London world, of what would previously have been the separate spheres of court, city and country, still provided the natural background a century later for Leslie Stephen, not as Cambridge academic, but as editor of the *Cornhill Magazine*. Stephen, as an influential London literary figure, attacked the closed élitist world of the university and championed Thomas Hardy against the prudishness of Mudie's and its readers. Yet from this liberal and sophisticated environment women were excluded.

The lack of public space accorded to women involved a comparable lack of 'discursive space' from which they could write, talk, mingle in groups, fashion their own identities and search out traditions which belonged to them.[21] This fruitful interchange Woolf found in Bloomsbury; that it was a territory for women is vital to the life she drew from it. Indeed, she made her own parallel with the coffee-houses in her Reading Notes on Roy Campbell's *The Georgiad*, in which she commented on his 'grievance . . . against our whole literary hierarchy and stands':

> He holds that we are clique-ridden, and suffer cruelly from feminine dictatorship. But how can this be helped in an age when cinema, B.B.C., and circulating library establish ideas & reputation & vogue? Literature was once lodged in the coffee-room & tavern: it is now bound to be an annexe of the boudoir & country house & sales departments of the great stores. It is the law; and it is no use complaining. Men have had their turn. (MHP/B.16f. vol. 1)

The conviction that it was time for women to make their own mental and physical space had caused the two Stephen sisters to set up house in Bloomsbury where they might pursue professions for women instead of watching – as they did in their father's house in Kensington – men pursue their professions.

A *salon*, the word which Clive Bell uses for the two Bloomsbury haunts, Gordon and Fitzroy Squares, is historically a place in which men shine to amuse women. No doubt Clive Bell did believe that this was the function of Bloomsbury. But Bloomsbury was potentially more dissident and anarchic because it exposed male reverence for rationality and the intellect to a critique – set in motion by a recognition of the body's primacy in all spheres – which challenged traditional masculine hierarchies.

A sense of the carnivalesque is for Woolf inseparable from an awareness of the body as grotesque rather than classical entity,[22] a metaphor Woolf uses in the *Diary* when talking about Madame de Scudéry's novel, *La Princesse de Clèves*:

> This masterpiece has long been on my conscience. Me to talk of fiction & not to have read this classic! But reading classics is generally hard going. Especially classics like this one, which are classics because of their perfect taste, shapeliness, composure, artistry. Not a hair of its head is dishevelled. (*Diary*, 2. 169).

Peter Stallybrass explains the idea of the classical body as structuring 'from the inside as it were, the characteristically "high" discourses of philosophy, statecraft, theology and law, as well as literature, as they emerged from the Renaissance' (p. 22). It is

easy to see how Woolf's model anticipates this explanation, pro-
moting the idea of the body as intrusive, messy and disorderly,
while inaugurating freedom from the restraints of the classic.
Her mother's dying words had urged her to 'hold yourself straight,
my little Goat',[23] in conformity with the classic notion of the well-
ordered body.

The reinstatement of the 'grotesque body' with its carnivalesque
associations has been made famous by Virginia Woolf's description of an incident shortly after the marriage of Vanessa Stephen
and Clive Bell:

> Suddenly the door opened and the long and sinister figure of
> Mr Lytton Strachey stood on the threshold. He pointed his
> finger at a stain on Vanessa's white dress.
> 'Semen?' he said.
> Can one really say it? I thought and we burst out laughing.
> With that one word all barriers of reticence and reserve went
> down. A flood of the sacred fluid seemed to overwhelm us.
> Sex permeated our conversation. The word bugger was never
> far from our lips. We discussed copulation with the same ex-
> citement and openness that we had discussed the nature of
> good. It is strange to think how reticent, how reserved we had
> been and for how long. It seems a marvel now that so late as
> the year 1908 or 9 Clive had blushed and I had blushed too
> when I asked him to let me pass to go to the lavatory on the
> French Express. ('Old Bloomsbury', pp. 173–4).

The new discussions allowed the body to trespass on the sacred
ground staked out by the mind. Bloomsbury became the site of
the body's cultural legitimation.

When Virginia Woolf thought of writing a sequel to *A Room of
One's Own* she claimed that it was going to be 'about the sexual
life of women' (*Diary*, 4. 6). This was never in fact written, perhaps because the threat of war deflected her into a different path
in *Three Guineas*. But she was still thinking about the inhibitions
which surrounded writing about sex early in 1941 when she
congratulated Ethel Smyth on her proposal to write her autobiography, remarking that 'there's never been a womans autobiography. Nothing to compare with Rousseau. Chastity and
modesty I suppose have been the reason. . . . I should like an
analysis of your sex life. As Rousseau did his' (*Letters*, 6. 453).

She had revelled in the unexpurgated edition of Rousseau's *Confessions*, published in 1896. But even Ethel Smyth felt some inhibitions, as Woolf observed:

> I'm interested that you cant write about masturbation. That I understand. . . . But as so much of life is sexual—or so they say—it rather limits autobiography if this is blacked out. It must be, I suspect, for many generations, for women; for its like breaking the hymen—if thats the membrane's name—a painful operation, and I suppose connected with all sorts of subterranean instincts. (*Letters*, 6. 459–60).

Woolf remained true to the end of her life to the free speech created by the female space of Bloomsbury.

Yet Bloomsbury did not continue to be that special female space. Woolf's paper on 'Old Bloomsbury' complains of its being early taken over by 'buggers' (not for her a homophobic term). In the female space of Bloomsbury homosexuality was part of a revolution in communication. Initially she relished the new lack of inhibition surrounding that taboo subject:

> So there was now nothing that one could not say, nothing that one could not do, at 46 Gordon Square. It was, I think, a great advance in civilisation. It may be true that the loves of buggers are not—at least if one is of the other persuasion—of enthralling interest or paramount importance. But the fact that they can be mentioned openly leads to the fact that no one minds if they are practised privately. Thus many customs and beliefs were revised. Indeed the future of Bloomsbury was to prove that many variations can be played on the theme of sex, and with such happy results that my father himself might have hesitated before he thundered out the one word which he thought fit to apply to a bugger or an adulterer; which was Blackguard! ('Old Bloomsbury', pp. 174–5)

However, Woolf's discontent soon surfaced and remained with her despite her affection and admiration for Lytton Strachey and E.M. Forster. She did not at first recognise that her dissatisfactions arose from her alienation from the sexual orientation of many of the young men around her:

Those long sittings, those long silences, those long arguments—
they still went on in Fitzroy Square as they had done in Gordon
Square. But now I found them of the most perplexing nature.
They still excited me much more than any men I met with in
the outer world of dinners and dances—and yet I was, dared
I say it or think it even?—intolerably bored. Why, I asked,
had we nothing to say to each other? Why were the most gifted
of people also the most barren? Why were the most stimulat-
ing of friendships also the most deadening? Why was it all so
negative? Why did these young men make one feel that one
could not honestly be anything? The answer to all my questions was, obviously—as you will have guessed—that there
was no physical attraction between us.

The society of buggers has many advantages—if you are a
woman. It is simple, it is honest, it makes one feel, as I noted,
in some respects at one's ease. But it has this drawback—with
buggers one cannot, as nurses say, show off. Something is always
suppressed, held down. Yet this showing off, which is not
copulating, necessarily, nor altogether being in love, is one of
the great delights, one of the chief necessities of life. ('Old
Bloomsbury', p. 172).

With the later history of Bloomsbury, her restlessness waxed rather
than waned. She moaned that the 'pale star of the Bugger has
been in the ascendant too long' (*Diary*, 3. 10), and complained
that the conversation and jokes of her male friends resembled
stepping into a 'men's urinal' (*Diary*, 3. 299). Her views were
not kept private: 'My anti-bugger revolution has gone round the
world, as I hoped it would. I am a little touched by what appears
their contrition, & anxiety to condone their faults' (*Diary*, 3. 10).
She was always afraid that the melancholy little Cambridge poets would stage a take-over of the hard-won female space.

Clive Bell declared that Bloomsbury writing was for the common reader, but he means by that term what Johnson meant,
the man in the street rather than the academic. For Virginia Woolf
Bloomsbury licensed the conjuring into a circle of women readers
stretching far beyond its ostensible geographical and even mental limits. The body was their route into the mind.

## OBSCENITY: SIR JOHN HARINGTON AND WOOLF

Leslie Stephen claimed that 'the one great service which a critic can render is to keep vice, vulgarity, or stupidity at bay'.[24] His daughter's view was different: 'If the British spoke openly about W.C.'s & copulation, then they might be stirred by universal emotions. As it is, an appeal to feel together is hopelessly muddled by intervening greatcoats & fur coats'. (*Diary*, 1. 5). She had enquired in *Orlando* how the reposeful and elephantine Victorians could possibly be imagined propagating their kind. Like Montaigne and Donne, she recognised that Rabelais's 'ineradicable connection between human ideals and man's grossest functions'[25] spelled a new compatibility between the body and the book.

That compatibility was registered in its most outrageous form in the Elizabethan period in a work Virginia Woolf does not appear to have known, *The Metamorphosis of Ajax* (1596) by Sir John Harington. This lively, learned and audacious tract set out its author's proposals for the invention of a water-closet, and caused scandal in its time for its racy free speech on excremental matters as well as for its jibes at many of Harington's contemporaries. Harington himself, a privileged courtier who was Elizabeth I's godson and prized by her for his insouciant wit, had already distinguished himself in a high culture activity by translating Ariosto's romance epic, the *Orlando Furioso*, into 'English Heroical Couplets'. His later excursion into plumbing may have been stimulated by his construction of a fine Italian fountain in his own garden at Kelston in Somerset, in imitation of the one described in Ariosto. Woolf, who knew Ariosto's poem, which lies in the hinterland of *Orlando*,[26] may have read it in Harington's translation. Lytton Strachey, who used the eighteenth-century collection of Harington letters, notes and family papers entitled the *Nugae Antiquae* (1779) for *Elizabeth and Essex* (1928), may also have drawn Woolf's attention to an Elizabethan who embodies aspects of the alternative tradition for women which she located in the early modern period.

Harington's spirit is closely allied to Woolf's in various ways, not least in his determination to marry high and low culture within his own writing. In Harington's biography the translation of the *Orlando Furioso* makes a strange bedfellow with *The Metamorphosis of Ajax*, just as his jests continually puncture even his most earnest moments. For Harington – as for More, Erasmus,

Rabelais and many other Renaissance writers – seriousness and laughter are part of the same impulse. E.M. Forster said of Woolf that her comic spirit 'speeded up' the serious side of her writing. Of this she was herself aware, on occasion castigating herself for making too many jokes and therefore encouraging people not to take her critical writing seriously. She produced her books in pairs, so that *Flush*, the biography of Elizabeth Barrett Browning's dog (modelled on her own spaniel, Pinka), provided relief from the drudgery she experienced in composing *The Years*. Flush again provides kinship with Harington, who was passionately fond of his own spaniel Bungy, and had him depicted on the Frontispiece to his translation of Ariosto, with a motto coming out of his mouth from the poem itself.[27] Sir John wrote a long letter to Prince Henry describing the antics of his dog after it had been stolen by the Spanish Ambassador. Recognising the errant Bungy at a great dinner, Harington reasserted his rightful ownership by commanding him to perform the tricks he had taught him – to the delectation of the assembled company.[28] A hint of this tale perhaps lies behind the moment in Woolf's *Orlando* when a courtier at a great banquet 'whistled to his dog and made him beg for a marrow-bone'.[29] The mock-heroic mode of *Flush* undermines both serious biography and complements Virginia Woolf's own high-culture novel (*The Years*) written at the same time. A dog takes precedence over human beings. But the likeness between Woolf and Harington does not end with their determined mingling of high and low, comic and serious.

For Harington, as for Woolf, books have a physical life which it is important to nurture and cherish. The Elizabethan courtier was one of the first writers to see his own work through the press, writing careful instructions to the printer Richard Field on how his translation of Ariosto was to be set. He was deeply interested in printing, and in the larger market which it would create for writing. Apparently he even tried to set up his own printing press, for he received a rebuke from the Privy Council in May 1592 for poaching someone else's apprentice.[30] Harington had a strong sense of the physical acts involved in reading and writing. Despite his concern with print, many of his works were in a scribal hand, which he oversaw with much meticulous cunning, taking pains to conceal where a scribe would take over from his master in handwritten documents.

Harington is one of the few Elizabethans who depicts himself as a reader; he is also unusually explicit about how he wanted his writings to be read. He conceives of a new readership, often female, and both courts and instructs it, not, as Sidney does, in the proper attitudes to poetry, but in the physical act of reading. The opening epigram of Book IV in *Epigrams 1618* ('*To an ill Reader*') inveighs against a rival who has not heeded the strictures of the Epistle about intelligent reading:

> The verses, *Sextus*, thou doost read, are mine;
> But with bad reading thou wilt make them thine.

(IV. 1)

Another epigram, also '*To* Sextus, *an ill Reader*', complains:

> That Epigram that last you did rehearse,
> Was sharpe, and in the making, neat and tearse,
> But thou doost read so harsh, point so peruerse,
> It seemed now neither witty nor verse.
>> For shame poynt better, and pronounce it cleerer,
>> Or be no Reader, *Sextus*, be a Hearer.

(III. 6)

Poetry demands performance. Harington complains that his epigrams have not only been badly read, but with the wrong facial expressions:

> Who reades our verse, with visage sowre and grim.
> I wish him enuy me, none enuy him.

(IV. 2)

The body of the reader, whether digesting, evacuating or performing in more dramatic ways, is central to Harington's sense of himself as writer.

In thinking of a new readership, Harington joins company with the sixteenth-century Protestant preacher, Hugh Latimer, whose famous 'Sermon of the Plough' was to feature prominently in Woolf's projected 'Common History'. Harington is the child of radical Protestantism through his mother, Isabella Markham (one of Elizabeth's Maids-of-Honour who was with her in the Tower in the 1550s). Harington, in his translation of the *Orlando Furioso*, offers marginal directions to his readers on the interpretation of the poem as well as providing extended prose notes at the end of each Canto. This practice offers a secular parallel with the Coverdale and Geneva Bibles, which also guide the reader's response to the sacred text. Harington was well aware of the controversies surrounding the individual's access to free interpretation of the Bible, not only from his upbringing, but from his experience. One of his Epigrams is entitled 'Of reading Scripture' and declares that the Bible offers different levels of interpretation to each level of reader, just as he also felt his translation of Ariosto operated on different levels. Women are his new readers.

Harington wrote, like Latimer, not for those to whom Latin and Greek came easily, but for readers of the vernacular, whether in sacred or secular texts, many of whom were women. He saw less division between the categories of sacred and secular than a modern reader would perceive, or than some of his contemporaries would have recognised. As he declared in the little essay 'Of Reeding Poetry' which he appended to his translation of *Aeneid VI*: 'The same pen oft tymes wrytes holly himns that wrate wanton sonnets, and the same pensyll draws the pictures of Chryste and owr lady that drew venus and Cupid and neyther do amorows verses corrupt all reeders nor lascyvyows pictures provoke all beholders.'[31] The question of the effect of what is written on the reader, and the joint responsibility of reader and writer was his constant concern. This was not unusual for his time. What was unusual was the degree of conscious activity which he accorded to the reader, which was the fruit of his training as a translator, in which the act of reading was a significant partner in the act of writing. In this conviction of partnership Harington looks forward to Woolf, who urged the reader to be the writer's ally.

He certainly would have been her ally, as she would have been his, in rescuing the body from its shroud of silence. If Woolf wanted evidence of the Elizabethans talking frankly about the body, Harington provides it to excess. Some of his epigrams compete with Bloomsbury on both sex and filth.[32] Much as he admired Sidney, and imitated his *Apology for Poetry* – of which he possessed a manuscript – in an 'Apologie' of his own at the beginning of his translation of the *Orlando*, his aesthetic principles were less high-minded than Sidney's. Sidney thought poetry should teach and delight, but Harington was content with delight only, and believed that a little obscenity added to the enjoyment of reading. The idea of self-improvement as a motive for reading always finds him winking at the reader across the written page. In the closing epigram inscribed in the 1600 *Orlando* which he sent to his mother-in-law ('Misacmos of his Muse') Harington compares his muse to a woman of pleasure (Elizabethan euphemism for a courtesan):

> My Muse is like king Edwards Concubine
> Whose minde did to devotion so encline
> She duly did each day to church resort
> Saue if she wear intyst to Venus sport
>     So would my Muse write grauely nere the latter
>     She slips sometimes into some wanton matter.[33]

Books are for delight and reading about sex has always, Harington maintained, pleased the common reader – men such as himself, but more importantly, women.

Harington was conscious of writing to please women, both in his translation of Ariosto and in *The Metamorphosis of Ajax*, and he believed that they liked obscenity as long as it was funny. He translated the bawdy Canto 28 of the *Orlando Furioso* for the Queen's Ladies-in-waiting, and incurred their mistress's royal wrath, for she rusticated him with the equivocal command that he translate the rest of the poem. Harington's 'Apologie of Poetry' pretended to advise women not to read the offending tale: '(If you will follow my cousell) turne over the leafe and let it alone, although even that lewd tale may bring some men profit, and I have heard that it is already (and perhaps not unfitly) termed the comfort of cuckolds' (*OF*, pp. 11–12). He thought a good deal of cant was talked about obscenity in literature and that people's practices differed from their preaching. He quotes a Martial epigram about Lucretia reading: '*Lucretia* (by which he signifies any chast matron) will blush and be ashamed to read a lascivious booke, but how? not except *Brutus* be by, that is if any grave man should see her read it, but if *Brutus* turne his backe, she will to it agayne and read it all' (*OF*, p. 9). Harington declares that in Ariosto 'there is not a word of ribaldry or obscenousnes', but he quickly backtracks by invoking 'our *Chawcer* who both in words and sence incurreth far more the reprehension of flat scurrilitie, as I could recite many places, not only in his Millers tale, but in the good wife of Bathes tale and many more, in which onely the decorum he keepes is that that excuseth it and maketh it more tolerable' (*OF*, p. 12). Harington shares Montaigne's scorn for the polite hypocrisies of prudery.

In his *Apologie* for *The Metamorphosis of Ajax* Harington singled out women as the true recipients of his book, both in their function as guardians of cleanliness in the home, and in their capacity for greater sensitivity to sweet savours as opposed to the sourness he aimed to correct with his invention. The book should be shown to 'all maner of ladies, of the Court, of the country, of the City, great Ladies, lesser Ladies, learned, ignorant, wise simple, fowle welfavoured, (painted unpainted) so they be Ladies, you may boldly prefer it to them'.[34] He seems to have known, like Montaigne, that women's attitudes to the body were more down-to-earth than men wanted to believe. Women were the first to gain from his invention of the water-closet, which was installed for the Queen and her ladies at Greenwich Palace. But he also sensed that his peculiar mingling of exhortation and ribaldry, body and mind, would speak to women in their own language. Men could hardly forgive him for talking so scurrilously, yet so wittily and learnedly, about excrement.

Harington argued in *The Metamorphosis of Ajax* that there can be no high civilisation while there is no sanitation. In an Epigram 'To the Ladies of the Queenes Priuy-chamber, at the making of their perfumed priuy at Richmond', he envisages his book swinging from the lavatory chain and exults in the transformations it has wrought on the unsavoury scene of evacuation:

For aye to hang, my Master he ordaines.
Yet deeme the deed to him no derogation,
But doome to this deuice new commendation,
Sith here you see, feele, smell that his conueyance
Hath freed this noysome place from all annoyance.
Now iudge you, that the work mock, enuie, taunt,
Whose seruice in this place may make most vaunt:
    If vs, or you, to praise it, were most meet,
    You, that made sowre, or vs, that make it sweet?

(I. 44)

When he wants to be vindictive to the poet Joyner, Harington recalls Tasso's writing verse in prison 'for want of Pen and Inke, with pisse and ordure' (II. 44). The body and the book are inseparable in Harington's thought, and he knew perfectly well that this was a new venture in his own time, as it had been for his mentors, Montaigne and Rabelais.

Both Frenchmen were ardent advocates of reinstating the obscene into ordinary language in the interests of human freedom – and in Montaigne's case, of a freedom which would be particularly liberating for women. Montaigne protests: 'We have the ladies to blush when they hear that but named which they are not at all afraid to do' ('Of Presumption, III. 319). He wrote in 'Upon Some Verses of Virgil': 'What has the act of generation, so natural, so necessary, and so just, done to men, to be a thing not to be spoken of without blushing, and to be excluded from all serious and moderate discourse? We boldly pronounce kill, rob, betray, and that we dare only to do betwixt the teeth. Is it to say, the less we expend in words, we may pay so much the more in thinking?' (IV. 263). He concludes:

> 'Tis an act that we have placed in the franchise of silence, from which to take it is a crime even to accuse and judge it; neither dare we reprehend it but by periphrasis and picture. . . . Is it not here as in matter of books, that sell better and become more public for being suppressed? (IV. 264)

Censorship, as Milton claims in his argument for freedom of the press in the *Areopagitica* (1644), stimulates the desires it aims to repress. Montaigne associates the suppression of free speech about sex and the body with the suppression of free speech itself. He admired Lucretius and other classical writers for their outspokenness: 'Those worthy people stood in need of no subtlety to disguise their meaning; their language is downright, and full of natural and continued vigour; they are all epigram; not only the tail, but the head, body, and feet' ('Upon Some Verses of Virgil', IV. 301). Thomas Combe's *Anatomie* to Harington's tract criticises squeamishness about obscenity:

> But I smyle at some whose manners proove that thear mynds admit all wickednes, and yet forsooth theyr ears cannot brooke a litle scurrilytye. Ys it not pittye that men of so fyne ears

should *male audire.* Yf one name a merd they thinke they are mard but a fylthyer thing ther is that mard them. What doe they with Rabbles and Aretyne in theyr studyes? (*An Anatomie of the Metamorpho-sed Ajax*, p. 200)

Harington claims that there is no filth in the language of his book, whatever the filth of its subject: 'Beleeve it (worthie readers, for I write not to the unworthie) A Jax when he is at his worst, yeelds not a more offensive savour to the finest nostrils, then some of the faults I have noted do, to God and the world. Be not offended with me for saying it, more then I am with some of you for seeing it' (*An Apologie*, p. 183). His plea for free speech about the body constitutes a wider demand for a freer world with less censorship, explicit and implicit.

Harington put his own desire for more cheerful obscenity into practice both in his translation of Ariosto, in his Epigrams, and in his reading of Sidney's *Arcadia.* He altered the texts he perused – both Ariosto and Sidney – in the interests of making them more bawdy, erotic and readable. When he wrote his 'Apologie of Poetrie' as Preface to his translation of the *Orlando Furioso* he had at hand Sidney's *Apology for Poetry*, probably lent him in manuscript by his close friend, Sidney's brother Robert, with whom he remained on intimate terms throughout his life, the two men exchanging verses.[35] But although Harington copied Sir Philip Sidney's treatise in many respects, he differed from his authority in both theory and practice because he envisaged readers on a larger and more diverse scale. P.J. Croft points out that Sidney wrote the *Arcadia* for 'a courtly and educated audience, while the scribes entrusted with the mechanical task of copying that work naturally belonged to a lower stratum in the social hierarchy'. Harington organised the copying of a manuscript of the *Arcadia* by his own scribes, and Croft paints a beguiling picture of the master intervening both in the copying activity and in the transmission of the text in order to make it more amusing for the scribes. As he supervised their work, Harington embellished Sidney's text, expanding its erotic moments, and lowering its diction.[36] The same process is evident in his translation of Ariosto. K.M. Lea criticises Harington for coarsening some of Ariosto's subtleties, but not every critic would agree with this judgement, and Lea herself acknowledges the accessibility of the translator's text to a new readership of young Elizabethans.[37] Along with

the pace and immediacy of Harington's translation goes a good
deal of expanding of the risqué and amusing parts, and cutting
out of bits which Harington found boring.

Harington could talk as much as he liked about the moral responsibilities of writer and reader, but he plainly recognised that
although readers may be improved by what they read, improve-
ment is not what newly literate readers are looking for. Sidney
declared that poetry sugared the pill of didacticism, but he did
not doubt the curative value of the pill itself. Harington, more
dedicated to the idea of reading for fun, is more modern than
Sidney. As Croft remarks: 'Need we accept without reservation
that it is only the *modern* reader who might find the *Arcadia* a
strain?. . . [Harington's] response to the *Arcadia* seems to have
been, in some ways at least, recognisably our own' (pp. 69–70).
Other readers besides Harington have found Sidney's heroic
pastoral written in too high a style, one of the most notable being Virginia Woolf.

Woolf complained in her *Diary* for Monday 16 November 1931:
'I cant get on with Philip Sidney; & so my perfect crystal globe
has a shadow crossing it' (4. 53). At the end of December she
was still having trouble, as she wrote to Vita Sackville-West: 'And
what about Penshurst or Sissingt? I'm so behindhand—I was going
to write about Sidney, and cant get back into the mood' (*Letters*,
4. 420). When she did get back in the mood, her *Common Reader*
essay on '"The Countess of Pembroke's *Arcadia*'" perfectly captures the sense of a text getting away, of a high-culture romance
which needs a Harington to rewrite it for the enjoyment of scribes
as well as great ladies and gentlemen. Woolf baulks at Sidney's
ceremonious style: 'In prose, he bethinks himself, one must not
use the common words of daily speech' (*CR II*, p. 46). When
Harington expands Sidney's '"Thou vile Mopsa"' into 'Thow vile
Mopsa sayde he the drone of my hyve the Cobwebb of my howse
the polecatt of my Chaumber'[38] he has incorporated into Sidney's
original a low diction which would have kept Woolf awake as
well as the drooping scribe. Harington's spirit can never separate the physical realities of the human condition (cobwebs, stinking polecats, somnolence over a dull book) from the high culture
fantasies of the mind.

Virginia Woolf always revelled in exposing the pretensions of
high culture through frankness about the body. She describes
Roger Fry's Omega workshops in iconoclastic spirit:

The house in which Roger Fry set up his workshop is there today – a house with a past of its own, a Georgian past, a Victorian past. A lady remembered it in her childhood; the Pre-Raphaelites, she said, had congregated there, and either Rossetti's legs had appeared through the ceiling or the floor had given way and the dinner-table had crashed through into the cesspool beneath – which, she could not remember. It had a past, anyhow. But now the Georgian and the Victorian ghosts were routed. Two Post-Impressionist Titans were mounted over the doorway, and all was bustle and confusion.[39]

The Victorian and Georgian past is ousted not only by confusion and the Post-Impressionists, but by Woolf's mode of writing, in which reverence for Rossetti is rudely shattered by a crude physicality: legs where they ought not to be, and a dining table – epitome of civilisation in the male Cambridge College of *A Room of One's Own* – plunging into a cesspool. Her grotesque interventions obtrude laughter at the excremental into the sphere of the beautiful and the good, discussed in those opening Thursday evenings at Bloomsbury. Obscenity, the freedom to name the unnameable, creates its own politics of change as much as the new art itself. Woolf wrote in 1909 to Clive Bell that 'we [herself, Pernel and Lytton Strachey and Irene Noel] went on with the usual selection and we discussed love and sex and filth and Sir Joshua's pictures and ethics' (*Letters*, 1. 418).

Frankness about bodily functions remained one of Woolf's creeds. She spoke of one of her female Hogarth Press employees as 'direct & sensible; goes to the W.C. frankly' (*Diary*, 3. 249). Leonard Woolf shared this view, and describes in his autobiography his astonishment, on one occasion, at T.S. Eliot's behaviour:

How inhibited he was then can be seen from an absurd incident which happened at one of his very early visits to Monks House and in which I remember for the first time breaking the ice. He was walking with Virginia and me across the fields down to the river. I suddenly wanted to make water and fell behind to do so. Neither of my companions saw what I was doing, but I suppose it was very obvious what I was doing. Anyhow, when I caught them up again, I felt that Tom was uncomfortable, even shocked. I asked him whether he was and he said yes, and we then had what gradually became a perfectly frank conversation about conventions and formality. Tom said that he not only could not possibly have done what I did, that he would never dream of shaving in the presence even of his wife.[40]

The presence of the woman, Virginia Woolf, disconcerts and inhibits Eliot, creating a need to deny the body.

Literature, in Woolf's view, would never thrive until people felt easy talking about the body. Even in the lavatory she recorded conversations between women which might become new fictions:

> Yesterday in the ladies lavatory at the Sussex Grill at Brighton I heard: She's a little simpering thing. I dont like her. But then he never did care for big women. . . . They were powdering & painting, these common little tarts, while I sat, behind a thin door, p—ing as quietly as I could. (*Diary*, 5. 357).

She may not have been blessed with the male writing instrument, but her tradition was, after all, orality, the body's mouth(s), not its pens.[41]

In his satirical fantasy *Ignatius His Conclave* (1611) Donne imagines himself in an ecstasy from which he rises out of his body and takes a journey through hell, listening to the orations of Copernicus, Machiavelli, Paracelsus – all there for being 'innovators'. Ignatius is enthroned as Lucifer's right-hand man, and makes a long speech against his enemies, who include Elizabeth of England. Donne grows as tired of it as the modern reader is likely to do: 'Truly I thought this Oration of *Ignatius* very long; and I began to think of my body which I had so long abandoned, lest it should putrifie, or grow mouldy, or be buried; yet I was loath to leave the Stage till I saw the Play ended.'[42] In a curious way this recapitulates the end of an earlier 'Extasie' where his own oration seems tedious to the poet and he begs his mistress to bring it to its natural conclusion: 'But O alas, so long, so farre / Our bodies why doe wee forbeare?' (p. 47). Donne, listening wearily to Ignatius, becomes as anxious as the lover about the state of his body.

Virginia Woolf, writing to Violet Dickinson in 1903, observed:

I have a great affection for you so on my account oil well those works of God and nature, lent you here for a brief space, but to be accounted for later on that day when the secrets of all souls, and the entrails of all Bodies shall stand before their Creator. (*Letters*, 1. 104).

The capital letter and the word 'entrails' say it all. Isn't it the soul, not the body, that ought to have a capital letter? And what do ladies know about entrails? Whatever they know ought not to be spoken, let alone written, as the scandalised Elizabethan court purveyed to Sir John Harington when he thrust under its unwilling nose his plans for converting stinking privies into sweet-smelling water-closets. Surely Rodmell, the home of the ethereal Bloomsbury aesthete lady, Mrs Woolf, didn't smell of the cess-pool?[43]

## BODIES, POLITICS AND THE UNLITERARY

Illness, declared Virginia Woolf, gives the reader courage to redisover a naked Shakespeare beneath the swathes of academic dress in which he was purveyed to the public:

> Rashness is one of the properties of illness—outlaws that we are—and it is rashness that we need in reading Shakespeare. It is not that we should doze in reading him, but that, fully conscious and aware, his fame intimidates and bores. . . . Shakespeare is getting flyblown; a paternal government might well forbid writing about him, as they put his monument at Stratford beyond the reach of scribbling fingers.

The reader in a sickbed experiences first-hand communication with the writer, unmediated by the inhibiting presence of a male priesthood of learning: 'With all this buzz of criticism about, one may hazard one's conjectures privately, make one's notes in the margin; but, knowing that someone has said it before, or said it better, the zest is gone.' Illness gives the body powers of observation which make the mind rebel: 'Illness, in its kingly sublimity, sweeps all that aside and leaves nothing but Shakespeare and oneself' ('On Being Ill', p. 22). Uncovering the naked text Woolf identified as the particular function of the woman reader.

Her reinstatement of the body within her own literary consciousness was impelled by her own contact not with imaginary women
readers, but with the ordinary working women whom she encountered in connection with Leonard Woolf's political activities.

A rediscovery of the political Virginia Woolf,[44] active in the
Fabian society and the Women's Guild, has gone some way
towards obliterating the image of the genteel and invalidish
Bloomsbury lady of which she was conscious in her own lifetime, and which derived from a view of Bloomsbury as a refuge
for aesthetes. Woolf protested against this view of Bloomsbury
in a letter to Ben Nicolson, artist son of Vita Sackville-West, written
in response to his criticisms of her biography of Roger Fry.
Nicolson claimed that the Bloomsbury Group – and of course
Fry himself – had no concern for the political urgencies of the
time. Woolf, writing with the Blitz around her, expostulated:

> There goes that damned siren, I said to myself, and dipped
> into your letter. You were making extracts from Roger's let-
> ters as you listened. 'Returning slowly though France he stopped
> in many of the towns and villages....' I began making extracts
> from your biography. 'Returning slowly from Italy with Jeremy
> Hutchinson, Ben Nicolson reached Venice in May 1935...'.
> Here the raiders came over head. I went and looked at them.
> Then I returned to your letter. 'I am so struck by the fools
> paradise in which he and his friends lived. He shut himself
> out from all disagreeable actualities and allowed the spirit of
> Nazism to grow without taking any steps to check it....' Lord,
> I thought to myself, Roger shut himself out from disagreeable
> actualities did he? Roger who faced insanity, death and every
> sort of disagreeable—what can Ben mean? Are Ben and I fac-
> ing actualities because we're listening to bombs dropping on
> other people? (*Letters*, 6. 413)

She herself had also faced insanity, death, and the disagreeables
of constant ill-health. Her impassioned response to Nicolson occupies three separate letters.

Nicolson accused Fry of '"retreating into his tower to uphold
certain ethical standards"' rather than trying to '"persuade as
many other people as possible to think and behave in the same
way"'. Virginia Woolf again erupts: 'Who on earth, I thought,
did that job more incessantly and successfully than Roger Fry?

Didn't he spend half his life, not in a tower, but travelling about England addressing masses of people, who'd never looked at a picture and making them see what he saw? And wasn't that the best way of checking Nazism?' She accuses Nicolson of wanting a scapegoat for the war, while admitting that she wants one herself; if his is Bloomsbury, hers could be aristocratic families such as his own who educate their sons at Eton and Oxford.

Woolf refuses to be lumped with Roger Fry in some indiscriminate collective 'Bloomsbury Group':

In fact I am not responsible for anything Roger did or said. My own education and my own point of view were entirely different from his. I never went to school or college. My father spent perhaps £100 on my education. When I was a young woman I tried to share the fruits of that very imperfect education with the working classes by teaching literature at Morley College; by holding a Womens Cooperative Guild meeting weekly; and, politically, by working for the vote. (*Letters*, 6. 419)

The books that she mentions as the follow-up to her political activities are not her novels:

It is true I wrote books and some of those books, like the Common Reader, A Room of One's Own and Three Guineas (in which I did my best to destroy Sackvilles and Dufferins) have sold many thousand copies. That is, I did my best to make them reach a far wider circle than a little private circle of exquisite and cultivated people. And to some extent I succeeded.

Leonard Woolf, she points out, was also Bloomsbury, and had spent his life writing books on politics and economics, and urging the creation of the League of Nations in an attempt to arrest the progress of Nazism. Her own books are for common readers – not just one or two judicious persons, but the masses, unknown men and women. She retorts angrily to Nicolson: 'I entirely agree with you when you say "You must educate your public. Taste and appreciation can never improve until attitudes of mind are changed." I felt that very much the other day when I lectured the W.E.A. on poetry at Brighton. It seemed to me useless to tell people who left school at 14 and were earning their livings in

shops and factories that they ought to enjoy Shakespeare.' The
lecture she had given, on 27 April 1940, was 'The Leaning Tower'.

At the beginning of 'The Leaning Tower' Woolf muses on the
origins of genius, and suggests that 'books descend from books
as families descend from families'.[45] Looking back to 1815 she
considers that writers were hardly affected at all by the Napoleonic
wars; neither Scott nor Jane Austen 'heard Napoleon's voice as
we hear Hitler's voice as we sit at home of an evening' (p. 107).
The same situation prevailed in the nineteenth century; the family
likeness which she observes between writers is consequent on peace
and prosperity. The great change comes with the First World War.
But at this point she pauses at the writer's 'chair':

> By his chair we mean his upbringing, his education. It is a
> fact, not a theory, that all writers from Chaucer to the present
> day, with so few exceptions that one hand can count them,
> have sat upon the same kind of chair—a raised chair. They
> have all come from the middle class; they have had good, at
> least expensive, educations. . . . That was true of all nineteenth-
> century writers, save Dickens; it was true of all the 1914 writers,
> save D.H. Lawrence. (p. 111)

Education, in her view, is the single determining fact in creating
their writing:

> It cannot be a mere chance that this mute class of educated
> people has produced so much that is good as writing; and
> that the vast mass of people without education has produced
> so little that is good. It is a fact, however. Take away all that
> the working class has given to English literature and that
> literature would scarcely suffer; take away all that the edu-
> cated class has given, and English literature would scarcely
> exist. (p. 112)

She proceeds: 'A boy brought up alone in a library turns into a
book worm; brought up alone in the fields he turns into an earth
worm. To breed the kind of butterfly a writer is you must let
him sun himself for three or four years at Oxford or Cambridge—
so it seems' (p. 112). Such a boy resides on a tower built by his
parents' class and money. The traditions which create good writing
are easily discernible:

Put a page of their writing under the magnifying-glass and you will see, far away in the distance, the Greeks, the Romans; coming nearer, the Elizabethans; coming nearer still, Dryden, Swift, Voltaire, Jane Austen, Dickens, Henry James. (p. 113)

But by the 1930s the tower had begun to lean, and those on it to feel uneasy in their position, so that when Woolf contrasts Wordsworth with MacNeice and C. Day Lewis, she hears politicians not poets. As she looks forward to the post-war generation she was never herself to witness, she asks: 'Will there be no more towers and no more classes and shall we stand, without hedges between us, on the common ground?' (p. 121). 'I look upon myself as one of the common sort', said Montaigne in his tower, surrounded by Latin and Greek texts. Why did he? 'I do not value myself upon any other account than because I know my own value' ('Of Presumption', III. 324). In *A Room of One's Own* Woolf had quoted Quiller-Couch's belief that 'a poor child in England has little more hope than had the son of an Athenian slave to be emancipated into that intellectual freedom of which great writings are born.' For Woolf the plight of working men embraces all women, 'who have had less intellectual freedom than some of the Athenian slaves' (*RO*, p. 106). But thanks to the Great War, some doors had opened for women.

Woolf's post-war Utopia is a classless society. She quotes the parent who wanted to send her child to the village school while retaining the educational advantages of the public school: 'She wanted the new world and the old world to unite, the world of the present and the world of the past' (p. 123). Virginia Woolf moves into her most savage attack on the society in which she was raised:

England has crammed a small aristocratic class with Latin and Greek and logic and metaphysics and mathematics until they cry out like the young men on the leaning tower, 'All that I would like to be is human'. She has left the other class, the immense class to which almost all of us must belong, to pick up what we can in village schools; in factories; in workshops; behind counters; and at home. When one thinks of that criminal injustice one is tempted to say England deserves to have no literature. (p. 123)

England has tried to bridge the gap in one particular way:

> This book was not bought; it was not hired. It was borrowed
> from a public library. England lent it to a common reader,
> saying 'It is time that even you, whom I have shut out from
> all my universities for centuries, should learn to read your
> mother tongue. I will help you.' If England is going to help
> us, we must help her. But how? Look at what is written in the
> book she has lent us. 'Readers are requested to point out any
> defects that they may observe to the local librarian.' This is
> England's way of saying: 'If I lend you books, I expect you to
> make yourselves critics'. (p. 124)

She hoped that the new generation would be able to choose its
education, a phrase which in the late twentieth century has lost
its political innocence. Readers must become critics so that they
can also become writers. The way to that end is through om-
nivorous reading. 'Nor let us shy away from the kings because
we are commoners. That is a fatal crime in the eyes of Aeschylus,
Shakespeare, Virgil, and Dante, who, if they could speak—and
after all they can—would say, "Don't leave me to the wigged
and gowned. Read me, read me for yourselves."' It doesn't matter reading with a crib (translation): 'Of course—are we not commoners, outsiders?'

Woolf's most striking contact with those outsiders had been
in June 1913 when she and Leonard attended the Conference in
Newcastle of the Women's Co-operative Guild. She became painfully aware, through first-hand experience, of the artificialities
of middle-class involvement in working-class politics, and set
out her embarrassments with admirable frankness in the letter
which stands as Preface to Margaret Llewelyn Davies's *Life as
We Have Known It* (1931) – the first-hand accounts by women in
the Co-operative Movement of their experiences in the Guild
(founded in 1883). In that Preface Woolf recalls, from a distance
of seventeen years, her unease, as spectator, at the speeches of
women passionately committed to improving the lot of themselves and their families:

> If every reform they demand was granted this very instant it
> would not touch one hair of my comfortable capitalistic head.
> Hence my interest is merely altruistic. It is thin spread and

moon coloured. There is no life blood or urgency about it. However hard I clap my hands or stamp my feet there is a hollowness in the sound which betrays me. I am a benevolent spectator.[46]

She tries to analyse this alienation and roots it in the body: 'After all the imagination is largely the child of the flesh. One could not be Mrs. Giles of Durham because one's body had never stood at the wash-tub; one's hands had never wrung and scrubbed and chopped up whatever the meat may be that makes a miner's supper' (p. xxiii). We are back in the world of the charwoman's rhyme which she had invoked as 'real' poetry against the melancholia of the youthful Cambridge poets. The bodies of the women at the Newcastle conference have been subjected to a discipline totally different from her own: 'Their bodies were thickset and muscular, their hands were large, and they had the slow emphatic gestures of people who are often stiff and fall tired in a heap on hard-backed chairs' (p. xxiv). She tries to explain her feelings to the organisers of the conference, Miss Kidd and Lilian Harris:

It had been a revelation and a disillusionment. We had been humiliated and enraged. To begin with, all their talk, we said, or the greater part of it, was of matters of fact. They want baths and money. To expect us, whose minds, such as they are, fly free at the end of a short length of capital to tie ourselves down again to that narrow plot of acquisitiveness and desire is impossible. We have baths and we have money. Therefore, however much we had sympathised our sympathy was largely fictitious. It was aesthetic sympathy, the sympathy of the eye and of the imagination, not of the heart and of the nerves; and such sympathy is always physically uncomfortable. (pp. xxvii–viii)

She identifies the source of her heartlessness: a lack of connection with the body. Ironically, the consciousness of that lack of connection expresses itself in physical discomfort.

Woolf proceeds to compare working women and ladies, admiring the strength and fortitude and capacity for 'tragedy and humour' which the working women possess: 'But, at the same time, it is much better to be a lady; ladies desire Mozart and

Einstein—that is, they desire things that are ends, not things that are means' (p. xxviii). Nevertheless she accords working women a quality which ladies lack, power with words: 'The quality they have, judging from a phrase caught here and there, from a laugh, or a gesture seen in passing, is precisely the quality that Shakespeare would have enjoyed. One can fancy him slipping away from the brilliant salons of educated people to crack a joke in Mrs. Robson's back kitchen' (p. xxix). In Orlando's gorgeous Elizabethan mansion the shabby poet (Shakespeare) sits at the servants' dinner table over his mug of ale while noblemen dine with the Queen (*O*, p. 14). Those Guild working women had access to a language no longer available even to Bloomsbury:

> How many words must lurk in those women's vocabularies that have faded from ours! How many scenes must lie dormant in their eye which are unseen by ours! What images and saws and proverbial sayings must still be current with them that have never reached the surface of print, and very likely they still keep the power which we have lost of making new ones (pp. xxix–xxx).

When she contemplated her drafts for her final work, her 'Common History', she saw in the figure of 'Anon' at the back door of the great house, the vitality of those working women. She comments on their written accounts of their lives and reading:

> That inborn energy which no amount of childbirth and washing up can quench had reached out, it seemed, and seized upon old copies of magazines; had attached itself to Dickens; had propped the poems of Burns against a dish cover to read while cooking. They read at meals; they read before going to the mill. (p. xxxv)

Reading creates ideas, arguments and ideals: 'But how could women whose hands were full of work, whose kitchens were thick with steam, who had neither education nor encouragement nor leisure remodel the world according to the ideas of working women? ... It was the Guild then that drew to itself all that restless wishing and dreaming' (p. xxxvii). Woolf reads the accounts in the light of the faces she remembers from the conference, but wonders if other readers without those memories will be able to realise the true nature of writings which 'as literature . . . have many limitations' (p. xxxix). According to that high culture definition of 'literature' the women's writings offer 'no view of life as a whole, and no attempt to enter into the lives of other people. Poetry and fiction seem far beyond their horizon' (p. xxxix). At this point Woolf traces connections with an earlier age:

> Indeed, we are reminded of those obscure writers before the birth of Shakespeare who never travelled beyond the borders of their own parishes, who read no language but their own, and wrote with difficulty, finding few words and those awkwardly. And yet since writing is a complex art, much infected by life, these pages have some qualities even as literature that the literate and instructed might envy. (p. xxxx)

She gives a sense of this quality in some random quotations, and concludes: 'These voices are beginning only now to emerge from silence into half articulate speech. These lives are still half hidden in profound obscurity. To express even what is expressed here has been a work of labour and difficulty. The writing has been done in kitchens, at odds and ends of leisure, in the midst of distractions and obstacles' (p. xxxi). She is in the world of *A Room of One's Own* but also of her own common reader, where Agnes Paston has had no leisure to develop the self-consciousness which would nurture inner life. The women of the Guild are a step further on, reading as if for life, in snatched moments. Even as the body obstructs 'literature', it moves the pen to create a world which transcends that high culture category, a world which would lead to Shakespeare more certainly than could the cloisters of Cambridge and the poetry of Woolf's nephew Julian Bell and his friends, of whose writing she exclaimed: 'Common sense and Cambridge are not enough' (*Diary*, 3. 329). Woolf knew that she was often condemned as heartless and bloodless, but in reading Renaissance literature she recognised that the body was a vital part of the alternative tradition of writing which was to be the main theme of her new 'Common History'.

Woolf's literary criticism invokes the body as the medium through which high culture must be returned to an earth-bound, invigorating centre, which belongs to women more than to men. If the mainstream of philosophy and religion had created traditions which relegated the body to an area outside culture,[47] its re-instatement which Virginia Woolf found in the Elizabethans and their French counterparts, Montaigne and Rabelais, serves to create a new space for women as writers and readers.

## THE PRESS AND THE FIRE

John Donne the younger published his father's work on suicide, *Biathanatos*, to avoid its destruction in the Civil War, paying heed to Donne's admonition to Robert Carr: 'Reserve it for me, if I live, and if I die, I only forbid it the Presse, and the Fire: publish it not, but yet burn it not; and between these, do what you will with it.'[48] With the onset of war in 1939 Virginia Woolf felt that her life as a writer was doomed. The Hogarth Press would cease to operate, and there would be no more readers. As she collected her manuscript *Diary* from her blitzed house she was also reading another devastating account of fire. On New Year's Day 1941 she recorded in her *Diary*: 'On Sunday night, as I was reading about the great fire, in a very accurate detailed book, London was burning. . . . This book was salvaged from 37; I brought it down from the shop, with a handful of Elizabethans for my book, now called "Turning a Page". A psychologist would see that the above was written with someone, & a dog, in the room. To add in private: I think I will be less verbose here per-haps—but what does it matter, writing too many pages. No printer to consider, no public' (*Diary*, 5. 351). The account of the great fire is one of the most spectacular narratives in Pepys's diary.[49] As Woolf reads Pepys's *Diary*, the difference between the hand-written record and the printed one is foremost in her mind. Without the press she was turned in on her own *Diary*, that pri-vate repository without print or public. She had written in 'The Patron and the Crocus' in the first *Common Reader* that writer and reader are twins cleaving together: without the one the other dies. But as she meditated on a male-dominated culture which had brought the war, she was also ruminating on her 'Common History' and the fate of the common reader.

The idea for her 'Common History' came to Virginia Woolf on 12 September 1940. She and Leonard were cut off from the Hogarth Press, which was islanded in Mecklenburgh Square, evacuated because of an unexploded bomb. In her rural exile at

Rodmell she 'suddenly conceived the idea of a new book', and felt that she could whip her brain into creativity 'if Hitler doesn't drop a splinter into my machine' (*Letters*, 6. 430–31). The machine is both the mind which writes the book, and also the Press which prints it. The devastation of London appalled her. The city of London she loved as the heart of the writing trade, Dr Johnson's, Richardson's and Pepys's London, in which she and Leonard had bought their own printing press.

The Hogarth Press had from its inception stood for freedom of speech. Woolf wrote to Ethel Smyth in ill-concealed despair in January 1941 that she still had plenty of ideas but couldn't bear the thought of arranging them to please another publisher: 'Didn't we start the Hogarth Press 25 years ago so as to be quit of editors & publishers? Its my nightmare, being in their clutches: but a nightmare, not a sane survey' (*Letters*, 6. 459). That liberty had been intimately connected with her awareness of the book as a body in itself: a material object which had its own life. The Hogarth Press had conveyed its message through the redesigning of books, which, with coloured Japanese and Czechoslovakian paper covers, looked more like Left-bank vagrants than sober Fleet Street citizens. Translation, from Russian, French, German – that mode of writing which multiplies and transforms the original voice, and whose radical effects on ideas of authorship were so well understood by Donne and his Renaissance contemporaries – had been an important part of the Hogarth Press venture from its inception. The Press had been conceived by the Woolfs as an organ for new voices in poetry, fiction, politics, and psychoanalysis.[50] That this would bring new readers was part of the excitement of the whole project.

In the correspondence between Flaubert and George Sand which Virginia Woolf so admired, George Sand attacks Flaubert for eclecticism about his readers: 'The mandarins do not need knowledge and even the education of a limited number of people has no longer reason for existing unless there is hope of influence on the masses.' The key to George Sand's rage is her own sense of being one of the masses because she is a woman: 'When I have drained my cup of bitterness, I shall feel better. I am a woman, I have affections, sympathies, and wrath. I shall never be a sage, nor a scholar.'[51] This outburst is reminiscent of Virginia Woolf's passionate defence of Bloomsbury (in August 1940) against Ben Nicolson's attack that she and her friends had done nothing to prevent the rise of Nazism. Sand accuses Flaubert of adopting a position in relation to the Franco-Prussian war which will lead to totalitarianism, clearly envisaged by her even though not named in that way. Her outburst seems prophetic, as she foresees a world from which intellectuals and artists withdraw, leaving the people to the mercies of their leaders. But it is significant that her letter to Flaubert stresses her gender (something she seldom does, and indeed often speaks of women as if she were not a woman, just as he addresses her as 'master'). Sand's identity is fashioned on exclusion. Like Woolf, being a woman means to George Sand that she will never be part of a company of sages and scholars.

Resistance to war called forth similar outbursts from both women writers, Sand to the Franco-Prussian war, and Woolf to the imminent Second World War. For Virginia Woolf the passions of 1916 were recapitulated in 1939. She had written during the First World War to Margaret Llewelyn Davies:

> I've been reading Carlyle's Past & Present, and wondering whether all his rant has made a scrap of difference practically. . . . I become steadily more feminist, owing to the Times, which I read at breakfast and wonder how this preposterous masculine fiction keeps going a day longer—without some vigorous young woman pulling us together & marching through it— Do you see any sense in it? (*Letters*, 2. 76).

The same revulsion animated her throughout the 1930s. Her loathing of Nazism was expressed as early as 1934: 'Meanwhile these brutal bullies go about in hoods & masks, like little boys dressed up, acting this idiotic, meaningless, brutal, bloody, pandemonium. . . . And for the first time I read articles with rage, to find him called a real leader' (*Diary*, 4. 223–4).[52] *The Common Reader* volumes, with their repudiation of the single authoritarian voice of literary leadership, were, as she pointed out to Ben Nicolson, her own act of political resistance, a woman's resistance to masculine domination.

As Woolf contemplated the loss of her own Press, which had so often prevented 'brooding', making her feel that even if she couldn't write she could build up a business, she was also working on *Between the Acts*, a novel whose fabric is constructed of fragments of half-remembered texts.[53] The idea of the 'common' had fascinated her from the inception of her critical enterprise. As she salvaged her books, her Press, her shattered London life, her new 'Common History' took form alongside *Between the Acts*, a novel nurtured by the confined village world of Rodmell. In the letter which talked of Chaucer's London Woolf observed: 'How odd it is being a countrywoman after all these years of being Cockney!' (*Letters*, 6. 460). Women are prominent in *Between the Acts*[54] as they were to be in the projected 'Common History', shadowed in the draft essay 'Anon'. To Lady Simon Virginia Woolf wrote: 'We live in the heart of the lower village world, to whom Leonard lectures on potatoes and politics. The gentry dont call' (*Letters*, 6. 464). In the midst of the life of ordinary people, Montaigne's '*le vulgaire*', she worked on her 'Common History':

> Did I tell you I'm reading the whole of English literature through? By the time I've reached Shakespeare the bombs will be falling. So I've arranged a very nice last scene: reading Shakespeare, having forgotten my gas mask, I shall fade far away, and quite forget.... They brought down a raider the other side of Lewes yesterday.... Thank God, as you would say, one's fathers left one a taste for reading! Instead of thinking, by May we shall be—whatever it may be: I think, only 3 months to read Ben Jonson, Milton, Donne, and all the rest! (1st February 1941, *Letters*, 6. 466).

The raider is almost a printer's joke, so easily does the word transform itself into reader. The echo of Keats' 'Ode to a Nightingale' in the preceding sentence recalls the early essay on 'Reading', but Virginia Woolf's heart is still in the Renaissance with Milton and Donne. Islanded in her village – she called it a 'desert island' – she both escaped into her books, but also returned through them to another time, in which print was only just beginning to make its impact on culture: the Elizabethan period. In her new 'Common History' she wanted to approach the Elizabethans through a history of the gradual movement from oral culture to the printed word, from listener to reader.

About that movement she had always felt ambivalent, believing that print created new readers who did not belong to the charmed circle of educated men, while at the same time accepting that the author who placed his (inevitably *his*) name on the spine of a book obliterated a long oral tradition in which women

were prominent: 'The printing press brought the past into existence. It brought into existence the man who is conscious of the
past the man who sees his time, against a background of the
past; the man who first sees himself and shows himself to us.
The first blow has been aimed at Anon when the authors name
is attached to the book. The individual emerges' ('Anon', p. 385).
She must have remembered that she had used almost exactly
the same words in her essay on Pepys, whose modernity she
identified as a sense of his own place in relation to past and
future. But she also recognised that a consciousness of the presence of 'Anon', that misty figure to whom she as writer connected herself, depended upon print, as her own voice had
depended on the freedom of the Hogarth Press, without which
there was only the private scribbling of the *Diary*.

Without print, Woolf felt that that republic of common readers
would be lost, and that without readers her own writing would
relapse into the private scribbling of the amateur: 'All this writing—what a deluge of words I've let loose—on paper only: I
mean not printed' (*Diary*, 5. 342, 6 December 1940). She wrote
ruefully to Ethel Smyth: 'I scribble to you as I scribble in my
diary' (*Letters*, 6. 453). The sense that the Blitz marked the end
of her life as an author was overpowering. She went, no doubt
unwisely, to view the bombed Tavistock Square (the home of
the Hogarth Press before she and Leonard had moved to
Mecklenburgh Square): 'I cd just see a piece of my studio wall
standing: otherwise rubble where I wrote so many books' (*Diary*,
5. 331). On 26 February 1941, three weeks before her death, she
wrote in her diary: 'Shall I ever write again one of those sentences that gives me intense pleasure?' (*Diary*, 5. 357). Pleasure,
that subversive female motive for writing to which she clung in
1940 when she read Madame de Sévigné's private letters, was
incomplete in her experience if it could not be shared with readers.
Where Madame de Sévigné, writing by hand, had needed only
one reader, her daughter, Woolf knew that her whole life as a
professional writer depended on her books reaching not just her
friends and relations, but that wide anonymous readership made
available to her through the mediation of her own printing press.

Print culture had served to silence a multiplicity which Woolf
wanted to recover and oppose to the single authoritarian male
professional voice. She observed, as she contemplated the transition from oral to written word which lies at the heart of her

literary project, the downgrading (in Walter Ong's words) of the 'wise old man and the wise old woman, repeaters of the past, in favor of younger discoverers of something new'.[55] As she read her handwritten *Diary* in the Sussex village with the floods rising round her, and Pepys's account of another destroyed London, she rediscovered aspects of a female oral tradition which she associated with her aunt, Caroline Emelia Stephen, and for which she had searched diligently through her reading of literature of the past.

The civilisation where these traditions of oral and print culture crossed, Virginia Woolf had long identified as Elizabethan, salvaging the Elizabethans from her bombed house. The movement to the playhouse had been the final glorious flowering of an old spoken culture, 'and the play itself was still anonymous'. For the audience, plays were a revelation of 'the expressive power of words after their long inadequacy' ('Anon', p. 395).[56] The common product, the work in which the reader had no sense of property, gives way to something she had written about as early as the first *Common Reader*, the solitary reader in a room of her own. In the draft fragment for her 'Common History', 'The Reader', Woolf ends with Burton, musing on the melancholy of the human soul, and contemplating, like Donne before him, suicide.[57]

The Hogarth Press had for more than a quarter of a century sent out her free voice to the common reader. The fire, from which Donne's *Biathanatos* and Pepys's *Diary* had been preserved, had in the end, by destroying the printing press, destroyed also the writer, for without it Woolf felt she would not again reach her common readers. But her work had been done, and she recorded her satisfaction in it in October 1940: 'I was glad to see the C.R. all spotted with readers at the Free Library to wh. I think of belonging' (*Diary*, 5. 329). Those readers were not her Bloomsbury friends and London acquaintances, but new readers, the women and working men for whom Tyndale had translated the English Bible and for whom Caxton had printed books in English.

Adrienne Rich claims that 're-vision—the act of looking back, of seeing with fresh eyes, of entering an old text from a new critical direction—is for women more than a chapter in cultural history: it is an act of survival'.[58] Virginia Woolf read the Elizabethans with the same Darwinian instinct for survival, writing in March 1940: 'Then I think I'll read an Elizabethan—like swinging from bough to bough' (*Diary*, 5. 276). As she contemplated the devastation of her physical environment she again hoped to renew her spirit with a return to the Renaissance, perhaps remembering how she had herself celebrated being reborn in the life of the pen. She had written five days earlier: 'I'm beginning Sense & Sensibility—& reading about Apes' (*Diary*, 5. 274). She thought of writing a *Common Reader* essay on Darwin. *Sense and Sensibility*, she declared to be 'masterly'. But the word roused old passions, and she altered it, making Austen 'mistressly in her winding up' (*Diary*, 5. 277). Language needed revision as much as the literary traditions it had created. She knew that some Elizabethans, and some of their seventeenth-century literary descendants, Bunyan, Dorothy Osborne, Pepys and many others, had survived in worlds which they themselves helped to change. As Woolf planned further reading, she recaptured the faith of Bunyan's Valiant in effort, defiance and personality which had animated Bernard's final speech in *The Waves*: 'For in God's name, I've done my share, with pen and talk, for the human race' (*Diary*, 5. 276).

The woman novelist, the Elizabethans and theories of evolution were inseparable in Woolf's mind from the alternative literary history along the female line for which she searched not as novelist, but as literary critic and historian. Readers and writers evolve. The historic moment of rebirth for women as readers and writers, and for men ill at ease with their own inherited masculine culture, she located in the sixteenth and seventeenth centuries, which she remapped as her own special Renaissance.

At the end of 'The Leaning Tower' Woolf sounded the clarion-call which had rung through all her writing: 'Literature is no one's private ground. Literature is common ground' (p. 125). Women, like working men, were to trespass on that ground which had become so carefully enclosed. Woolf's life both as writer and reader embodied an act of constant trespass in search of other trespassers. After a lifetime of travelling in the realms of gold, she saw from her window as she laid down her book, not just male poets and their common readers gathering in the garden outside, but the faces – at first obscure, then more clearly defined – of women writers and, behind them, in an ever-growing throng, women readers.

# Notes

## CHAPTER 1: VIRGINIA WOOLF'S RENAISSANCE

1. Jane Marcus, 'Sapphistry: Narration as Lesbian Seduction in *A Room of One's Own*', in *Virginia Woolf and the Languages of Patriarchy* (Bloomington, 1987): 163–87. Cf. Margaret S.M. Ezell, 'The Myth of Judith Shakespeare: Creating the Canon of Women's Literature', *NLH*, 21, 3 (1990): 579–92, pp. 583–5.
2. Sandra M. Gilbert and Susan Gubar, *No Man's Land: The Place of the Woman Writer in the Twentieth Century*, vol. I (New Haven 1987), 196, and vol. III (New Haven, 1994): 3–56 *passim*; Louise A. DeSalvo, 'Shakespeare's *Other* Sister', in Jane Marcus (ed.), *New Feminist Essays on Virginia Woolf* (1981): 61–81. Susan M. Squier and Louise A. DeSalvo (eds), 'Virginia Woolf's [*The Journal of Mistress Joan Martyn*]', *Twentieth Century Literature*, 25, 3/4 (1979), 237–64; Beth C. Schwartz, 'Thinking Back Through Our Mothers: Virginia Woolf Reads Shakespeare', *ELH*, 58:2 (1991), 721–46.
3. Nelly Furman, 'Textual Feminism', in Sally McConnell-Ginet, Ruth Borker and Nelly Furman (eds), *Women and Language in Literature and Society* (New York, 1980): 45–54, p. 50.
4. 'Professions for Women', in Michèle Barrett, *Virginia Woolf: Women & Writing* (1979): 57–63, p. 58. The essay was based on the speech Woolf delivered in on 21 January 1931 to the London/National Society for Women's Service. The first 'novel-essay' in the draft novel, *The Pargiters*, was based on this speech, of which the full draft, with author's alterations, is printed at the beginning of *The Pargiters*, ed. by Mitchell A. Leaska (Hogarth Press, 1978): xxvii–xliv.
5. 'Women and Fiction', in Barrett, *Virginia Woolf: Women & Writing*: 42–52, p. 58. The essay, which in draft form had provided the text of her two lectures to students at Newnham and Girton in October 1928, was published in the *The Forum* in March 1929, and posthumously in *Granite and Rainbow*.
6. Woolf, 'A Sketch of the Past', in Jeanne Schulkind (ed.), *Virginia Woolf: Moments of Being* (Sussex, 1976), p. 129.
7. *The Diary of Virginia Woolf*, vol. 4: 1931–35, ed. by Anne Olivier Bell and Andrew McNeillie (Harmondsworth, 1983), p. 25. All quotations from Virginia Woolf's *Diaries* from 1915–1941 are taken from this 5-volume edition.
8. Virginia Woolf, 'Anon', in Brenda Silver (ed.), '"Anon" and "The Reader": Virginia Woolf's Last Essays', *Twentieth Century Literature*, 25, 3/4 (1979), 356–9, pp. 382–9. Besides the two essays Silver also transcribed the manuscript of Woolf's 'Notes for Reading at Random', which I use in this study.
9. Joan Kelly-Gadol, 'Did Women Have a Renaissance?', in Renate

Bridenthal and Claudia Koonz (eds), *Becoming Visible: Women in European History*, (Boston, 1977): 137–64; Lillian S. Robinson, 'Sometimes, Always, Never: Their Women's History and Ours', *NLH*, 21, 2 (1990): 377–93.

10. See Alice Fox's pioneer study of Woolf's Renaissance criticism in relation to her fiction, *Virginia Woolf and the Literature of the English Renaissance* (Oxford, 1990).
11. T.S. Eliot, 'Tradition and the Individual Talent', *The Sacred Wood* (1920): 42–53.
12. Virginia Woolf, *A Room of One's Own* (Harmondsworth, 1972), p. 66.
13. Anthony Grafton and Lisa Jardine, *From Humanism to the Humanities* (1986), p. 45.
14. Margaret L. King and Albert Rabil Jr. (eds), *Her Immaculate Hand* (Binghamton, NY, 1983).
15. Virginia Woolf, 'Professions for Women', in Barrett, *Virginia Woolf: Women & Writing*, p. 57.
16. Draft of [Speech before the London/National Society for Women's Service, January 21 1931], reproduced in *The Pargiters*, p. xxix.
17. Woolf, 'Professions for Women', p. 58.
18. Woolf, *The Pargiters*, (first novel-essay), p. 6.
19. Woolf, 'The Elizabethan Lumber Room', *The Common Reader*: First series, ed. Andrew McNeillie (1984), p. 43.
20. Woolf, 'Professions for Women', pp. 59, 60, 63.
21. Hélène Cixous, 'The Laugh of Medusa', in Elaine Marks and Isabelle Courtivron (eds), *New French Feminisms* (Hemel Hempstead, 1981): 245–64, p. 250.
22. Margaret M. McGowan, *Montaigne's Deceits: The Art of Persuasion in the Essais* (1974), p. 146, describes 'Montaigne's distrust, and even hatred, of the professional'.
23. Donald M. Frame, *Montaigne: A Biography* (New York, 1965), p. 184.
24. *Diary, Hyde Park Gate 1903?*, in Virginia Woolf, *A Passionate Apprentice: The Early Journals 1897–1909*, ed. Mitchell A. Leaska (1990), p. 178. For Lady Anne Clifford's self-definition in a patriarchal society see Barbara K. Lewalski, 'Re-writing Patriarchy and Patronage: Margaret Clifford, Anne Clifford, and Aemilia Lanyer', in *The Yearbook of English Studies*, 21 (1991): 87–106, pp. 86–97.
25. Virginia Woolf, 'Donne After Three Centuries', *The Common Reader*: Second Series (1932), p. 34.
26. Mario Schiff, *Marie de Gournay* (Paris, 1910), p. 2; Marjorie Henry Ilsley, *A Daughter of the Renaissance* (The Hague, 1963), p. 17; Alan M. Boase, *The Fortunes of Montaigne* (1935), p. 53.
27. Marie le Jars de Gournay, *Grief Des Dames* (1626), reprinted in Schiff, *Marie de Gournay*, p. 91.
28. Virginia Woolf, *The Common Reader*: First Series, ed. Andrew McNeillie (1984), Preface, p. 1.
29. Samuel Johnson, 'Gray', *Lives of the English Poets* (1964): II. 453–64, p. 463.
30. Barbara Currier Bell and Carol Ohmann, 'Virginia Woolf's Criticism: A Polemical Preface', *Critical Inquiry*, 1 (1974): 361–71, discuss

Woolf's politicising of her own critical discourse, but take Woolf's 'common reader' for a straight reproduction of Johnson's ungendered judicious reader.

31. 'Byron and Mr Briggs' [draft Preface to *CR I*], in Andrew McNeillie (ed.), *The Essays of Virginia Woolf*, vol. 3: 1912–1918 (1988), Appendix II, p. 482. Quotations from Virginia Woolf's essays are from this edition unless otherwise specified.

32. Cf. Hermione Lee, *Virginia Woolf* (1996), pp. 415–17.

33. T.S. Eliot, 'The Function of Criticism', in *Selected Essays* (1932): 23–34, p. 24.

34. S.P. Rosenbaum, 'An Educated Man's Daughter: Leslie Stephen, Virginia Woolf and the Bloomsbury Group', in Patricia Clements and Isobel Grundy (eds), *Virginia Woolf: New Critical Essays* (1983): 32–56, p. 43; Lee, *Virginia Woolf*, p. 71.

35. Leslie Stephen, 'The Novels of De Foe', *Hours in a Library* (1917), I. 1–43, p. 1.

36. Elaine Showalter, 'Towards a Feminist Poetics', in Elaine Showalter (ed.), *The New Feminist Criticism* (1986): 125–43, p. 131.

37. 'The Serpentine', *PA*, p. 211, and n60; the event and suicide note were recorded in *Evening News and Evening Mail*, p. 3, col. 2, 23 September 1903.

38. Nigel Nicolson and Joanne Trautmann (eds), *The Flight of the Mind The Letters of Virginia Woolf*, vol. 1: 1888–1912 (Virginia Stephen) (1975), 140. All quotations from Virginia Woolf's letters are from this edition.

39. Woolf, 'Women and Fiction', p. 44.

40. 'Report on Teaching at Morley College', July 1905, original typescript Monks House Papers/A 22, reprinted as Appendix B in Quentin Bell, *Virginia Woolf: A Biography*, Volume I: *Virginia Stephen 1882–1912* (1972): 202–4, p. 203.

41. DeSalvo, 'Shakespeare's Other Sister', 61–81, discusses this story in a context of Woolf's creation of an alternative myth to that of Judith Shakespeare in *A Room of One's Own*.

42. Squier and DeSalvo (eds), 'Virginia Woolf's [*The Journal of Mistress Joan Martyn*]', p. 240.

43. Bell, *Virginia Woolf: A Biography*, I. 6–7. Cf. Lee, *Virginia Woolf*, pp. 66–8. Virginia Woolf, 'Caroline Emelia Stephen', *The Guardian*, 21 April 1909, reprinted in *Essays*, 1. 267–9.

44. Catherine F. Smith, 'Three Guineas: Virginia Woolf's Prophecy', in Jane Marcus (ed.), *Virginia Woolf and Bloomsbury* (1987): 225–41, pp. 228–9.

45. Marcus, *Virginia Woolf and the Languages of Patriarchy*, pp. 105, 81, on Caroline Emelia Stephen's insistence that nursing needed to be professionalised rather than carried out as a voluntary and charitable activity by bountiful ladies.

46. *Quaker Strongholds* (1890) and *Light Arising: Thoughts on the Central Radiance* (1908).

47. *RO*, p. 76. For an exploration of this theme in Woolf's thought, see Jane Marcus's seminal essay, 'Thinking Back through Our Mothers', in Jane Marcus (ed.), *Art and Anger: Reading Like a Woman* (Columbus, Ohio, 1988): 73–100.

48. From *Light Arising: Thoughts on the Central Radiance*, p. 75, quoted in Woolf, 'Caroline Emelia Stephen', *Essays*, 1. 268, and 269, n5; see Jane Marcus, 'The Niece of a Nun: Virginia Woolf, Caroline Stephen, and the Cloistered Imagination', in Jane Marcus (ed.), *Virginia Woolf: A Feminist Slant* (Lincoln, Nebraska, 1983): 7–26; Cf. S.P. Rosenbaum, *Victorian Bloomsbury* (1987), p. 23.
49. Cf. Marcus, *Virginia Woolf and the Languages of Patriarchy*, p. 85: 'Katherine Stephen boasted that she had converted her aunt to the cause of women's education by showing her the students' private rooms at Newnham.'
50. Marcus, *Virginia Woolf and the Languages of Patriarchy*, p. 27.
51. Virginia Woolf, *Women & Fiction: The Manuscript Versions of A ROOM OF ONE'S OWN*, transcribed and edited by S.P. Rosenbaum (Oxford, 1992), pp. 3–4.
52. Merry E. Weisner, 'Women's Defense of Their Public Role', in Mary Beth Rose (ed.), *Women in the Middle Ages and the Renaissance: Literary and Historical Perspectives* (Syracuse, 1985): 1–27, pp. 11–12.
53. Natalie Zemon Davis, 'Printing and the People', *Society and Culture in Early Modern France* (Cambridge, 1987): 189–226, pp. 192, 214, 213.
54. Stephanie H. Jed, *Chaste Thinking: The Rape of Lucretia and the Birth of Humanism* (Bloomington, 1989), p. 13.
55. James Raven, *Judging New Wealth*, (Oxford, 1992), p. 5.
56. Elizabeth Eisenstein, *The Printing Revolution in Early Modern Europe* (Cambridge, 1983), pp. 151, 24–30, 45.
57. Harold Love, *Scribal Publication in Seventeenth-Century England* (Oxford, 1993), p. 50.
58. Richard C. Newton, 'Jonson and the (Re)-Invention of the Book', in Claude J. Summers and Ted-Larry Pebworth (eds), *Classic and Cavalier: Essays on Jonson and the Sons of Ben* (Pittsburgh, 1982): 31–55, p. 36.
59. Jonathan Goldberg, *Writing Matter: From the Hands of the English Renaissance* (Stanford, 1990), pp. 53, 119, 234–7, 138, 136–7.
60. Eisenstein, *The Printing Revolution in Early Modern Europe*, pp. 124–5.
61. See Ruth Hughey (ed.), *The Arundel Harington Manuscript of Tudor Poetry* (Columbus, Ohio, 1960).
62. Walter Ong, *Orality and Literacy: The Technologizing of the Word* (1982), pp. 111–12.
63. Mary E. Gaither, 'The Hogarth Press 1917–46', in J. Howard Woolmer, *A Checklist of the Hogarth Press 1917–1946*, (Revere, Pennsylvania, 1986), p. xvii.
64. John Lehmann, *Thrown to the Woolfs* (1978), p. 70.
65. Virginia Woolf, *Roger Fry* (Harmondsworth, 1979), p. 165.
66. Terry Eagleton, *The Rape of Clarissa* (Oxford, 1982), p. 3.
67. D. F. McKenzie, *Bibliography and the Sociology of Texts* (British Library, 1986), p. 16.

CHAPTER 2: VIRGINIA WOOLF AND MONTAIGNE

1. First published in *Academy & Literature*, 25 February 1905, reprinted in *Essays*, I. 24–7, p. 25. In their annotation to the Woolfs' visit to Montaigne's chateau on 23 April 1931, the editors of the *Diary*, 4. 21, n6, observe that Leonard Woolf venerated Montaigne 'as the first civilised modern man', but it appears that the phrase was Virginia's.
2. Gillian Beer, *Arguing with the Past*, (1989), p. 188.
3. David Hume, 'On the Rise and Progress of the Arts and Sciences', in *Essays Moral, Political and Literary* [1741, 1742], (Oxford, 1963), pp. 134–5. See Graham Good, *The Observing Self: Rediscovering the Essay* (1988), p. 4, for the essay as a 'female' form.
4. Woolf quotes Montaigne in French from *Oeuvres complétes de Michel de Montaigne*, ed. Arthur Armaingaud (Paris: L. Conard, 1924), but the echoes in her own writing come from *Essays of Montaigne*, trans. Charles Cotton [1693], ed. William Carew Hazlitt for the Navarre Society (1923), in five volumes, which Woolf reviewed in the *TLS* January 1924, and which was revised and published in *The Common Reader: First Series*: 58–68. Montaigne is quoted throughout this work from the five-volume Navarre Society edition.
5. André Gide, *Montaigne* (1929), pp. 77–8. Terence Cave, 'Problems of Reading in the *Essais*', in I.D. McFarlane and Ian MacLean (eds), *Montaigne, Essays in Memory of Richard Sayce* (Oxford, 1982): 133–66, p. 153: 'It is as if the text were situated exactly at the mid-point between the writings it echoes and its potential readers, looking in both directions simultaneously' (p. 153). This brilliant essay has influenced all my thinking on Montaigne. See also Cathleen M. Bauschatz, 'Montaigne's Conception of Reading in the Context of Renaissance Poetics and Modern Criticism', in Susan R. Suleiman and Inge Crossman (eds), *The Reader in the Text: Essays on Audience and Interpretation* (Princeton, 1980): 264–91.
6. *The Essays of Virginia Woolf*, 3. 142. 'Reading', although published posthumously in *The Captain's Death-Bed and Other Essays* (1950), was probably written in 1919, at the beginning of the period when Woolf embarked on the project of *The Common Reader*.
7. *The Poems and Verses of John Keats*, ed. John Middleton Murry (1949), p. 211.
8. Nelly Furman, 'The politics of language: beyond the gender principle?' in Gayle Greene and Coppélia Kahn (eds), *Making a Difference: Feminist Literary Criticism* (1985): 59–79, p. 65.
9. Cixous, 'The Laugh of Medusa', in Marks and Courtivron (eds), *New French Feminisms*, pp. 245, 257, 250.
10. Furman, 'Textual Feminism', in McConnell-Ginet *et al.*, *Women and Language in Literature and Society*, p. 51.
11. Victoria Kahn, 'Habermas, Machiavelli, and the Humanist Critique of Ideology', *PMLA*, 105 (1990): 464–76, pp. 465, 469–70.
12. Terence Cave, *The Cornucopian Text: Problems of Writing in the French Renaissance* (Oxford, 1979), pp. 272–4. Cf. Timothy J. Reiss, 'Montaigne

and the Subject of Polity', in Patricia Parker and David Quint (eds), *Literary Theory / Renaissance Texts* (Baltimore, 1986): 115–49, pp. 133–4; also in the same collection Stephen Greenblatt, 'Psychoanalysis and Renaissance Culture': 210–24.

13. Ian Maclean, *The Renaissance Notion of Woman* (Cambridge, 1980); see also Alice A. Jardine, *Gynesis: Configurations of Woman and Modernity* (Ithaca, 1985), p. 45.

14. Donald M. Frame, *Montaigne's Discovery of Man* (New York, 1955), pp. 3–4, 131–4, 164–7.

15. Carol Clark, 'Talking About Souls: Montaigne on Human Psychology', in McFarlane and MacLean (eds), *Montaigne*: 57–76, p. 69.

16. Unpublished recollection (1989) by M.C. Bradbrook, now in the Girton College archive.

17. Walter J. Ong, *Rhetoric, Romance, and Technology* (Ithaca, 1971), pp. 15, 17, and ch. 5, 'Latin Language Study as a Renaissance Puberty Rite': 113–41, *passim.*

18. Genevieve Lloyd, *The Man of Reason* (1984), pp. 44–50, discusses Descartes' attitude to women in his choice of the vernacular for the *Discourse on Method.*

19. See Mary Ellen Lamb, 'The Cooke Sisters: Attitudes toward Learned Women', in Margaret Hannay (ed.), *Silent But for the Word: Tudor Women as Patrons, Translators and Writers of Religious Works* (Kent, Ohio, 1985): 107–25, pp. 115–17, for a discussion of Florio's dedication as implicitly misogynistic.

20. Richard H. Popkin, *The History of Scepticism from Erasmus to Spinoza* (Berkeley and Los Angeles, 1979), p. 44.

21. Walter J. Ong, *Ramus, Method and the Decay of Dialogue* (Cambridge, Mass., 1958), pp. 11–12; *Rhetoric, Romance and Technology*, pp. 17, 281.

22. Peter Sharratt, 'Peter Ramus and the Reform of the University: the Divorce of Philosophy and Eloquence', in Peter Sharratt (ed.), *French Renaissance Studies 1540–70* (Edinburgh, 1976): 4–20; Grafton and Jardine, *From Humanism to the Humanities*, pp. 196–7.

23. Montaigne, 'Of Repentance', IV. 208; 'Of the Institution of Children', I. 229–32. Roger Trinquet, *La Jeunesse de Montaigne* (Paris, 1972), pp. 350–80, *passim.*

24. Montaigne, 'Of the Institution of Children', I. 216–17; 'Of the Affection of Fathers to their Children', II. 314–15.

25. Sharratt, 'Peter Ramus and the Reform of the University: the Divorce of Philosophy and Eloquence', p. 18. James. J. Supple, *Arms Versus Letters: The Military and Literary Ideals of the 'Essais' of Montaigne* (Oxford, 1984), p. 268.

26. Ong, *Rhetoric, Romance, and Technology*, pp. 136–8.

27. Grafton and Jardine, *From Humanism to the Humanities*, pp. 29–57.

28. *The Oxford Book of War Poetry*, ed. Jon Stallworthy (Oxford, 1984), p. 269.

29. See Supple, *Arms Versus Letters*, pp. 11–12, 186–7, for Montaigne's ironic standpoint in this particular essay, and for a comprehensive discussion of the essayist's relation to aristocratic militarism.

30. Malcolm Smith, *Montaigne and the Roman Censors* (Genève, 1981), pp. 16–17, 23–35. Montaigne's works, like Gide's, were admired in his lifetime, but put on the Catholic Index after his death: in the essayist's case in 1676, in Gide's, in 1952, a year after his death.
31. Ben Jonson, *Discoveries* (1641) (Edinburgh, 1966), p. 31.
32. Jardine, *Gynesis: Configurations in Woman and Modernity*, p. 154, speaks of a denial of any absolute idea of truth as 'a valorization of nonmastery. And, as we know, a lack of mastery has, historically, always connoted the feminine'.
33. Cave, 'Problems of Reading in the *Essais*', in McFarlane and MacLean (eds), *Montaigne*, pp. 141, 152–3, 156.
34. John Gross, *The Rise and Fall of the Man of Letters* (1969), quoted in McNeillie, introduction to *The Common Reader: First Series*.
35. Margaret Whitford, 'Luce Irigaray's Critique of Rationality', in Morwenna Griffiths and Margaret Whitford (eds), *Feminist Perspectives in Philosophy* (1988): 109–30.
36. Jane Marcus, '"Taking the Bull by the Udders": Sexual Difference in Virginia Woolf—a Conspiracy Theory', in Marcus (ed.), *Virginia Woolf and Bloomsbury*: 146–69, pp. 155–62, demonstrates Woolf's strategies for undermining the single authoritarian lecturing voice.
37. Virginia Woolf, *Three Guineas* (Harmondsworth, 1977), pp. 102–3.
38. David Palmer, *The Rise of English Studies* (1965), pp. 6–11, 43, 44–5, 54–6, 78, 116, 136. Chris Baldick, *The Social Mission of English Studies 1848 1932* (Oxford, 1983), pp. 61, 67–9.
39. McGowan, *Montaigne's Deceits*, pp. 5–6.
40. Quoted in Barbara Lewalski, 'Of God and Good Women: The poems of Aemilia Lanyer', in Hannay (ed.), *Silent But for the Word*: 203–24, p. 208.
41. M.A. Screech, *Montaigne and Melancholy* (1983), pp. 134–6, discusses Montaigne's *'entre nous'*.
42. Jean Grimshaw, *Feminist Philosophers* (Brighton, 1986), p. 74, observes: 'It is problematic ... for women to seek simple inclusion in many philosophical theories or ideals, since these are often defined in opposition to what is female. But it is also problematic simply to assert the value of the feminine or to characterise it in ways which simply recapitulate versions of old polarisations between masculine and feminine.'
43. Maclean, *The Renaissance Notion of Woman*, pp. 1–27. See also Patricia Parker, *Literary Fat Ladies* (1987), p. 181. For a discussion of the relation of Aristotle's categories to twentieth-century philosophical thought see Jardine, *Gynesis: Configurarions of Woman and Modernity*, p. 72, referring particularly to the work of Hélène Cixous. Jonathan Dollimore, 'Different Desires: Subjectivity and Transgression in Wilde and Gide', *Textual Practice*, I: 1 (1987): 48–67, p. 56, and *Sexual Dissidence* (Oxford, 1991), pp. 64–8.
44. Cotton's translation of Montaigne's 'cabinet' is 'closet', but Carew Hazlitt alters the translation to 'water-closet', and I have kept this anchronistic reading as it seems to me true to the spirit of the essay, and Virginia Woolf would particularly have relished the change.

45. See D. Coleman, 'Montaigne's "Sur des Vers de Virgile": Taboo subject, Taboo author', in R.R. Bolgar (ed.), *Classical Influences on European Culture, A.D. 1500–1700* (Cambridge, 1976): 135–40, for Montaigne's concealed questioning of gender division through his references to Martial: 'Homosexuality plus the opening up of whole new dimensions around male and female rôles in sexual matters is left in the reader's mind' (p. 139).
46. Holograph Reading Notes, Berg, XXIII.
47. Jacob Burckhardt, *The Civilization of the Renaissance in Italy* (New York, 1954), pp. 292–6.
48. Maclean, *The Renaissance Notion of Woman*, p. 8.
49. Supple, *Arms Versus Letters*, pp. 237–9, 242–3. McGowan, *Montaigne's Deceits*, p. 133.
50. Emily Davies, *The Higher Education of Women* (1866), ed. Janet Howarth (London and Ronceverte, 1988), pp. 162–3.
51. McGowan, *Montaigne's Deceits*, p. 129, 143. Maclean, *The Renaissance Notion of Woman*, p. 86, observes: 'An area of humanistic thought which promises to open the way for a new interpetation of woman is historicism. If this were to be applied to an ancient or even theological text, it would reveal the relativity between statements about woman and the cultural identity of their author'. Maclean sees some evidence – in the form of an attack on the Scholastic synthesis outlined in his book – of revisionary thinking about women in the period 1580–1630 (p. 87).
52. Jardine, *Gynesis: Configurations of Woman and Modernity*, p. 147, discusses in Heidegger, Nietzsche and Freud the way in which 'this stand against the historically solid alliance between truth and experience has been a stand against humanism' and claims that this is 'a positive step for women, in most ways'.
53. Woolf, 'The Elizabethan Lumber Room', *CR I*. 43–4.

CHAPTER 3: VIRGINIA WOOLF READS JOHN DONNE

1. Thomas Docherty, *John Donne, Undone* (1986), esp. pp. 52–71; Stanley Fish, 'Masculine Persuasive Force: Donne and Verbal Power', in Elizabeth D. Harvey and Katharine Eisaman Maus (eds), *Soliciting Interpretation: Literary Theory and Seventeenth-Century English Poetry* (Chicago, 1990): 223–52, p. 228; John Carey, *John Donne: Life, Mind and Art* (1981), pp. 91, 117 and *passim*; Carey's view of Donne was early countered by Annabel Patterson in 'Misinterpretable Donne: The Testimony of the Letters', *John Donne Journal*, 1 (1982): 37–53.
2. 'Donne's Poetical Works', *The National Magazine and Monthly Critic*, IX (1838): 374–8, in A.J. Smith (ed.), *John Donne: The Critical Heritage* (1975), p. 367.
3. Kathleen Tillotson, 'Donne's Poetry in the Nineteenth Century (1800–72)', in John R. Roberts (ed.), *Essential Articles for the Study of John Donne's Poetry* (Hassocks, 1975): 20–33, p. 31.
4. Wilbur Sanders, *John Donne's Poetry* (Cambridge, 1971), pp. 104, 105.

5. Carey, *John Donne: Life, Mind and Art*, pp. 105–6.
6. Joan Bennet, 'The Love Poetry of John Donne: A Reply to Mr. C.S. Lewis', *Seventeenth Century Studies presented to Sir Herbert Grierson*, (Oxford, 1938): 85–104, p. 91, and, in the same volume, C.S. Lewis, 'Donne and Love Poetry in the Seventeenth Century': 64–84, pp. 75–6.
7. Alexander Sackton, 'Donne and the Privacy of Verse', *SEL*, 7 (1967): 67–82; Alan McColl, 'The Circulation of Donne's Poems in Manuscript', in A.J. Smith (ed.), *John Donne: Essays in Celebration* (1972): 28–46, pp. 32–4.
8. Izaak Walton, *The Life of John Donne, DD*. (1865), p. 35; Ilona Bell, '"UNDER YE RAGE OF A HOTT SONN & YR EYES": John Donne's Love Letters to Ann More', in Claude J. Summers and Ted-Larry Pebworth (eds), *The Eagle and the Dove* (Columbia, 1986): 25–52, p. 41.
9. Bell, '"UNDER YE RAGE OF A HOTT SONN & YR EYES": John Donne's Love Letters to Ann More', pp. 33, 35.
10. John Donne, *A Sermon of Commemoration of the Lady Danvers, late Wife of Sir John Danvers, Preach'd at Chilsey, where she was lately buried*', (Together with other Commemorations of Her; By her Sonne G: Herbert), (1627), p. 152.
11. Helen Gardner (ed.), *The Elegies and the Songs and Sonnets* (Oxford, 1965), Appendix C: 248–58, 'Lady Bedford and Mrs Herbert', p. 251: 'It is possible that on other occasions she [Lucy Bedford] showed him others of her "compositions", or that they wrote poems on similar themes or answering each other.'
12. Arthur F. Marotti, 'John Donne and the Rewards of Patronage', in Guy Fitch Lytle and Stephen Orgel (eds), *Patronage in the Renaissance* (Princeton, 1981): 207–34, p. 224.
13. Love, *Scribal Publication in Seventeenth-Century England*, p. 151.
14. Donne, *Poetical Works*, ed. Herbert J. C. Grierson (Oxford, 1921), p. 288. All quotations from Donne's poetry are from this edition.
15. The relevant manuscripts are listed in Peter Beal, *Index of English Literary Manuscripts* (1987), I. 292–6, and 414–71. The extra stanza, beginning 'Lie stille, my dove, why dost thou rise?' was set by John Dowland, *A Pilgrim's Solace* (London 1612), and Orlando Gibbons, *The First Set of Madrigals and Motets* (London 1612), and has been thought not to be by Donne, although in manuscript miscellanies dating from the 1630s it was sometimes included as a first stanza (C.F. Main, 'New Texts of Donne', *SB*, 9 (1957): 225–33, pp. 229–30). In BL Add. MS 25,707, the stanza is in a different hand in the margin, with a mark to show that it should go at the beginning of the poem. But what is interesting is the variety of headings given to the poem with the additional stanza, and the disagreements they evince about whether the main poetic voice is that of:
   i) a man: 'A Gentleman to his Mrs, being a bedd with him that she wold not rise', (Sloane MS 1792, ff. 11v–12. Beal, I. 479)
   ii) a woman: 'At last they enioye one the other, but his business enforseth him to make an early hast, Her lines upon it', and a narrative which involves his answering her: 'At the next enoiyment

shee quits his rizing with an erlyer. His lines' (Rosenbach Founda-
tion, MS 243/4, p. 73, Beal I. 480).

iii) Donne himself and a lady: 'Dr Dunne at his Mistris rysing'
(Folger MS V. a. 262, p. 102, Beal, I. 478), and 'Dr Dunne of his mrs
rising' (Folger, MS V. a. 345, p. 237, Beal, I. 478).

16. Samuel Johnson, 'Cowley,' *Lives of the English Poets* (1964), I. 15; see
William R. Keast, 'Johnson's Criticism of the Metaphysical Poets',
in Roberts (ed.), *Essential Articles for the Study of John Donne*: 11–19.

17. *The Notebooks of Samuel Taylor Coleridge, 1794–1804*, in Smith (ed.),
*John Donne: The Critical Heritage*, p. 270.

18. Journal C, *The Journals and Miscellaneous Notebooks of Ralph Waldo
Emerson*, in Smith (ed.), *John Donne: The Critical Heritage*, p. 304.

19. Lewis, 'Donne and Love Poetry in the Seventeenth Century', p. 64.
See Tillotson, 'Donne's Poetry in the Nineteenth Century (1800–72)',
p. 30, for some nineteenth-century versions of this tradition.

20. For a different view, see Edward le Comte, 'Jack Donne: From Rake
to Husband', in Peter Amadeus Fiore (ed.), *Just So Much Honor*,
(University Park, 1972): 9–32.

21. The original letter, quoted in my text, is from Donne to Sir Robert
More, his brother-in-law, in *The Loseley Manuscripts*, ed. by Alfred
John Kempe (1835), p. 345; quoted in Edmund Gosse, *The Life and
Letters of John Donne* (1899), II. 48, and by Woolf in Berg XX, with
the note 'of his wife'.

22. Maureen Sabine, *Feminine Engendered Faith: The Poetry of John Donne
and Richard Crashaw* (1992), p. 44 and *passim*.

23. See Patricia Thomson, 'John Donne and the Countess of Bedford',
*MLR*, 44 (1949): 329–40, p. 333; for reading aloud in this period see
William Nelson, 'From "Listen, Lordings" to "Dear Reader"', *Uni-
versity of Toronto Quarterly*, 46 (1976–7): 111–24.

24. John Donne, *Letters to Severall Persons of Honour*, published by John
Donne [the younger], (1651), p. 272.

25. Gosse, *Life and Letters of John Donne*, I. 8.

26. *Tixall Letters: or the Correspondence of the Aston Family*, ed. Arthur
Clifford, (1815), I. 147.

27. David Norbrook, 'The Monarchy of Wit and the Republic of Letters: Donne's Politics', in Harvey and Maus (eds), *Soliciting Interpretation*: 3–36, p. 6, queries 'the assumption that Donne and his
contemporaries were fundamentally irrationalists, their minds daz-
zled by spectacular images of authority, [which] has influenced the
reading of Donne's poetry and prose.'

28. W. Milgate, 'The Early References to John Donne', *N&Q*, 195 (1950):
229–3, 246–7, 290–2, 381–3; p. 383, concludes that Donne's individuality was the most striking impression left on his contemporaries.
See also Josephine Miles, 'Ifs, Ands, Buts for the Reader of Donne',
in Fiore, *Just so Much Honor*: 272–91.

29. John Donne, 'Sermon Preached upon Whitsunday' [? At St. Paul's,
1622], in G.R. Potter and E.M. Simpson (eds), *The Sermons of John
Donne* (Berkeley, 1959): V. 58–76, p. 71.

30. Brenda R. Silver, *Virginia Woolf's Reading Notebooks* (Princeton, 1983),

p. 228, quoting from MHP/B2o.

31. Donne, *Letters to Severall Persons of Honour*, p. 25.
32. See Josephine Miles, 'Ifs, Ands, Buts, for the Reader of Donne', p. 276, on the prose language structures which dominate Donne's poetry.
33. 'The Flea', p. 36; 'The Good-morrow', p. 1; 'Lovers infiniteness', p. 16.
34. Richard B. Wollman, 'The "Press and the Fire": Print and Manuscript Culture in Donne's Circle', *SEL*, 33 (1993): 85–97, p. 87, 89–91. I am indebted to this excellent article throughout this section, although Wollman does not talk about women readers.
35. Donne, *Letters to Severall Persons of Honour*, pp. 44–5.
36. Lynette McGrath, '"Let Us Have Our Libertie Againe": Amelia Lanier's 17th-Century Feminist Voice', *Women's Studies*, 20 (1992): 331–48, pp. 345, 341; cf. Elaine V. Beilin, *Redeeming Eve: Women Writers of the English Renaissance* (Princeton, 1987), pp. 177–207; Lewalski, 'Re-writing Patriarchy and Patronage: Margaret Clifford, Anne Clifford, and Aemilia Lanyer', pp. 97–106.
37. Lewalski, 'Of God and Good Women: The poems of Aemilia Lanyer', in Hannay (ed.), *Silent But for the Word*, pp. 220–4.
38. Quoted in Thomson, 'Donne and the Countess of Bedford', p. 335. See also Love, *Scribal Publication in Seventeenth-Century England*, pp. 51–2.
39. Love, *Scribal Publication in Seventeenth-Century England*, p. 219; Arthur F. Marotti, *John Donne, Coterie Poet* (Madison, 1986).
40. Woolf, 'Indiscretions', *Essays*, 3. 463.
41. *The Essayes of Michael Lord of Montaigne*, trans. by John Florio (1928 [1603]), I. 1–11.
42. John Donne, *Devotions Upon Emergent Occasions*, ed. John Sparrow (Cambridge, 1923), p. 8.
43. Richard Helgerson, *Self-Crowned Laureates* (Berkeley and London, 1983), p. 33.
44. Gosse, *Life and Letters of John Donne* (1899), I. 17–18.
45. Barbara Kiefer Lewalski, *Writing Women in Jacobean England* (Cambridge, Mass., 1993), pp. 2–4, p. 11: 'Obviously these Jacobean women did not and could not change their world, but they were able to imagine and represent a better one.'
46. Sir Philip Sidney, *An Apology for Poetry*, ed. by Geoffrey Shepherd (Manchester, 1973), pp. 138–9.
47. Margaret Maurer, 'The Real Presence of Lucy Russell, Countess of Bedford, and the terms of John Donne's "Honour is so Sublime Perfection"', *ELH*, 47 (1980): 205–34, p. 214.
48. Donne, *Letters to Severall Persons of Honour*, p. 11. John Carey, 'John Donne's Newsless Letters', in *Essays and Studies*, 34, ed. Anne Barton (1981): 45–65, pp. 54–5; Claude Guillén, 'Notes toward the Study of the Renaissance Letter', in Barbara Kiefer Lewalski (ed.), *Renaissance Genres: Essays on Theory, History, and Interpretation* (Cambridge, Mass., 1986): 70–101, p. 79, underestimates the complexity of Donne's subject-matter in his verse letters to women.
49. Sackton, 'Donne and the Privacy of Verse', p. 80.
50. Donne, *A Sermon of Commemoration of the Lady Danvers*, p. 131.

51. R.C. Bald, *Donne and the Drurys* (Cambridge, 1959), p. 64, note *.
52. Kathleen Kelly, 'Conversion of the Reader in Donne's "Anatomy of the World"', in Summers and Pebworth (eds), *The Eagle and the Dove*: 147–56, p. 56.
53. Anna Jameson, *The Loves of the Poets* (1829), I. ix.
54. John Donne, *Pseudo-martyr* (1610), p. 393.
55. Sabine, *Feminine Engendered Faith: The Poetry of John Donne and Richard Crashaw*, p. ix.·
56. *Dr. Faustus*, A- and B-texts (1604, 1616), ed. David Bevington and Eric Rasmussen (Manchester, 1993), II. i. 130.
57. Docherty, *John Donne, Undone*, p. 60.
58. John Donne, *Biathanatos* (1647), Preface.
59. In the Monk's House Catalogue the Oxford *Donne* published in 1929 has 'Leonard Woolf 1929' inscribed in his own hand. But Woolf's usual practice was to use more than one edition. Her own reading of Donne began many years earlier.
60. For a discussion of *Biathanatos* within a Libertine tradition and also of its dissemination in the later seventeenth century, see George Williamson, 'The Libertine Donne', *PQ* 13 (1934): 276–91.
61. Sparrow, *Devotions Upon Emergent Occasions*, pp. xx–xxii.
62. Annabel Patterson, 'All Donne', in Harvey and Maus (eds), *Soliciting Interpretations*: 37–67, p. 42.
63. *Paradoxes, Problems, Essayes, Characters*, Written by Dr. Donne (1652), p. 1.
64. See Louise A. DeSalvo, 'As "Miss Jan Says": Virginia Woolf's Early Journals', in Marcus (ed.), *Virginia Woolf and Bloomsbury*: 96–124, pp. 113–18, for a placing of this statement in a context of rebellion against Leslie Stephen's agnosticism.

## CHAPTER 4: LETTERS AS RESISTANCE

1. Margaret W. Ferguson, 'A Room Not Their Own: Renaissance Women as Readers and Writers', in Clayton Koelb and Susan Noakes (eds), *The Comparative Perspective on Literature* (Ithaca, 1988): 93–116; Frances Mossiker, *Madame de Sévigné: A Life and Letters* (New York, 1985), p. 22. See also Sidonie Smith, *A Poetics of Women's Autobiography: Marginality and the Fictions of Self-Representation* (Bloomington, 1987), p. 5.
2. Dorothy Osborne, *Letters to Sir William Temple*, ed. Kenneth Parker (Harmondsworth, 1987), p. 75.
3. MHP/B/2p, also MHP/B3c.
4. Francis Osborn[e], *Advice to a Son* (Oxford, 1658), p. 17. Guillén, 'Notes toward the Study of the Renaissance Letter', pp. 83–4, observes that Donne's verse letters often share this characteristic, but suggests also that orality is traditionally part of a literary use of voice in letters by men. Guillén recognises that letters mark an important transitional stage in the 'passage from orality to writing' which is why they are significant for women in the Renaissance period.

5. *The Letters and Literary Remains of Edward Fitzgerald*, ed. William Aldis Wright (1989), I. 374.
6. Elizabeth Goldsmith, 'Authority, Authenticity, and the Publication of Letters by Women', in Goldsmith (ed.), *Writing the Female Voice: Essays on Epistolary Literature* (Boston, 1989): 46–59, p. 54.
7. Louise K. Horowitz, 'The Correspondence of Madame de Sévigné: Lettres or Belles-Lettres?', *French Forum*, 6:1 (1981): 13–25, p. 17.
8. Madame de Sévigné, *Lettres*, Texte établi et annoté par Gerard-Gailly (Paris, 1953), I. 248: 'Mon Dieu, ma bonne, que vos lettres sont aimables! il y a des endroits dignes de l'impression: un de ces jours vous trouverez qu'un de vos amis vous aura trahie.' The translations in the text are my own.
9. MHP/B.2c, quoted in Silver, introduction to 'Notes for Reading at Random', p. 370.
10. 'Madame de Sévigné', *The Death of the Moth and Other Essays* (1942): 37–41, pp. 40–41.
11. Catharine R. Stimpson, 'The Female Sociograph: The Theater of Virginia Woolf's Letters', in Donna C. Stanton (ed.), *The Female Autograph* (Chicago, 1984): 168–79. Stimpson observes that Woolf's letters 'exemplify a particular women's text, one that is neither wholly private nor wholly public. They occupy a psychological and rhetorical middle space between what she wrote for herself and what she produced for a general audience'. Moreover, in form they also occupy a middle ground 'between the "literal" and the "literary," those two frayed poles with which some stake out the territories of discourse' (pp. 168, 175). Annabel Patterson, *Censorship and Interpretation* (Madison, 1984), p. 204: 'The letter poses the problem of how literary and extraliterary motives intersect in genre formation.'
12. Silver, introduction to 'Notes for Reading at Random', in '"Anon" and "The Reader"', p. 370.
13. *Lettres*, II. 858: 'Mon fils me traduira la satire contre les folles amours [et] devroit la faire lui-même, ou du moins en profiter.'
14. *Lettres*, I. 249: 'Il disoit les plus folles choses du monde, et moi aussi; c'étoit une scène digne de Molière.'
15. *Lettres*, I. 183: 'Voilà un beau songe, voilà un beau sujet de roman ou de tragédie.' Horowitz, 'The Correspondence of Madame de Sévigné: Lettres or Belles-Lettres?', p. 22.
16. Woolf, 'The Reader', in Silver, '"Anon" and "The Reader"', p. 428.
17. Patricia Meyer Spacks, 'Female Resources: Epistles, Plot and Power', in Goldsmith (ed.), *Writing the Female Voice*, pp. 67, 75.
18. Alan Duguld McKillop, *Samuel Richardson: Printer and Novelist* (Chapel Hill, 1936), p. 184.
19. Sainte-Beuve, 'Madame de Sévigné', *Fin de Portraits Littéraires: Portraits de femmes, Oeuvres*, (Paris, 1960): II. 991–1007, p. 1007.
20. Christopher Hill, 'Clarissa Harlowe and Her Times', in *Puritanism and Revolution* (1958): 367–94, p. 380.
21. Samuel Richardson, *Familiar Letters on Important Occasions* [1741], introduced by Brian C. Downs (1958).
22. Janet Gurkin Altman, *Epistolarity: Approaches to a Form* (Columbus,

Ohio, 1982), p. 212; Horowitz, 'The Correspondence of Madame de Sévigné: Lettres or Belles-Lettres?', p. 25: 'Letter writing shares several distinct goals: the transfer of information, the need to communicate and maintain a certain relationship (however altered), but also the experience of writing free of professional status and obligation.'

23. 'Dorothy Osborne's Letters', *CR II*, p. 64.
24. *Letters of the Lady Brilliana Harley*, ed. by Thomas Taylor Lewis (1854), p. 7.
25. *Lettres*, II. 755: 'Enfin je me réveillai beaucoup par cette dispute: sans cela j'étois morte.'
26. *Lettres*, I. 124: 'Qui m'a paru abîmée en Dieu; elle étoit à la messe comme en extase'; 'Je crois que le milieu de ces extrémités est toujours le meilleur.'
27. *Lettres*, II. 892: 'La tendresse que je l'ai pour vous, ma chère bonne, me semble mêlée avec mon sang, et confondue dans la moelle de mes os; elle est devenue moi-même, je le sens comme je le dis.'
28. *Lettres*, II. 455: 'Pour moi, je ne veux qu'une feuille de votre écriture . . . car je préfère votre santé à toutes choses, à ma propre satisfaction, qui peut être solide quand vous vous porterez bien.'
29. *Lettres*, I. 191–2: 'Si vous songez à moi, ma pauvre bonne, soyez assurée aussi que je pense continuellement à vous: c'est ce que les dévots appellent une pensée habituelle; c'est ce qu'il faudroit avoir pour Dieu, si l'on faisoit son devoir. Rien ne me donne de distraction; je suis toujours avec vous; je vois ce carrosse qui avance toujours et qui n'approchera jamais de moi; je suis toujours dans les grands chemins; il me semble même que j'ai quelquefois peur qu'il ne verse.'
30. Donne, *Letters to Severall Persons of Honour*, p. 11.
31. Harriet Ray Allentuch, 'My Daughter/Myself: Emotional Roots of Madame de Sévigné's art', *MLQ*, 43: 2(1982): 121–37, p. 123: 'Madame de Sévigné sought the emotional experience of passion with her daughter; to state less would require the amputation of much of her writing'.
32. *Lettres*, I. 203: 'Je suis bien assurée qu'il me viendra des lettres; je ne doute point que vous [ne m']ayez écrit; mais je les attends, et je ne les ai pas: il faut se consoler, et s'amuser en vous écrivant.'
33. Patterson, *Censorship and Interpretation*, pp. 8–10, 95.
34. Woolf, 'Notes for Reading at Random', in Silver, '"Anon" and "The Reader"', pp. 378, 379, n8. The note to compare Lady Ann Bacon with Madame de Sévigné is in the A version (A6, 8–9) of 'Anon', see Silver, '"Anon" and "The Reader"', p. 412, n42.
35. Mary A. Favret, *Romantic Correspondence: Women, Politics and the Fiction of Letters* (Cambridge, 1993), discusses the revolutionary potential of letters in the Romantic period, which has, I suggest, some precedent in seventeenth-century letters by women.
36. James Spedding, *The Letters and Life of Francis Bacon*, (1861) I. 113.
37. Elspeth Graham, Hilary Hinds, Elaine Hobby and Helen Wilcox (eds), *Her Own Life: Autobiographical Writings by Seventeenth-Century Englishwomen*, (1989), pp. 2, 10, 16: 'To write was an act of resistance in itself' (p. 118).

38. P.J. Croft, *The Poems of Robert Sidney* (Oxford, 1984), pp. 77–8.
39. Margaret Cavendish, Duchess of Newcastle, *Sociable Letters* (1664), p. 14.
40. *The George Sand–Gustave Flaubert Letters*, trans. by Aimée L. McKenzie (1922), p. 121–2.
41. Ong, *Orality and Literacy*, p. 163.
42. *The George Sand–Gustave Flaubert Letters*, p. 11.
43. Jane Marcus, '"No More Horses": Woolf on Art and Propaganda', *Women's Studies*, 4: 2–3 (1977), p. 274, quoted in Stimpson, 'The Female Sociograph: The Theater of Virginia Woolf's Letters', p. 171.


CHAPTER 5: DIARIES: PEPYS AND WOOLF


1. *The Diary of Samuel Pepys*, ed. Robert Latham and William Matthews (1970–83), IX. 564–5.
2. Patricia Meyer Spacks, 'Selves in Hiding', in Estelle C. Jelinek, *Women's Autobiography: Essays in Criticism* (Bloomington, 1980): 112–32, p. 112.
3. Louis A. Renza, 'The Veto of the Imagination: A Theory of Autobiography', in James Olney (ed.), *Autobiography: Essays Theoretical and Critical* (Princeton, 1980): 268–95, pp. 280–1.
4. Edwin Chappell, *The Secrecy of the Diary*: A Paper read before the Samuel Pepys Club, 24 November 1933, privately printed, pp. 3, 4, 6.
5. Robert Louis Stevenson, 'Samuel Pepys', *Cornhill Magazine*, XLIV (July 1891): 31–46, p. 36. Walter Ong, *Interfaces of the Word* (Ithaca, 1977), pp. 79, 102–3, on the diary as a form which requires the writer to 'fictionalize' readers.
6. Osborne, *Advice to a Son*, p. 10.
7. Woolf, 'Papers on Pepys', (first published in the *TLS*, 4 April 1918), *Essays*, 2. 235.
8. Monks House Catalogue, 2nd lot: 'Books from the library of the late V. and L. Woolf', under 'Family Items from LS', p. 6: 'Pepys (Samuel) Diaries and Correspondence. 4 vols. 8vo. 1/2 morocco 5th Ed. 1856. LS – some notes and figures.' This was presumably the copy used by Leslie Stephen for his entry on Pepys in the *Dictionary of National Biography*.
9. Clive Bell, *Old Friends* (1956), p. 97.
10. Coleridge, *Marginalia*, reproduced in *N&Q*, First Series, VI, no. 149 (1852): 213–16, p. 214.
11. Christopher Hill, 'Samuel Pepys (1633–1703)', *Collected Essays* (Brighton, 1985), I. 258–73, p. 258.
12. Louise A. DeSalvo, '1897: Virginia Woolf at Fifteen', in Marcus (ed.), *Virginia Woolf: A Feminist Slant*: 78–108, for an account of Woolf's reading at this period, which does not, however, discuss her reading of Pepys.
13. The book was H. B. Wheatley (ed.), *Occasional Papers Read by Members at the Meetings of the Samuel Pepys Club*, vol. I: 1903–14 (Chiswick, 1917).

14. Woolf, 'Anon', in Silver, '"Anon" and "The Reader"', pp. 389, 414, n49. The Pepys quotation is from MHP/B2c; Nora Eisenstein, 'Virginia Woolf's Last Words on Words: *Between the Acts* and "Anon"', in Marcus, *New Feminist Essays on Virginia Woolf*: 253–66, pp. 257–62.
15. Jed, *Chaste thinking: The Rape of Lucretia and the Birth of Humanism*, pp. 14, 83–7.
16. Shakespeare's *Collected Works* in three volumes are in the Pepys library. There is no mention in the *Diary* of Pepys's having seen *Much Ado* although he saw Glapthorne's imitation of it, *Wit in a Constable* (1640) on 23 May 1662: 'The first time that it is acted; but so silly a play I never saw I think in my life' (III. 90 and n2).
17. 'A Character of King Charles II', in *The Complete Works of George Savile, first Marquess of Halifax*, ed. Walter Raleigh (Oxford, 1912): 187–208, p. 202.
18. Marjorie Astin, *Mrs Pepys Her Book* (1929), Foreword, p. 5.
19. Dale Spender, *The Diary of Elizabeth Pepys* (1991), p. 201.
20. Marcus, *Virginia Woolf and the Languages of Patriarchy*, p. 84.
21. John Morgan, *Godly learning: Puritan Attitudes towards Reason, Learning and Education, 1560–1640* (Cambridge, 1986), p. 21.
22. Pepys, *Diary*, IX. 21–2 and n2, and 58; Stevenson, 'Samuel Pepys', p. 33; Francis Barker, *The Tremulous Private Body* (1984), pp. 1–14 and *passim*.
23. Hill, 'Samuel Pepys (1633–1703)', p. 269.
24. Ong, *Interfaces of the Word*, p. 80.
25. H. Porter Abbott, *Diary Fiction: Writing as Action* (Ithaca, 1984), p. 86.
26. Marcus, *Virginia Woolf and the Languages of Patriarchy*, p. 99.
27. Henry B. Wheatley, 'The Growth of the Fame of Samuel Pepys', in *Occasional Papers of the Samuel Pepys Club*, vol. I: 1903–1917: 156–73, p. 168.

## CHAPTER 6: BUNYAN AND VIRGINIA WOOLF

1. Rosenbaum, *Victorian Bloomsbury*, p. 22, points out not only how strong Evangelical Puritanism was within Virginia Woolf's Clapham sect ancestry, but also its influence on other members of the Bloomsbury group. Maynard Keynes's grandfather had been a minister in Bunyan's church.
2. Silver, *Virginia Woolf's Reading Notebooks*, pp. 121, 67–8, 21–4.
3. *Catalogue of Books from the Library of Leonard and Virginia Woolf*, Monk's House Catalogue, p. 8.
4. Margaret Olafson Thickstun, 'From Christiana to Stand-fast: Subsuming the Feminine in *The Pilgrim's Progress*', *SEL*, 26 (1986): 439–53. Cf. Kathleen M. Swaim, 'Mercy and the Feminine Heroic in the Second Part of *Pilgrim's Progress*', *SEL*, 30 (1990): 386–409.
5. Carole Levin, 'John Foxe and the Responsibilities of Queenship', in Rose (ed.), *Women in the Middle Ages and the Renaissance*: 113–33.
6. John R. Knott, Jr., '"Thou must live upon my Word": Bunyan and

the Bible', in N. H. Keeble (ed.), *John Bunyan: Conventicle and Parnassus* (Oxford, 1988): 153–70, p. 153.

7. John Foxe, *Acts and Monuments* (1641) [*Book of Martyrs*], III. 796: 'This prison was within a Court where the Prebends chambers were, being a vault beneath the ground, and being before the window inclosed with a pale of height; by estimation, foure foot and a half, and distant from the same three foot, so that she looking from beneath, might onely see such as stood at the pale. . . . Her lying in that prison was onely upon a little short straw between a paire of stocks and a stone wall.' This edition of Foxe carries the title by which the book was always known, and which will be used in this text: the *Book of Martyrs*. For the conditions of Bunyan's own imprisonment, see Christopher Hill, *A Turbulent, Seditious, and Factious People: John Bunyan and his Church 1628–1688* (Oxford, 1988), pp. 120–2.

8. Hill, *A Turbulent, Seditious, and Factious People*, pp. 158 n3, 214.

9. Roger Pooley, '*Grace Abounding* and the New Sense of Self', in Anne Laurence, W.R. Owens and Stuart Sim (eds), *John Bunyan and his England 1628–88* (London and Ronceverte, 1990): 105–14.

10. John Bunyan, *A Relation of My Imprisonment*, in *Grace Abounding to the Chief of Sinners*, ed. Roger Sharrock (Oxford, 1962), pp. 117–18.

11. John Brown, *John Bunyan (1628–1688): His Life, Times and Work*, revised Frank Mott Harrison (1928), pp. 114–17; see Hill, *A Turbulent, Seditious, and Factious People*, p. 14.

12. Stephen Greenblatt, *Renaissance Self-Fashioning: From More to Shakespeare* (Chicago, 1980), p. 98.

13. William Haller, *Foxe's Book of Martyrs and the Elect Nation* (1963), p. 178.

14. Quoted in Nigel Smith, 'Bunyan and the Language of the Body in Seventeenth-Century England', in Laurence *et al.*, *John Bunyan and his England 1628–88*: 161–74, p. 163.

15. Bunyan, *Grace Abounding*, p. 105.

16. E.P. Thompson, *The Making of the English Working Class* (1963), p. 31.

17. John R. Knott, Jr., *The Sword of the Spirit: Puritan Responses to the Bible* (Chicago, 1980), p. 25.

18. *The Byble: that is/the holy Scripture of the Olde and New Testament*, trans. Myles Coverdale ([Cologne or Marburg?], 1535).

19. Quoted in Gordon Campbell, 'Fishing in Other Men's Waters: Bunyan and the Theologians', in Keeble (ed.), *John Bunyan: Conventicle and Parnassus*: 137–51, p. 140.

20. Roger Sharrock, '"When I first took my Pen in hand": Bunyan and the Book', in Keeble (ed.), *John Bunyan: Conventicle and Parnassus*: 71–90, p. 83, points out that Bunyan was at pains to emphasise throughout his writings the extreme poverty of his personal circumstances, indeed possibly to exaggerate them, within a tradition of the abasement of the poor man who is raised through the graciousness of the Lord.

21. *The Holie Bible: conteyning the olde Testament and the newe* (1568).

22. Knott, *The Sword of the Spirit*, p. 6; Thomas Hyatt Luxton, 'The Pilgrim's Passive Progress: Luther and Bunyan on Talking and Doing, Word and Way', *ELH*, 53 (1986): 73–98, p. 84.
23. Owen C. Watkins, *The Puritan Experience* (1972), p. 210; Knott, *The Sword of the Spirit*, pp. 24, 29. Showalter, 'Towards a Feminist Poetics', p. 129, notes the use of the same Biblical metaphor in feminist criticism. Rosenbaum, *Victorian Bloomsbury*, p. 22, connects Leonard Woolf's Hebraism with a tradition of Evangelical Puritanism.
24. John Bunyan, *The Pilgrim's Progress*, ed. N.H. Keeble (Oxford, 1984), pp. 128, 277 n128; see Valentine Cunningham, 'Glossing and Glozing: Bunyan and Allegory', in Keeble, *John Bunyan: Conventicle and Parnassus*: 217–40, p. 230, for a different interpretation of Christian's use of the Psalms in this passage.
25. Sharrock, '"When I first took my Pen in hand": Bunyan and the Book', p. 87: Bunyan added the marginal glosses after the first edition. When Bunyan made the decision to gloss his allegory with Biblical texts, he followed a device used by all the early translators of the Bible in which the reader is pointed to parallel texts – (Coverdale: 1535 and Great Bible: 1539) – and/or given interpretative comment (Geneva: 1560 and Bishops' Bible: 1568). Such guidance subtly directs the reader's interpretation of the central text. The consequent releasing of multiple meanings is evident in Bunyan's use of Psalm 38:4 to gloss the first paragraph of *The Pilgrim's Progress*, not least because of a difference between the various Bibles Bunyan might have known in the numbering of the Psalms. The Coverdale Bible follows the Vulgate: Psalm 38 is numbered 37. Bunyan's gloss of Psalm 38 [Coverdale 37] would thus include by implication a reference to Psalm 39 [Coverdale 38]. Although it is not certain which Bible Bunyan used (see Campbell, 'Fishing in Other Men's Waters', p. 139), the Coverdale Bible would have appealed to him because it relies on Tyndale's translations and employs a deliberately colloquial language for a newly literate readersip.
26. Watkins, *The Puritan Experience*, p. 211, stresses Puritan dependence on the reader's familiarity with Biblical texts.
27. The Geneva Bible (1560) replaces the native 'wickednesses' with the Latinate 'iniquities', suggesting that the translators already in 1560 envisaged a more educated readership.
28. Knott, '"Thou must live upon my Word"', p. 164, lists the many possible Biblical sources for the idea of pilgrimage, but he omits the particular case of this translation.
29. The Geneva Bible makes the point even more clearly: 'And the Lord aunswered me, and said: Write the vision, and make it plaine upon tables, that *he may runne that readeth it.*'
30. It is possible that Bunyan at some point read Sir Thomas Wyatt's paraphrases of the Penitential Psalms (printed in 1549). If so he would have found in Wyatt's linking stanzas for Psalm 38, a similar concealed reference to Coverdale 39. Rebholz believes that Wyatt used the Coverdale translation:

Like as the *pilgrim* that in a long way
Fainting for heat, provoked by some wind
In some fresh shade lieth down at mids of day,
So doth of David the wearied voice and mind
Take breath of sighs when he had sung this lay
Under such shade as sorrow hath assigned;
And as the t'one still minds his voyage end,
So doth the t'other to mercy still pretend.

*Sir Thomas Wyatt: The Complete Poems*, ed. by R. A. Rebholz (Harmondsworth, 1978), p. 206, my italics. Here Wyatt, like Bunyan in *The Pilgrim's Progress*, has separated the Psalmist from his own metaphor of the pilgrim: they are two distinct people, narrator and wayfarer, the dreamer and Christian. Wyatt sees the Psalmist's burden as one of articulation.

31. Stanley Fish, *Self-Consuming Artefacts* (Berkeley, 1972), p. 240.
32. Marcus, *Virginia Woolf and the Languages of Patriarchy*, p. 94, points out that Mrs Manresa's name recalls Manresa in Spain where the *Spiritual Exercises* of St Ignatius were composed, so that the Tyndale allusion contributes to a web of theological associations which are all, in Woolf's novel, connected with women's history and relation to language.
33. Thickstun, 'From Christiana to Stand-fast: Subsuming the Feminine in *The Pilgrim's Progress*', p. 451.
34. N.H. Keeble, '"Here is her Glory, even to be under Him": The Feminine in the Thought and Work of John Bunyan', in Laurence *et al.*, *John Bunyan and his England 1628–88*: 131–48, p. 133; Elspeth Graham, 'Authority, Resistance and Loss: Gendered Difference in the Writings of John Bunyan and Hannah Allen', in the same volume: 115–30, p. 125.
35. Deborah Cameron, *Feminism and Linguistic Theory* (1985), pp. 91–113. Adrienne Munich, 'Notorious signs, feminist criticism and literary tradition', in Greene and Kahn, *Making a Difference: Feminist Literary Criticism*: 238–59, p. 252, observes: 'Marginality empowers the feminist reader to prise open mythologies that govern patriarchal texts. A feminist critic may not write or even seek a woman's language, but she can exile herself from language's patrimony. Hence her own writing can establish a different bond with traditional texts.' See also Gilbert and Gubar, *No Man's Land: The Place of the Woman Writer in the Twentieth Century*, on Woolf's 'desire to revise not woman's language but woman's relation to language' (I. 230).
36. Marcus, 'Thinking Back through Our Mothers', in Marcus (ed.), *Art and Anger*: 73–100, pp. 88–9, argues that the feminine metaphor is Woolf's invention, a view which underestimates Woolf's learning in this area.
37. Cora Kaplan, 'Pandora's box: subjectivity, class and sexuality in socialist feminist criticism', in Greene and Kahn, *Making a Difference*: 146–76, p. 148.
38. Monks House Catalogue, pp. 51, 30.

39. Elizabeth Mary Wright, *The Life of Joseph Wright* (1932), I. 20, 19, 26–8.
40. Wright, *The Life of Joseph Wright*, I. 37, 281, 282.
41. Naomi Black, 'Virginia Woolf and the Women's Movement', in Marcus (ed.), *Virginia Woolf: A Feminist Slant*: 180–97. Marcus, 'Thinking Back through Our Mothers', pp. 74, 77, draws important parallels between Walter Benjamin's position as Jewish intellectual in Germany and Woolf's sense of sharing as a woman the position of outsider which her husband experienced as a Jew.
42. Berg, X, quoting Wright, *The Life of Joseph Wright*, I. 266.
43. Woolf's Reading Notes on *The Pilgrim's Progress* are all in Berg XXIII.
44. N.H. Keeble, '"Of him thousands daily Sing, and talk": Bunyan and his Reputation', in Keeble (ed.), *John Bunyan: Conventicle and Parnassus*: 251–60.
45. The editors of the *Diary* note that this entry conflates two subsequent books whose history was intricately intertwined: *The Years* (1937) and *Three Guineas* (1938). In a later marginal note to the entry just quoted Woolf wrote: '(This is Here & Now I think. May. 34)'. The speech to the National Society for Women's Service, of which Pippa Strachey was Secretary, forms the first Essay in *The Pargiters*, and is quoted in Chapter I.
46. Report of the Archbishop's Commission on the Ministry of Women (Church Assembly, 1935), p. 29.
47. Virginia Woolf, *Three Guineas* (Harmondsworth, 1977), pp. 187–8.
48. Sharrock, '"When I first took my Pen in hand": Bunyan and the Book', p. 89.
49. Woolf, 'Anon', in Silver (ed.), '"Anon" and "The Reader,"': Virginia Woolf's Last Essays', p. 384.
50. Woolf, 'Notes for Reading at Random', in Silver, '"Anon" and "The Reader"', pp. 373–9.
51. Silver, '"Anon" and "The Reader"', p. 400. The prolonged discussion of Latimer in 'Anon' represents an addition to the 'C' version of the manuscript, following a single marginal note in the B version, and Silver suggests that Woolf probably rewrote the essay in order to incorporate Latimer into it.
52. Woolf, *The Pargiters*, p. xxxv.
53. Hugh Latimer, *Fruitful Sermons* (London: Thomas Cotes, 1635). Woolf's Notes are in Berg, XVI. See N.H. Keeble, '"Take away preaching, and take away salvation": Hugh Latimer, Protestantism and prose style', in Neil Rhodes (ed.), *English Renaissance Prose: new essays in criticism* (Binghampton, NY: Centre for Medieval Texts and Studies, forthcoming 1997).
54. Watkins, *The Puritan Experience*, p. 2 and *passim*; Graham, 'Authority, Resistance and Loss', p. 126.
55. Sharrock, '"When I first took my Pen in hand": Bunyan and the Book', p. 74.
56. Susan Stanford Friedman, 'Post/Poststructuralist Feminist Criticism: The Politics of Recuperation and Negotiation', *NLH*, 22, 2 (1991): 465–90, p. 487, n4.

57. Cunningham, 'Glossing and Glozing: Bunyan and Allegory', p. 236.
58. Woolf, *The Pargiters*, pp. xxvii–xxviii.
59. Letter to Mrs N. Senior, September 18, 1874, in C. Edmund Maurice, *Life of Octavia Hill* (1913), p. 308, quoted in *Three Guineas*, p. 185 n35. Marcus, 'Thinking Back through Our Mothers', p. 75, points to Woolf's sense of herself as 'redeemer' and 'deliverer' of lost lives, but does not explore the Biblical implications of such language.
60. Martin Luther, Letter to Eoben Hess, March 29, 1523, in *Werke*, Weimar Edition, *Briefwechsel*, III. 50., quoted in Roland Mushat Frye, *God, Man, and Satan* (Princeton, 1960), p. 8.
61. V. Milo Kaufmann, *The Pilgrim's Progress and Traditions in Puritan Meditation* (New Haven, 1966), p. 133.
62. Mary Astell, *The Christian Religion As Profess'd by a Daughter of the Church of England* (1705), p. 139, quoted in Florence M. Smith, *Mary Astell* (New York, 1916), p. 6. This passage was copied by Woolf into her Reading Notes, Berg, X.
63. Smith, *Mary Astell*, p. 21; *TG*, p. 30.
64. Sharrock, '"When I first took my Pen in hand"', pp. 90, 76.
65. Showalter, 'Towards a Feminist Poetics', p. 131.

## CHAPTER 7: THE BODY AND THE BOOK

1. Woolf, 'On Being Ill', *The Moment and Other Essays* (1949): 14–24, pp. 14, 15. This essay was published by T. S. Eliot in *The New Criterion*, January 1926, and subsequently printed by the Woolfs for the Hogarth Press in a special limited edition of 250 copies in 1930.
2. Donne, *Devotions Upon Emergent Occasions*, pp. 11–12. Donne's *Devotions* are often read as a political statement, but Mary Arshagouni, 'The Politics of John Donne's *Devotions Upon Emergent Occasions*: or, New Questions on the New Historicism', *Renaissance and Reformation*, XXVII, 3 (1991): 233–48, argues that the work represents a turning away from politics into a more private and personal world.
3. Donne, *Paradoxes, Problemes, Essayes, Characters*: 33–7, pp. 33–5.
4. R.C. Bald, *John Donne: A Life* (Oxford, 1970), p. 37. See also for the intersection of Donne's use of birth metaphors with medical history, Elizabeth D. Harvey, *Ventriloquized Voices: Feminist Theory and Renaissance Texts* (1992), pp. 76–115.
5. Carey, *John Donne: Life, Mind and Art*, pp. 135–8.
6. M.A. Screech, 'Medicine and Literature: Aspects of Rabelais and Montaigne (with a glance at the Law)', in Sharratt (ed.), *French Renaissance Studies*: 156–69.
7. Suzanne W. Hull, *Chaste Silent & Obedient: English Books for Women 1475–1640* (San Marino, 1982), pp. 61–2, and *passim*.
8. Margaret Todd, *The Life of Sophia Jex-Blake* (1918), annotated in MHP/ B.16f. vol. 1, and Berg XXVI and VII.
9. Janet Wolff, *Feminine Sentences: Essays on Women and Culture* (Oxford, 1990), p. 122.
10. See Noelle Caskey, 'Interpreting Anorexia Nervosa', and Ellen L.

Bassuk, 'The Rest Cure: Repetition or Resolution of Victorian Women's Conflicts?', in Susan Rubin Suleiman (ed.), *The Female Body in Western Culture* (Cambridge, Mass., 1986): 175–89 and 139–51 respectively.

11. Jane Marcus, '"Taking the Bull by the Udders": Sexual Difference in Virginia Woolf – a Conspiracy Theory', in Marcus (ed.), *Virginia Woolf and Bloomsbury*: 147–69, p. 149: 'The salient sub-text in every Woolf novel is the voice of the working-class women, the heroic charwomen mythologised into a collective Nausicaa washing the dirty linen of the patriarchal family, her perpetual subject.'

12. Bell, *Virginia Woolf: A Biography*, I. Appendix C, 'Virginia Woolf and the Authors of *Euphrosyne*', pp. 205–6.

13. 'Old Bloomsbury', in Schulkind (ed.), *Virginia Woolf: Moments of Being*, p. 160.

14. Bell, *Old Friends*, pp. 129–30; Leonard Woolf, *Beginning Again: An autobiography of the years 1911 to 1918* (1978), p. 22.

15. Frances Spalding, *Vanessa Bell* (1983), p. 50.

16. Memoir III, quoted in Spalding, *Vanessa Bell*, p. 49.

17. 'Old Bloomsbury', p. 168; S.P. Rosenbaum, *Victorian Bloomsbury*, p. 3; Rosenbaum's cover features a picture of the (all male) Reading Society described by Clive Bell.

18. 'Am I a Snob?', in Schulkind (ed.), *Virginia Woolf: Moments of Being*, p. 188.

19. Woolf, '[Phyllis and Rosamond]', in Susan Dick (ed.), *The Complete Shorter Fiction of Virginia Woolf* (1985): 17–29, p. 24.

20. Peter Stallybrass and Allon White, *The Politics and Poetics of Transgression* (1986), pp. 95–6.

21. Stallybrass and White, *The Politics and Poetics of Transgression*, p. 80; Ellen Moers, *Literary Women* (1977), p. 64, quoted in Wolff, *Feminine Sentences*, p. 25; Wolff, pp. 23, 39–42;

22. Mikhail Bakhtin, *Rabelais and His World*, trans. Helen Iswolsky (Bloomington, 1984), pp. 317–22.

23. Woolf, 'A Sketch of the Past', in Schulkind, *Virginia Woolf: Moments of Being*, p. 84.

24. Leslie Stephen, 'Thoughts on Criticism, by a Critic' (*Cornhill Magazine*, 1876), in *Men, Books, and Mountains*, ed. by S.O.A. Ullmann (1956), p. 231.

25. Stephen Greenblatt, 'Filthy Rites', *Daedalus*, 111: 3 (1982): 1–16, p. 12.

26. Pauline Scott, 'From *Orlando Furioso* to *Orlando*: Reconfiguring the Ground of Gender Identification', unpublished paper presented at the MLA session on 'Virginia Woolf and the Renaissance', April 1994.

27. The motto was 'Fin che Venga' ('Until he cometh') from Olivero's crest. In his Notes to Canto 43 of the *Orlando Furioso* Harington wrote: 'Marrie for the shagheard dogge that could daunce to please Ladies so well and had such pretie qualities, I dare undertake my servant Bungy (whose picture you may see in the first page of the book and is knowne to the best Ladies of England) may compare with any Pilgrims dogge that served such a saint this seven yeare, onely he wants that qualitie to shake duckets out of his ears' (*Ludovico*

Ariosto's *Orlando Furioso translated into English Heroical Verse by Sir John Harington*, ed. with an introduction by Robert McNulty (Oxford, 1972), p. 515). All future references are to this edition.

28. Sir John Harington, *Nugae Antiquae* (1779), II. 123–4.
29. Virginia Woolf, *Orlando* (Harmondsworth, 1963), p. 27.
30. Ian Grimble, *The Harington Family* (1957), p. 119.
31. 'Of Reeding Poetry', in *The Sixth Book of Virgil's Aeneid VI*, translated by Sir John Harington, 1604, ed. Simon Cauchi (Oxford, 1991), p. 96; Rich, *Harington & Ariosto*, p. 78.
32. R.H. Miller, 'Unpublished Poems by Sir John Harington', *ELR*, 14:2 (1984): 148–58, p. 150.
33. Sir John Harington, 'Epigrams' in a scribal hand with letter and holograph signature, addressed to Lady Jane Rogers, bound in to the 1600 edition of the *The Orlando Furioso* in English Heroical Verse, 1591.
34. Sir John Harington, *An Apologie, Sir John Harington's A New Discourse of a Stale Subject, called The Metamorphosis of Ajax*, ed. Elizabeth Story Donno (1962), p. 219.
35. Michael G. Brennan, 'Sir Robert Sidney and Sir John Harington of Kelston', *N&Q*, NS, 34, 2:(1987): 232–7.
36. P.J. Croft, 'Sir John Harington's Manuscript of Sir Philip Sidney's *Arcadia*', in Stephen Parks and P.J. Croft, *Literary Autographs* (Los Angeles, 1983): 39–75, p. 63.
37. Kathleen M. Lea, 'Harington's Folly', in *Elizabethan and Jacobean Studies Presented to Frank Percy Wilson* (Oxford, 1959): 43–58, pp. 50, 56.
38. Quoted in Croft, 'Sir John Harington's Manuscript of Sir Philip Sidney's "Arcadia"', p. 65.
39. Virginia Woolf, *Roger Fry* (Harmondsworth, 1940) p. 165.
40. Leonard Woolf, *Downhill All the Way* (1967), pp. 108–9.
41. Goldberg, *Writing Matter: From the Hands of the English Renaissance*, p. 99: 'The training of the boy to be a pen—and the training of the pen to be a mouth—along with the emphasis on the softness and malleability of the hand, suggests feminization even as it founds the privileged male subject.' For a different interpretation of this passage in Virginia Woolf's *Diary* see John Carey, *The Intellectuals and the Masses* (1992), pp. 209–10.
42. John Donne, *Ignatius His Conclave*, in *Paradoxes, Problemes, Essayes, Characters*, (1653): 107–216, p. 176. The satire was written in 1610; two editions in Latin, and a third in English, appeared in 1611. It was reprinted in 1634, 1635 and 1652.
43. Kennedy, *A Boy at the Hogarth Press*, p. 39.
44. Marcus, '"No more horses": Virginia Woolf on art and propaganda', in *Art and Anger*, pp. 101–21; Black, 'Virginia Woolf and the Women's Movement', in Marcus, *Virginia Woolf: A Feminist Slant*, pp. 180–97. For Virginia Woolf's differences from Leonard Woolf on political issues, see Laura Moss Gottlieb, 'The War between the Woolfs', in Marcus (ed.), *Virginia Woolf and Bloomsbury*: 242–52.
45. Woolf, *The Moment and Other Essays* (1949): 105–25, p. 106.
46. Virginia Woolf, introductory letter to Margaret Llewelyn Davies, *Life*

*as We have Known It* (1977 [1931]): xvii–xxxxi, p. xxi.

47. Stallybrass and White, *The Politics and Poetics of Transgression*, p. 22.
48. *Letters to Severall Persons of Honour*, p. 22, and John Donne the younger, 'Epistle Dedicatory to the Lord Phillip Harbert [*sic*]'.
49. Also noted by Silver, '"Anon" and "The Reader"', p. 414, n49.
50. Gaither, '*The Hogarth Press: 1917–1946*', in Woolmer, *A Checklist of the Hogarth Press 1917–1946*, pp. xxiv, xviii, xxx–xxxi, and p. 83 [1930], no. 223; Lee, *Virginia Woolf*, pp. 371–3.
51. *The George Sand–Gustave Flaubert Letters*, p. 224.
52. See Judith L. Johnston, 'The Remediable Flaw: Revisioning Cultural History in *Between the Acts*', in Marcus (ed.), *Virginia Woolf and Bloomsbury*: 253–77, for the relation of this novel to the threat of Hitler.
53. Ong, *Orality and Literacy*, pp. 125, 133: 'Manuscript culture had taken intertextuality for granted. Still tied to the commonplace tradition of the old oral world, it deliberately created texts out of other texts, borrowing, adapting, sharing the common, originally oral, formulas and themes even though it worked them up into fresh literary forms impossible without writing'.
54. Lyndall Gordon, *Virginia Woolf, A Writer's Life* (1984), p. 267.
55. Ong, *Orality and Literacy*, p. 41.
56. Helgerson, *Self-Crowned Laureates*, p. 36: 'In the theater the professional dramatist was visible, if at all, only as an actor. And when, on rare occasions, his work got into print, it was likely to be anonymous.'
57. Silver, '"Anon" and "The Reader"', p. 435, notes a difference between the manuscript and typescript versions of 'The Reader': 'The MS dicussion of Burton's book tells us that we "find at the centre of this labyrinth of words, a man sitting alone in his college room, thinking about"—the sentence is left incomplete. In the TS, he is thinking about suicide.'
58. Adrienne Rich, *On Lies, Secrets, and Silence: Selected Prose 1966–1978* (1980), p. 35. Judith Fetterley, *The Resisting Reader* (Bloomington, 1978), pp. viii, xxii–xxiii.

# Select Bibliography

Abbott, H. Porter. *Diary Fiction: Writing as Action*. Ithaca: Cornell University Press, 1984.

Allentuch, Harriet Ray. 'My Daughter/Myself: Emotional Roots of Madame de Sévigné's art'. *MLQ*, 43: 2, 1982: 121–37.

Altman, Janet Gurkin. *Epistolarity: Approaches to a Form*. Columbus, Ohio: Ohio State University Press, 1982.

Arshagouni, Mary. 'The Politics of John Donne's *Devotions Upon Emergent Occasions*: or, New Questions on the New Historicism'. *Renaissance and Reformation*, XXVII, 3, 1991: 233–48.

Astin, Marjorie. *Mrs Pepys Her Book*. London: Noel Douglas, 1929.

Bakhtin, Mikhail. *Rabelais and His World*. Trans. Helen Iswolsky. Bloomington: Indiana University Press, 1984.

Bald, R. C. *Donne and the Drurys*. Cambridge: Cambridge University Press, 1959.

—— *John Donne: A Life*. Oxford: Clarendon Press, 1970.

Baldick, Chris. *The Social Mission of English Studies 1848–1932*. Oxford: Clarendon Press, 1983.

Barker, Francis. *The Tremulous Private Body: Essays on Subjection*. London and New York: Methuen, 1984.

Barrett, Michèle. *Virginia Woolf: Women & Writing*. London: The Women's Press, 1979.

Bassuk, Ellen L. 'The Rest Cure: Repetition or Resolution of Victorian Women's Conflicts?'. In Suleiman, ed. *The Female Body in Western Culture*: 139–51.

Bauschatz, Cathleen M. 'Montaigne's Conception of Reading in the Context of Renaissance Poetics and Modern Criticism'. In Suleiman and Crossman, eds. *The Reader in the Text: Essays on Audience and Interpretation*: 264–91.

Beal, Peter. *Index of English Literary Manuscripts*. London: Mansell, 1987.

Beer, Gillian. *Arguing with the Past*. London and New York: Routledge, 1989.

Beilin, Elaine V. *Redeeming Eve: Women Writers of the English Renaissance*. Princeton: Princeton University Press, 1987.

Bell, Anne Olivier, and McNeillie, Andrew. *The Diary of Virginia Woolf*. Harmondsworth: Penguin, 1977–84. 5 volumes.

Bell, Barbara Currier, and Ohmann, Carol. 'Virginia Woolf's Criticism: A Polemical Preface'. *Critical Inquiry*, 1, 1974: 361–71.

Bell, Clive. *Old Friends*. London: Cassell, 1956.

Bell, Ilona. '"UNDER YE RAGE OF A HOTT SONN & YR EYES": John Donne's Love Letters to Ann More'. In Summers and Pebworth, eds. *The Eagle and the Dove*: 25–52.

Bell, Quentin. *Virginia Woolf: A Biography*. London: Hogarth Press, 1972. 2 volumes.

Bennet, Joan. 'The Love Poetry of John Donne: A Reply to Mr. C.S. Lewis'. In *Seventeenth Century Studies presented to Sir Herbert Grierson*: 85–104.

Bible, The Geneva. 1560.

Bible, *The Holie Bible: conteyning the olde Testament and the newe*. London: 1568.

*The Byble: that is/the holy Scripture of the Olde and New Testament*. Trans. Myles Coverdale. [Cologne or Marburg?], 1535.

Black, Naomi. 'Virginia Woolf and the Women's Movement'. In Marcus, ed. *Virginia Woolf: A Feminist Slant*: 180–97.

Boase, Alan M. *The Fortunes of Montaigne*. London: Methuen, 1935.

Brennan, Michael G. 'Sir Robert Sidney and Sir John Harington of Kelston'. *N&Q*, NS, 34: 2, 1987: 232–7.

Bridenthal, Renate, and Koonz, Claudia, eds. *Becoming Visible: Women in European History*. Boston: Houghton Mifflin, 1977.

Brown, John. *John Bunyan (1628–1688): His Life, Times and Work*. Revised by Frank Mott Harrison. London: Hulbert, 1928.

Bunyan, John. *A Relation of My Imprisonment*. In *Grace Abounding to the Chief of Sinners*. Ed. Roger Sharrock. Oxford: Clarendon Press, 1962.

—— *Doctrine of the Law and Grace unfolded*. London: Nathaniel Ponder, 1685.

—— *Some Gospel-truths Opened*. Wright: 1656.

—— *The Pilgrim's Progress*. Ed. N.H. Keeble. Oxford and New York: Oxford University Press, 1984.

Burckhardt, Jacob. *The Civilization of the Renaissance in Italy*. New York: Random House, 1954.

Cameron, Deborah. *Feminism and Linguistic Theory*. London: Macmillan 1985.

Campbell, Gordon. 'Fishing in Other Men's Waters: Bunyan and the Theologians'. In Keeble, ed. *John Bunyan: Conventicle and Parnassus*: 137–51.

Carey, John. *The Intellectuals and the Masses*. London: Faber & Faber, 1992.

—— *John Donne: Life, Mind and Art*. London: Faber & Faber 1981.

—— 'John Donne's Newsless Letters'. In *Essays and Studies*, 34. Ed. Anne Barton, 1981: 45–65.

Caskey, Noelle. 'Interpreting Anorexia Nervosa'. In Suleiman, ed. *The Female Body in Western Culture*: 175–89.

Catalogue: Books from the Library of the late V. and L. Woolf. MHP, University of Sussex, Virginia Woolf Archive.

Cave, Terence. *The Cornucopian Text: Problems of Writing in the French Renaissance*. Oxford: Clarendon Press, 1979.

—— 'Problems of Reading in the *Essais*'. In McFarlane and MacLean, eds. *Montaigne: Essays in Memory of Richard Sayce*: 133–66.

Cavendish, Margaret, Duchess of Newcastle. *Sociable Letters*. London: printed by William Wilson, 1664.

Chappell, Edwin. *The Secrecy of the Diary: A Paper read before the Samuel Pepys Club, November 24th 1933*. Privately printed.

Cixous, Hélène. 'The Laugh of Medusa'. In Marks and Courtivron, eds. *New French Feminisms*: 245–64.

Clark, Carol. 'Talking About Souls: Montaigne on human psychology'. In McFarlane and MacLean, eds. *Montaigne: Essays in memory of Richard Sayce*: 57–76.

Clements, Patricia, and Grundy, Isobel, eds. *Virginia Woolf: New Critical Essays*. London: Vision, 1983.

Coleman, D. 'Montaigne's "Sur des vers de Virgile": Taboo Subject, Taboo Author'. In R.R. Bolgar, ed. *Classical Influences on European Culture, A.D. 1500–1700*. Cambridge: Cambridge University Press, 1976: 135–40.

Coleridge, Samuel Taylor. *Marginalia*. In *N&Q*, First Series, VI: 149, 1852: 213–16.

Croft, P.J. *The Poems of Robert Sidney*. Oxford: Clarendon Press, 1984.

——. 'Sir John Harington's Manuscript of Sir Philip Sidney's *Arcadia*'. In Stephen Parks and P.J. Croft. *Literary Autographs*. Los Angeles: University of California, William Andrews Clark Memorial Library, 1983: 39–75.

Cunningham, Valentine. 'Glossing and Glozing: Bunyan and Allegory'. In Keeble, *John Bunyan: Conventicle and Parnassus*: 217–40.

Davies, Emily. *The Higher Education of Women* (1866). Ed. Janet Howarth. London and Ronceverte: Hambledon Press, 1988.

Davis, Natalie Zemon. *Society and Culture in Early Modern France*. Cambridge: Polity Press, 1987.

DeSalvo, Louise A. 'Shakespeare's *Other* Sister'. In Marcus, ed. *New Feminist Essays on Virginia Woolf*: 61–81.

——. '1897: Virginia Woolf at Fifteen'. In Marcus, ed. *Virginia Woolf: A Feminist Slant*: 78–108.

——. 'As "Miss Jan Says": Virginia Woolf's Early Journals'. In Marcus, ed. *Virginia Woolf and Bloomsbury*: 96–124.

Dick, Susan, ed. *The Complete Shorter Fiction of Virginia Woolf*. London: Hogarth Press, 1985.

Docherty, Thomas. *John Donne, Undone*. London and New York: Methuen, 1986.

Dollimore, Jonathan. 'Different Desires: Subjectivity and Transgression in Wilde and Gide'. *Textual Practice*, I: 1, 1987: 48–67.

——. *Sexual Dissidence*. Oxford: Oxford University Press, 1991.

Donne, John. *A Sermon of Commemoration of the Lady Danvers, late Wife of Sir John Danvers*, Preach'd at Chilsey, where she was lately buried'. Together with other Commemorations of Her; By her Sonne G: Herbert. London: Printed by I. H. for *Philemon Stephens* and *Christopher Meredith*, 1627.

——. *Biathanatos*: A Declaration of that Paradoxe & Thesis, that *Selfe-homicide* is not so Naturally Sinne, that it may never be otherwise. London: Printed by John Dawson, 1647.

——. *Devotions Upon Emergent Occasions*. Ed. John Sparrow. Cambridge: Cambridge University Press, 1923.

——. *Ignatius His Conclave*. In *Paradoxes, Problemes, Essayes, Characters*, 1653: 107–216.

——. *Letters to Severall Persons of Honour*, published by John Donne [the younger]. Printed by J. Flesher, for Richard Marriot, 1651.

———. *The Loseley Manuscripts*. Ed Alfred John Kempe. London: John Murray 1835.

———. *Paradoxes, Problemes, Essayes, Characters*, Written by Dr. Donne. London: Printed by T: N: for Humphrey Moseley, 1653.

———. *Poetical Works*. Ed. Herbert J.C. Grierson. Oxford: Oxford University Press, 1921.

———. *Pseudo-martyr*. London: Printed by W. Stansby for Walter Burre, 1610.

———. *The Sermons of John Donne*. Ed. G.R. Potter and E.M. Simpson and Thomas R. Potter. Berkeley and Los Angeles: University of California Press, 1959. 10 volumes.

———. *John Donne: The Critical Heritage*. Ed. by A. J. Smith. London: Routledge & Kegan Paul, 1975.

Eagleton, Terry. *The Rape of Clarissa*. Oxford: Basil Blackwell, 1982.

Eisenstein, Elizabeth. *The Printing Revolution in Early Modern Europe*. Cambridge: Cambridge University Press, 1983.

Eisenstein, Nora. 'Virginia Woolf's Last Words on Words: *Between the Acts* and "Anon"'. In Marcus. *New Feminist Essays on Virginia Woolf*: 253–66.

Eliot, T.S. *Selected Essays*. London: Faber & Faber, 1932.

———. *The Sacred Wood*, 1920.

Ezell, Margaret S.M. 'The Myth of Judith Shakespeare: Creating the Canon of Women's Literature'. *NLH*, 21, 3: 1990: 579–92.

Favret, Mary A. *Romantic Correspondence: Women, politics and the fiction of letters*. Cambridge: Cambridge University Press, 1993.

Ferguson, Margaret W. 'A Room Not Their Own: Renaissance Women as Readers and Writers'. In Clayton Koelb and Susan Noakes, eds. *The Comparative Perspective on Literature*. Ithaca, 1988: 93–116.

Fetterley, Judith. *The Resisting Reader*. Bloomington and London: Indiana University Press, 1978.

Fiore, Peter Amadeus, ed. *Just So Much Honor*. University Park and London: Pennsylvania State University Press, 1972.

Fish, Stanley. *Self-Consuming Artefacts*. Berkeley and Los Angeles: University of California Press, 1972.

Fitzgerald, Edward. *The Letters and Literary Remains of Edward Fitzgerald*. Ed. by William Aldis Wright. London: Duckworth, 1989. 3 volumes.

Flaubert, Gustave, and Sand, George. *The George Sand–Gustave Flaubert Letters*. Trans. Aimée L. McKenzie. Introduction by Stuart P. Sherman. London: Duckworth, 1922.

Fox, Alice. *Virginia Woolf and the Literature of the English Renaissance*. Oxford: Clarendon Press, 1990.

Foxe, John. *Acts and Monuments*. London: printed for the Company of Stationers, 1641. 3 volumes.

Frame, Donald M. *Montaigne: A Biography*. New York: Harcourt, Brace and World, 1965.

———. *Montaigne's Discovery of Man*. New York: Columbia University Press, 1955.

Friedman, Susan Stanford. 'Post/Poststructuralist Feminist Criticism: The Politics of Recuperation and Negotiation'. *NLH*, 22, 2: 1991: 465–90.

Frye, Roland Mushat. *God, Man, and Satan*. Princeton: Princeton University Press, 1960.

Furman, Nelly. 'Textual Feminism'. In McConnell-Ginet, Borker and Furman, eds. *Women and Language in Literature and Society*: 45–54.

———. 'The politics of language: beyond the gender principle?'. In Greene and Kahn, eds. *Making a Difference: Feminist Literary Criticism*: 59–79.

Gardner, Helen, ed. *The Elegies and the Songs and Sonnets*. Oxford: Clarendon Press, 1965.

Gide, André. *Montaigne*. London and New York: Blackamore Press, 1929.

Gilbert, Sandra M. and Gubar, Susan, *No Man's Land: The Place of the Woman Writer in the Twentieth Century*, 3 volumes. New Haven: Yale University Press, 1987, 1989, 1994.

Goldberg, Jonathan. *Writing Matter: From the Hands of the English Renaissance*. Stanford: Stanford University Press, 1990.

Goldsmith, Elizabeth, ed. *Writing the Female Voice: Essays on Epistolary Literature*. Boston: Northwestern University Press, 1989.

Good, Graham. *The Observing Self: Rediscovering the Essay*. London and New York: Routledge, 1988.

Gordon, Lyndall. *Virginia Woolf, A Writer's Life*. London: Oxford University Press, 1984.

Gosse, Edmund. *The Life and Letters of John Donne*. London: William Heinemann, 1899. 2 volumes.

Gottlieb, Laura Moss. 'The War between the Woolfs'. In Marcus, ed. *Virginia Woolf and Bloomsbury*: 242–52.

Gournay, Marie le Jars de. *Grief Des Dames*, 1626. Reprinted in Mario Schiff. *Marie de Gournay*. Paris: Librairie Honoré Champion, Editeur, 1910.

Grafton, Anthony and Jardine, Lisa. *From Humanism to the Humanities* London: Gerald Duckworth, 1986.

Graham, Elspeth. 'Authority, Resistance and Loss: Gendered Difference in the Writings of John Bunyan and Hannah Allen'. In Laurence et al., eds. *John Bunyan and his England 1628–1688*: 115–30.

———, Hinds, Hilary, Hobby, Elaine, and Wilcox, Helen, eds. *Her Own Life: Autobiographical Writings by Seventeenth-Century Englishwomen*. London: Routledge, 1989.

Greenblatt, Stephen. 'Filthy Rites'. *Daedalus*, 111 no. 3, 1982: 1–16.

———. 'Psychoanalysis and Renaissance Culture'. In Parker and Quint, eds. *Literary Theory/Renaissance Texts*: 210–24.

———. *Renaissance Self-Fashioning: From More to Shakespeare*. Chicago and London: University of Chicago Press, 1980.

Greene, Gayle, and Kahn, Coppélia, eds. *Making a Difference: Feminist Literary Criticism*. London: Methuen, 1985.

Grierson, Herbert J.C. *Seventeenth Century Studies presented to Sir Herbert Grierson*. Oxford: Clarendon Press, 1938.

Griffiths, Morwenna, and Whitford, Margaret, eds. *Feminist Perspectives in Philosophy*. London: Macmillan, 1988.

Grimble, Ian. *The Harington Family*. London: Jonathan Cape, 1957.

Grimshaw, Jean. *Feminist Philosophers*. Brighton: Harvester Wheatsheaf, 1986.

Guillén, Claude. 'Notes toward the Study of the Renaissance Letter'. In

Lewalski, ed. *Renaissance Genres: Essays on Theory, History, and Interpretation*: 70–101.

Halifax, George Savile, first Marquess of. 'A Character of King Charles II'. In *The Complete Works of George Savile, first Marquess of Halifax*. Ed. Walter Raleigh. Oxford: Clarendon Press, 1912: 187–208.

Haller, William. *Foxe's Book of Martyrs and the Elect Nation*. London: Jonathan Cape, 1963.

Hannay, Margaret, ed. *Silent But for the Word: Tudor Women as Patrons, Translators, and Writers of Religious Works*. Kent, Ohio: Kent State University Press, 1985.

Harington, Sir John. 'Epigrams' in a scribal hand with letter and holograph signature, bound in to the 1600 edition of the *The Orlando Furioso in English Heroical Verse by John Harington Esquire*. Imprinted at London by Richard Field, 1591.

———. *Ludovico Ariosto's Orlando Furioso translated into English Heroical Verse by Sir John Harington*. Ed. Robert McNulty. Oxford: Clarendon Press, 1972.

———. *Nugae Antiquae*. London: printed for J. Dodsley, Pall-Mall, & T. Shrimpton, Bath, 1779. 3 volumes.

———. *Orlando Furioso in English Heroical Verse. By John Harington Esquire*. Imprinted at London by Richard Field, 1591.

———. *Sir John Harington's A New Discourse of a Stale Subject, called The Metamorphosis of Ajax*. Ed. Elizabeth Story Donno. London: Routledge & Kegan Paul, 1962.

———. *The Sixth Book of Virgil's Aeneid VI*. Translated by Sir John Harington, 1604. Ed. Simon Cauchi. Oxford: Clarendon Press, 1991.

Harley, Lady Brilliana. *Letters of the Lady Brilliana Harley*. Ed. by Thomas Taylor Lewis. London: printed for the Camden Society, 1854.

Harvey, Elizabeth D. *Ventriloquized Voices: Feminist Theory and Renaissance Texts*. London: Routledge, 1992.

———, and Maus, Katharine Eisaman, eds. *Soliciting Interpretations*. Chicago and London: University of Chicago Press, 1990.

Helgerson, Richard. *Self-Crowned Laureates*. Berkeley and London: University of California Press, 1983.

Hill, Christopher. 'Clarissa Harlowe and Her Times'. In *Puritanism and Revolution*, 1958: 367–94.

———. 'Samuel Pepys (1633–1703)'. In *Collected Essays*. Brighton: Harvester Wheatsheaf, 1985: I. 258–73.

———. *A Turbulent, Seditious, and Factious People: John Bunyan and his Church 1628–1688*. Oxford: Clarendon Press, 1988.

Horowitz, Louise K. 'The Correspondence of Madame de Sévigné: Lettres or Belles-Lettres?'. *French Forum*, 6:1, 1981: 13–25.

Hughey, Ruth, ed. *The Arundel Harington Manuscript of Tudor Poetry*. Columbus, Ohio: Ohio State University Press, 1960. 2 volumes.

Hull, Suzanne W. *Chaste Silent & Obedient: English Books for Women 1475–1640*. San Marino: Henry E. Huntingdon Library and Art Gallery, 1982.

Hume, David. *Essays Moral, Political and Literary*. London: Oxford University Press, 1963.

Ilsley, Marjorie Henry. *A Daughter of the Renaissance*. The Hague: Mouton, 1963.

Jameson, Anna. *The Loves of the Poets*. London: Henry Colburn, 1829.

Jardine, Alice A. *Gynesis: Configurations of Woman and Modernity*. Ithaca and London: Cornell University Press, 1985.

Jed, Stephanie H. *Chaste Thinking: The Rape of Lucretia and the Birth of Humanism*. Bloomington and Indianapolis: Indiana University Press, 1989.

Jelinek, Estelle C. *Women's Autobiography: Essays in Criticism*. Bloomington: Indiana University Press, 1980.

Johnson, Samuel. *Lives of the English Poets*. London: Oxford University Press, 1964. 2 volumes.

Johnston, Judith L. 'The Remediable Flaw: Revisioning Cultural History in *Between the Acts*'. In Marcus, ed. *Virginia Woolf and Bloomsbury*: 253–77.

Jonson, Ben. *Discoveries* (1641). Edinburgh: University Press, 1966.

Kahn, Victoria. 'Habermas, Machiavelli, and the Humanist Critique of Ideology'. *PMLA*, 105, no. 3, 1990: 464–76.

Kaplan, Cora. 'Pandora's box: subjectivity, class and sexuality in socialist feminist criticism'. In Greene and Kahn, *Making a Difference: Feminist Literary Criticism*: 146–76.

Kaufmann, V. Milo. *The Pilgrim's Progress and Traditions in Puritan Meditation*. New Haven and London: Yale University Press, 1966.

Keast, William R. 'Johnson's Criticism of the Metaphysical Poets'. In Roberts, ed. *Essential Articles for the Study of John Donne*: 11–19.

Keats, John. *The Poems and Verses of John Keats*. Edited by John Middleton Murry. London: Eyre & Spottiswoode, 1949.

Keeble, N.H., ed. *John Bunyan: Conventicle and Parnassus*. Oxford: Clarendon Press, 1988.

——. '"Here is her Glory, even to be under Him": The Feminine in the Thought and Work of John Bunyan'. In Laurence *et al.*, *John Bunyan and his England 1628–88*: 131–48.

Kelly, Kathleen. 'Conversion of the Reader in Donne's "Anatomy of the World"'. In Summers and Pebworth, eds. *The Eagle and the Dove*: 147–56.

Kelly-Gadol, Joan. 'Did Women Have a Renaissance?'. In Bridenthal and Koonz, eds. *Becoming Visible: Women in European History*: 137–64.

Kennedy, Richard. *A Boy at the Hogarth Press*. London: Whittington Press, 1972.

King, Margaret L., and Rabil, Albert Jr., eds. *Her Immaculate Hand*. Binghamton, NY: Centre for Medieval and Early Renaissance Studies, 1983.

Knott, John R. Jr. *The Sword of the Spirit*: Puritan Responses to the Bible. Chicago and London: University of Chicago Press, 1980.

——. '"Thou must live upon my Word": Bunyan and the Bible'. In Keeble, ed. *John Bunyan: Conventicle and Parnassus*: 153–70.

Lamb, Mary Ellen. 'The Cooke Sisters: Attitudes toward Learned Women'. In Hannay, ed. *Silent But for the Word: Tudor Women as Patrons, Translators, and Writers of Religious Works*: 107–25.

Latimer, Hugh. *Fruitful Sermons*. London: Thomas Cotes, 1635.
Laurence, Anne, Owens, W.R., and Sim, Stuart. *John Bunyan and his England 1628–88*. London and Ronceverte: Hambledon Press, 1990.
Lea, Kathleen M. 'Harington's Folly'. In *Elizabethan and Jacobean Studies Presented to Frank Percy Wilson*. Oxford: Clarendon Press, 1959: 43–58.
Le Comte, Edward. 'Jack Donne: From Rake to Husband'. In Fiore, ed. *Just So Much Honor*: 9–32.
Lee, Hermione. *Virginia Woolf*. London: Chatto & Windus, 1996.
Lehmann, John. *Thrown to the Woolfs*. London: Weidenfeld & Nicolson, 1978.
Levin, Carole. 'John Foxe and the Responsibilities of Queenship'. In Rose, ed. *Women in the Middle Ages and the Renaissance*: 113–33.
Lewalski, Barbara Kiefer. *Writing Women in Jacobean England*. Cambridge, Mass: Harvard University Press, 1993.
——, ed. *Renaissance Genres: Essays on Theory, History, and Interpretation*. Cambridge, Mass: Harvard University Press, 1986.
——. 'Re-writing Patriarchy and Patronage: Margaret Clifford, Anne Clifford, and Aemilia Lanyer'. In *The Yearbook of English Studies*, 21, 1991: 87–106.
——. 'Of God and Good Women: The poems of Aemilia Lanyer'. In Hannay, ed. *Silent But for the Word: Tudor Women as Patrons, Translators and Writers of Religious Works*: 203–24.
Lewis, C.S. 'Donne and Love Poetry in the Seventeenth Century'. In *Seventeenth-Century Studies, presented to Sir Herbert Grierson*: 64–84.
Lloyd, Genevieve. *The Man of Reason: 'Male' and 'Female' in Western Philosophy*. London: Methuen, 1984.
Love, Harold. *Scribal Publication in Seventeenth-Century England*. Oxford: Clarendon Press, 1993.
Luxton, Thomas Hyatt. 'The Pilgrim's Passive Progress: Luther and Bunyan on Talking and Doing, Word and Way'. *ELH*, 53, 1986: 73–98.
Lyttle, Guy Fitch, and Orgel, Stephen. *Patronage in the Renaissance*. Princeton: Princeton University Press, 1981.
McColl, Alan. 'The Circulation of Donne's Poems in Manuscript'. In Smith, ed. *John Donne: Essays in Celebration*: 28–46.
McConnell-Ginet, Sally, Borker, Ruth, and Furman, Nelly. eds. *Women and Language in Literature and Society*. New York: Praeger, 1980.
McFarlane, I.D., and MacLean, Ian, eds. *Montaigne: Essays in Memory of Richard Sayce*. Oxford: Clarendon Press, 1982.
McGowan, Margaret M. *Montaigne's Deceits: The Art of Persuasion in the Essais*. London: University of London Press, 1974.
McGrath, Lynette. '"Let Us Have Our Libertie Againe": Amelia Lanier's 17th-Century Feminist Voice'. *Women's Studies*, 20, 1992: 331–48.
McKenzie, D.F. *Bibliography and the Sociology of Texts*. The Panizzi Lectures, 1985. London: British Library, 1986.
McKillop, Alan Duguld. *Samuel Richardson: Printer and Novelist*. Chapel Hill: University of North Carolina Press, 1936.
Maclean, Ian. *The Renaissance Notion of Woman*. Cambridge: Cambridge University Press, 1980.

McNeillie, Andrew, ed. *The Essays of Virginia Woolf*. London: Hogarth Press, 1986–8. 3 volumes.

Main, C.F. 'New Texts of Donne'. *SB*, 9, 1957: 225–33.

Marcus, Jane. *Virginia Woolf and the Languages of Patriarchy*. Bloomington: Indiana University Press, 1987.

——, ed. *Virginia Woolf: A Feminist Slant*. Lincoln, Nebraska: University of Nebraska Press, 1983.

——, ed. *Art and Anger: Reading Like a Woman*. Columbus, Ohio: Ohio State University Press for Miami University, 1988.

——, ed. *New Feminist Essays on Virginia Woolf*. London: Macmillan, 1981.

——, ed. *Virginia Woolf and Bloomsbury*. London: Macmillan, 1987.

Marks, Elaine, and Courtivron, Isabelle, eds. *New French Feminisms*. Hemel Hempstead: Harvester, 1981.

Marlowe, Christopher. *Dr. Faustus*, A- and B-texts, 1604, 1616. Ed. David Bevington and Eric Rasmussen. Manchester: Manchester University Press, 1993.

Marotti, Arthur F. 'John Donne and the Rewards of Patronage'. In Lyttle and Orgel. *Patronage in the Renaissance*: 207–34.

——. *John Donne, Coterie Poet*. Madison: University of Wisconsin Press, 1986.

Maurer, Margaret. 'The Real Presence of Lucy Russell, Countess of Bedford, and the terms of John Donne's "Honour is so Sublime Perfection"'. *ELH*, 47, 1980: 205–34.

Maurice, Edmund C. *Life and Letters of Octavia Hill*. London: Macmillan, 1913.

Miles, Josephine. 'Ifs, Ands, Buts for the Reader of Donne'. In Fiore, *Just So Much Honor*: 272–91.

Milgate, W. 'The Early References to John Donne'. *N&Q*, 195, 1950: 229–3, 246–7, 290–2, 381–3.

Miller, R H. 'Unpublished Poems by Sir John Harington'. *ELR*, 14:2, 1984: 148–58.

Moers, Ellen. *Literary Women*. New York: Doubleday Anchor Press, 1977.

Montaigne, Michel de. *Essays of Montaigne*. Trans. Charles Cotton. Ed. William Carew Hazlitt. London: Navarre Society, 1923 [1693]. 5 volumes.

——. *The Essayes of Michael Lord of Montaigne*. Trans. John Florio. London: J.M. Dent, 1928 [1603].

Morgan, John. *Godly learning: Puritan Attitudes towards Reason, Learning and Education, 1560–1640*. Cambridge: Cambridge University Press, 1986.

Mossiker, Frances. *Madame de Sévigné: A Life and Letters*. New York: Columbia University Press, 1985.

Munich, Adrienne. 'Notorious signs, feminist criticism and literary tradition'. In Greene and Kahn. *Making a Difference: Feminist Literary Criticism*: 238–59.

Nelson, William. 'From "Listen, Lordings" to "Dear Reader"'. *University of Toronto Quarterly*, 46, 1976–7: 111–24.

Newton, Richard C. 'Jonson and the (Re)-Invention of the Book'. In Summers and Pebworth, eds. *Classic and Cavalier: Essays on Jonson and the Sons of Ben*: 31–55.

Nicolson, Nigel, and Trautmann, Joanne, eds. *The Letters of Virginia Woolf*. London: Hogarth Press, 1975–80. 6 volumes.

Norbrook, David. 'The Monarchy of Wit and the Republic of Letters: Donne's Politics'. In Harvey and Maus, eds. *Soliciting Interpretations*: 3–36.

Olney, James, ed. *Autobiography: Essays Theoretical and Critical*. Princeton: Princeton University Press, 1980.

Ong, Walter J. *Interfaces of the Word: Studies in the Evolution of Culture*. Ithaca: Cornell University Press, 1977.

——. *Orality and Literacy: The Technologizing of the Word*. London: Methuen, 1982.

——. *Ramus, Method and the Decay of Dialogue*. Cambridge, Mass.: Harvard University Press, 1958.

——. *Rhetoric, Romance, and Technology*. Ithaca and London: Cornell University Press, 1971.

Osborne, Dorothy. *Letters to Sir William Temple*. Ed. Kenneth Parker. Harmondsworth: Penguin, 1987.

Osborn[e], Francis. *Advice to a Son*. Oxford: Printed by H. H. for Tho. Robinson, 1658.

*The Oxford Book of War Poetry*. Ed. Jon Stallworthy. Oxford and New York: Oxford University Press, 1984.

Palmer, David. *The Rise of English Studies*. London: Oxford University Press for the University of Hull, 1965.

Parker, Patricia. *Literary Fat Ladies*. London and New York: Methuen, 1987.

——, and Quint, David, eds. *Literary Theory/Renaissance Texts*. Baltimore and London: Johns Hopkins University Press, 1986.

Patterson, Annabel. *Censorship and Interpretation: The Conditions of Writing and Reading in Early Modern England*. Madison and London: University of Wisconsin Press, 1984.

——. 'All Donne'. In Harvey and Maus, eds. *Soliciting Interpretations*: 37–67.

——. 'Misinterpretable Donne: The Testimony of the Letters'. *John Donne Journal*, 1, 1982: 37–53.

Pepys, Samuel. *The Diary of Samuel Pepys*. Ed. Robert Latham and William Matthews. London: G. Bell, 1970–83. 11 volumes.

Pooley, Roger. '*Grace Abounding* and the New Sense of Self'. In Laurence et al. *John Bunyan and his England 1628–88*: 105–14.

Popkin, Richard H. *The History of Scepticism from Erasmus to Spinoza*. Berkeley: University of California Press, 1979.

Raven, James. *Judging New Wealth: Popular Publishing and Responses to Commerce in England, 1750–1800*. Oxford: Clarendon Press, 1992.

Reiss, Timothy J. 'Montaigne and the Subject of Polity'. In Parker and Quint, eds. *Literary Theory/Renaissance Texts*: 115–49.

Renza, Louis A. 'The Veto of the Imagination: A Theory of Autobiography'. In Olney, ed. *Autobiography: Essays Theoretical and Critical*: 268–95.

*Report of the Archbishop's Commission on the Ministry of Women*. Church Assembly, 1935.

Rich, Adrienne. *On Lies, Secrets, and Silence: Selected Prose 1966–1978.* London: Virago, 1980.

Rich, Townsend. *Harington & Ariosto.* New Haven: Yale University Press, 1940.

Richardson, Samuel. *Familiar Letters on Important Occasions* [1741]. Introduced by Brian C. Downs. London: Secker & Warburg, 1958.

Roberts, John R., ed. *Essential Articles for the Study of John Donne's Poetry.* Hassocks: Harvester, 1975.

Robinson, Lillian S. 'Sometimes, Always, Never: Their Women's History and Ours'. *NLH,* 21, 2 (1990): 377–93.

Rose, Mary Beth, ed. *Women in the Middle Ages and the Renaissance: Literary and Historical Perspectives.* Syracuse: Syracuse University Press, 1985.

Rosenbaum, S. P. *Victorian Bloomsbury: The Early Literary History of the Bloomsbury Group.* London: Macmillan, 1987.

———, ed. *Women & Fiction: The Manuscript Versions of A ROOM OF ONE'S OWN.* Oxford: Blackwell, 1992.

———. 'An Educated Man's Daughter: Leslie Stephen, Virginia Woolf and the Bloomsbury Group'. In Clements and Grundy, eds. *Virginia Woolf: New Critical Essays:* 32–56.

Rousseau, Jean Jacques. *The Confessions of Jean Jacques Rousseau.* Privately printed, 1896. 2 volumes.

Sabine, Maureen. *Feminine Engendered Faith: The Poetry of John Donne and Richard Crashaw.* London: Macmillan, 1992.

Sackton, Alexander. 'Donne and the Privacy of Verse'. *SEL,* 7, 1967: 67–82.

Sainte-Beuve. 'Madame de Sévigné'. In *Fin de Portraits Littéraires: Portraits de femmes, Oeuvres.* Paris: Librairie Gallimard, 1960: II. 991–1007.

Sanders, Wilbur. *John Donne's Poetry.* Cambridge: University Press, 1971.

Schiff, Mario. *Marie de Gournay.* Paris: Librairie Honoré Champion, Editeur, 1910.

Schulkind, Jeanne, ed. *Virginia Woolf: Moments of Being: unpublished autobiographical writings.* Brighton: Sussex University Press, 1976.

Schwartz, Beth C. 'Thinking Back Through Our Mothers: Virginia Woolf Reads Shakespeare'. *ELH,* 58, 2: 1991, 721–46.

Screech, M.A. *Montaigne and Melancholy.* London: Gerald Duckworth, 1983.

———. 'Medicine and Literature: Aspects of Rabelais and Montaigne (with a glance at the Law)'. In Sharratt, ed. *French Renaissance Studies:* 156–69.

Sévigné, Madame de. *Lettres.* Texte établi et annoté par Gérard-Gailly. Paris: Librairie Gallimard, 1953. 3 volumes.

Sharratt, Peter, ed. *French Renaissance Studies 1540–70.* Edinburgh: University Press, 1976.

Sharrock, Roger. '"When I first took my Pen in hand": Bunyan and the Book'. In Keeble, ed. *John Bunyan: Conventicle and Parnassus:* 71–90.

Showalter, Elaine, ed. *The New Feminist Criticism.* London: Virago Press, 1986.

Sidney, Sir Philip. *An Apology for Poetry.* Ed. by Geoffrey Shepherd. Manchester: Manchester University Press, 1973.

Silver, Brenda, ed. '"Anon" and "The Reader": Virginia Woolf's Last Essays'. *Twentieth Century Literature*, 25, 3/4 (1979): 356–80.
——. *Virginia Woolf's Reading Notebooks*. Princeton: Princeton University Press, 1983.
Smith, A.J., ed. *John Donne: The Critical Heritage*. London: Routledge & Kegan Paul, 1975.
——, ed. *John Donne: Essays in Celebration*. London: Methuen, 1972.
Smith, Catherine F. '*Three Guineas*: Virginia Woolf's Prophecy'. In Marcus, ed. *Virginia Woolf and Bloomsbury*: 225–41.
Smith, Florence M. *Mary Astell*. New York: Columbia University Press, 1916.
Smith, Malcolm. *Montaigne and the Roman Censors*. Genève: Librairie Droz, 1981.
Smith, Nigel. 'Bunyan and the Language of the Body in Seventeenth-Century England'. In Laurence *et al. John Bunyan and his England 1628–88*: 161–74.
Smith, Sidonie. *A Poetics of Women's Autobiography: Marginality and the Fictions of Self Representation*. Bloomington and Indianapolis: Indiana University Press, 1987.
Spacks, Patricia Meyer. 'Female Resources: Epistles, Plot and Power'. In Goldsmith, ed. *Writing the Female Voice: Essays on Epistolary Literature*: 63–76.
——. 'Selves in Hiding'. In Jelinek. *Women's Autobiography: Essays in Criticism*: 112–32.
Spalding, Frances. *Vanessa Bell*. London: Macmillan, 1983.
Spedding, James. *The Letters and Life of Francis Bacon*. London: Longman, Green, Longman, Roberts, 1861. 14 volumes.
Spender, Dale. *The Diary of Elizabeth Pepys*. London: Grafton, 1991.
Squier, Susan M., and DeSalvo, Louise A. 'Virginia Woolf's [*The Journal of Mistress Joan Martyn*]'. *Twentieth Century Literature*, 25, 3/4, 1979: 237–69.
Stallybrass, Peter, and White, Allon. *The Politics and Poetics of Transgression*. London: Methuen, 1986.
Stanton, Donna C., ed. *The Female Autograph*. Chicago, 1984.
Stephen, Leslie. *Hours in a Library*. London: John Murray, 1917 [1874]. 3 volumes.
——. 'Thoughts on Criticism, by a Critic'. *Cornhill Magazine*, 1876. In *Men, Books, and Mountains*. Ed. by S.O.A. Ullmann. London: The Hogarth Press, 1956: 213–32.
Stevenson, Robert Louis. 'Samuel Pepys'. *Cornhill Magazine*, XLIV, July, 1981: 31–46.
Stimpson, Catharine R. 'The Female Sociograph: The Theater of Virginia Woolf's Letters'. In Stanton, ed. *The Female Autograph*: 168–79.
Suleiman, Susan Rubin, ed. *The Female Body in Western Culture*. Cambridge, Mass: Harvard University Press, 1986.
—— and Crossman, Inge, eds. *The Reader in the Text: Essays on Audience and Interpretation*. Princeton: Princeton University Press, 1980.
Summers, Claude J., and Pebworth, Ted-Larry, eds. *The Eagle and the Dove*. Columbia: University of Missouri Press, 1986.

——, eds. *Classic and Cavalier: Essays on Jonson and the Sons of Ben*. Pittsburgh: University of Pittsburgh Press, 1982.

Supple, James J. *Arms Versus Letters: the military and literary ideals of the 'Essais' of Montaigne*. Oxford: at the Clarendon Press, 1984.

Swaim, Kathleen M. 'Mercy and the Feminine Heroic in the Second Part of *Pilgrim's Progress'*. *SEL*, 30, 1990: 386–409.

Thickstun, Margaret Olafson. 'From Christiana to Stand-fast: Subsuming the Feminine in *The Pilgrim's Progress'*. *SEL*, 26, 1986: 439–53.

Thompson, E.P. *The Making of the English Working Class*. London: Victor Gollancz, 1963.

Thomson, Patricia. 'John Donne and the Countess of Bedford'. *MLR*, 44, 1949: 329–40.

Tillotson, Kathleen. 'Donne's Poetry in the Nineteenth Century (1800–72)'. In Roberts, ed. *Essential Articles for the Study of John Donne's Poetry*: 20–33.

Todd, Margaret. *The Life of Sophia Jex-Blake*. London: Macmillan, 1918.

*Tixall Letters: or the Correspondence of the Aston Family*. Ed. Arthur Clifford. London: Printed for Longman *et al.*, 1815. 2 volumes.

Trinquet, Roger. *La Jeunesse de Montaigne*. Paris: A. G. Nizet, 1972.

Walton, Izaak. *The Life of John Donne, DD*. London: Henry Kent Causton, 1865.

Watkins, Owen C. *The Puritan Experience*. London: Routledge & Kegan Paul, 1972.

Weisner, Merry E. 'Women's Defense of Their Public Role'. In Rose, ed. *Women in the Middle Ages and the Renaissance: Literary and Historical Perspectives*: 1–27.

Wheatley, Henry B. 'The Growth of the Fame of Samuel Pepys'. In *Occasional Papers of the Samuel Pepys Club*. Printed for the Club at the Chiswick Press, 1917. Volume I: 1903–14: 156–73. 2 volumes.

Whitford, Margaret 'Luce Irigaray's Critique of Rationality' In Griffiths and Whitford (eds), *Feminist Perspectives in Philosophy*: 109–30.

Williamson, George. 'The Libertine Donne'. *PQ* 13, 1934: 276–91.

Wolff, Janet. *Feminine Sentences: Essays on Women and Culture*. Oxford: Basil Blackwell, 1990.

Wollman, Richard B. 'The "Press and the Fire": Print and Manuscript Culture in Donne's Circle'. *SEL*, 33 (1993): 85–97.

Woolf, Leonard. *Beginning Again: An Autobiography of the years 1911 to 1918*. London: Hogarth Press, 1958.

——. *Downhill All the Way: An Autobiography of the years 1919–1939*. London: Hogarth Press, 1967.

Woolf, Virginia. *The Common Reader: First Series*. Ed. by Andrew McNeillie. Hogarth Press, 1984 [1925].

——. *The Common Reader: Second Series*. London: Hogarth Press, 1932.

——. *The Complete Shorter Fiction of Virginia Woolf*. Ed. by Susan Dick. London: Hogarth Press, 1985.

——. *The Death of the Moth and Other Essays*. London: Hogarth Press 1942.

——. Introductory letter to Margaret Llewelyn Davies, *Life as We have Known It*. London: Virago Press, 1977 [1931].

——. *The Moment and Other Essays*. London: Hogarth Press, 1949.

——. *Orlando*. Harmondsworth, 1963 [1928].

——. *The Pargiters*. Ed. Mitchell A. Leaska. London: Hogarth Press, 1978.

——. *A Passionate Apprentice: The Early Journals 1897–1909*. Ed. Mitchell A. Leaska. London: Hogarth Press, 1990.

——. *Roger Fry*. Harmondsworth: Penguin Books, 1979 [1940].

——. *A Room of One's Own*. Harmondsworth: Penguin Books, 1972 [1929].

——. *Three Guineas*. Harmondsworth: Penguin, 1977 [1938].

——. *Women & Fiction: The Manuscript Versions of A ROOM OF ONE'S OWN*. Transcribed and edited by S. P. Rosenbaum. Oxford: Blackwell, 1992.

Woolmer, J. Howard. *A Checklist of the Hogarth Press 1917–1946*. Revere, Pennsylvania: Woolmer/Brotherson, 1986.

Wright, Elizabeth Mary. *The Life of Joseph Wright*. London: Oxford University Press, 1932. 2 volumes.

Wyatt, Sir Thomas. *Sir Thomas Wyatt: The Complete Poems*. Ed. R. A. Rebholz. Harmondsworth: Penguin, 1978.

# Index

271